A PENGUIN SPECIAL

S 170

BRITISH ECONOMIC POLICY
SINCE THE WAR

ANDREW SHONFIELD

BRITISH ECONOMIC
POLICY SINCE THE WAR

BY

ANDREW SHONFIELD

PENGUIN BOOKS

Penguin Books Ltd, Harmondsworth, Middlesex
U.S.A.: Penguin Books Inc., 3300 Clipper Mill Road, Baltimore 11, Md
AUSTRALIA: Penguin Books Pty Ltd, 762 Whitehorse Road,
Mitcham, Victoria

—

First published 1958

—

Made and printed in Great Britain
by Wyman & Sons Ltd,
London, Reading, and Fakenham

CONTENTS

Contents

ECONOMIC DIARY 1945–1958

ECONOMIC DIARY 1945–1958

1945	6 December	End of Lease-Lend; U.S. £1,000m. loan agreement signed in Washington.
1946	11 May	Bank of England Nationalization Act.
1947	4 January	Coal mines nationalized.
	January–February	Fuel crisis.
	23 August	Suspension of convertibility of sterling into dollars.
	4 October	Sir Stafford Cripps appointed Minister of Economic Affairs.
	15 November	Autumn Budget; Budget leak; Mr Hugh Dalton, Chancellor of Exchequer, resigns. Sir Stafford Cripps takes over.
1948	10 January	Capital construction cuts announced.
	13 March	U.S. Loan exhausted.
	10 April	Budget 1948/9. 'Once-for-all' capital levy.
	1 April	Electricity nationalized.
	27 May	Railways, road haulage, other transport undertakings transferred to state control.
	5 July	National Health Service started.
1949	18 September	Devaluation of £ from $4.03 to $2.80.
	24 October	Crisis economy measures, including capital expenditure cuts, announced.
1950	23 February	General Election. Labour returned.
	18 April	Budget 1950/1. Lower ranges of income tax reduced by 6d to 1s in the pound.
	19 October	Sir Stafford Cripps resigns; Mr Gaitskell Chancellor of the Exchequer.
1951	29 January	New rearmament programme announced.
	15 February	Vesting day, steel nationalization.
	10 April	Budget 1951/2. Income tax up 6d in the pound. Initial allowances for investment withdrawn.
	17 April	Capital issues restricted.
	21 June	Building programme cut to help defence.
	26 July	Dividend limitation; bank advances restricted; price controls; dollar import cuts.
	25 October	General Election; Conservatives returned.
	26 October	Mr R. A. Butler appointed Chancellor of Exchequer in Mr Churchill's Cabinet.
	7 November	Economy measures: first post-war increase in bank rate to $2\frac{1}{2}$ per cent; building cuts; excess profits tax; import restrictions.

1952	29 January	Balance-of-payments crisis: further import restrictions; capital investment cuts; hire-purchase restrictions.
	11 March	Budget: slight reductions in income tax. Bank rate up to 4 per cent.
1953	14 April	Budget: 6d off income tax. Initial allowances on capital expenditure restored.
	5 May	Steel allocation scheme ended.
	6 May	Transport Act, 1953: denationalization.
	14 May	Iron and Steel Act: denationalization.
	17 September	Bank rate reduced to $3\frac{1}{2}$ per cent.
1954	6 April	Budget: new investment allowances.
	13 May	Bank rate reduced to 3 per cent.
	July (first half)	All food rationing ended.
	19 August	Hire-purchase finance restrictions eased.
	10 November	Building licensing ended.
1955	27 January	Bank rate increased to $3\frac{1}{2}$ per cent.
	24 February	Bank rate increased to $4\frac{1}{2}$ per cent. Hire-purchase restrictions.
	6 April	Sir Anthony Eden Prime Minister.
	19 April	Budget 1955/6. Standard rate of income tax reduced 6d in the pound.
	26 May	General Election. Conservatives returned.
	25 July	Emergency measures: bank credit restricted; further hire-purchase restrictions.
	26 October	Supplementary Budget: further restrictions on capital investment, housing cuts.
	20 December	Mr Butler resigns; Mr Harold Macmillan appointed Chancellor of the Exchequer.
1956	16–17 February	Bank rate up to $5\frac{1}{2}$ per cent. Investment allowances suspended; more h.p. restrictions.
	4 December	Post-Suez crisis measures, including waiver of U.S. loan repayment.
1957	10 January	Mr Macmillan Prime Minister.
	13 January	Mr Thorneycroft Chancellor of the Exchequer.
	7 February	Bank rate reduced to 5 per cent.
	5 April	New defence policy, cuts in expenditure.
	9 April	Budget: income tax concessions on higher incomes.
	19 September	Further restrictions on bank credit. Bank rate increased to 7 per cent.
1958	6 January	Mr Thorneycroft resigns. Mr Heathcoat-Amory Chancellor of the Exchequer.

CHAPTER ONE

INTRODUCTION

THIS is a book about politics, looked at from an economic viewpoint. It is a sign of the confusion into which the subject has fallen that it is necessary to make a point of explaining that an economic theme is the natural raw material for a political argument. This marks the difference between 'political economy', as the nineteenth century knew it, and modern 'economics'. The modern word has a hard, pretentious, scientific ring about it – a sound which, however, becomes less impressive as one becomes aware of the extraordinarily limited field to which the mathematical certainties can be practically applied. For the rest, it is very much a matter of political judgement, backed by as much empirical fact as possible.

My thesis in this book is that Britain must learn to grow faster in wealth. That is a highly political contention. Some people believe that stability is more important than growth. Some people positively dislike growth, especially economic growth, because it involves change, especially social change. One finds economists ranged predictably on the two sides of this argument, according to temperament, just like the members of any amateur debating society. I also suggest that many military and political activities of a prestige character ought to be given up, in order to make this country better equipped to grow rapidly. Again, this is plainly a matter of political choice. I believe it to be an urgent one.

I am impressed by the case of France as evidence of what happens to a nation which continually tries to support a bigger political burden than its economy will readily bear, which clings to positions of international prestige, regardless of the fact that the essential structure of its national life is crumbling all around it. The inability of the state to will the financial means for carrying out the political decisions which it has taken leads eventually to a terrible atmosphere of hatred and contempt between people and government. The political decisions imply a heroic readiness for financial sacrifice, which simply is not there – because no one will admit that times have changed, that France no longer has a natural position of pre-eminence in the world, that even the modest pretensions of a second-class power cost a great deal to maintain nowadays. When the rare politician like Mendès-France comes along and tries to draw attention to some of these truths, the French parliament howls him down, in order not to have to listen to his voice. For all the vaunted shrewdness and realism of the French people in their daily lives, they have managed in their thinking about national affairs to retreat into a world of illusion. When every now and then they are woken from it with a jolt, they react with extraordinary bitterness – especially towards their allies, who ought, they feel, to have known better than to bring this humiliation on them.

Having once embarked on this course, it is extremely difficult to get out of the habit of blaming others for situations, which are the result simply of the disproportion between the political ends and the material means to fulfil them. The retreat continues from one illusion to the next – from the impossible war in Indo-China to the impossible war in North Africa, and now to the great mirage of oil in the Sahara desert, which is going to solve all France's problems all at once. French writers like Raymond Aron are themselves the most acute critics of this curious state of the French spirit, which leads on the Left to a total utopianism in politics, total in its refusal to have anything to do with the sordid realities of ordinary daily life. This is of course the perfect formula for ensuring that these realities become more sordid. On the Right of French politics there is an equally extreme historicism, which manifests itself in another kind of rigidity. Because almost every action of today is bound to represent a decline from some glory of France of the past, life becomes overspread with a kind of facile pessimism, whose chief manifestation is the refusal to face the future. The typical gesture that goes with this mood is the head in the hands and the statement: 'I will not think about it.' It is not surprising that there is no more narrow and unbudging conservatism than that of the French conservatives.

Some observers professed to see signs that Britain was moving into this Gallic mood of embitterment, of national nostalgia and intransigent unrealism, after the Suez incident at the end of 1956.

But although the initial shock of the experience was great – especially the discovery of Britain's weakness when isolated from America – the second phase was not, as had been feared, a lapse into a typically French state of resentment and sulks. Rather, the whole affair has been used to stimulate a lot of fresh thinking on previously accepted assumptions about Britain's position in the world. The hurt nostalgia, which was the first reaction to Suez, soon gave way to an activity of critical self-examination. It seems so far to involve less pain, less resistance, and above all less turgid argument of an elementary character than the similar attempt which is being conducted by a small group of forward-looking intellectuals on the other side of the Channel. This book is offered as a further contribution to the process of re-examination.

I have had a great deal of help in writing it from Zuzanna Shonfield, my wife. Much of the statistical and other factual material was collected and organized by her. Alan Day, Reader in Economics at London University, gave me the benefit of his critical comment on the manuscript. I also had much useful discussion from Mr Michael Shanks on the section dealing with trade union affairs. From Mr Alfred Hecht I received a number of favours, material as well as spiritual, which eased the problem of thinking and writing. I owe special thanks to Miss Ilsa Meryn for carrying through a most taxing task on the manuscript, the worst of which fell in the last week of December 1957, over Christmas. At an earlier stage I had the benefit of discussion with Professor Arthur Lewis of Manchester University on the long-term trend in the British economy, from the middle of the nineteenth century onwards. My indebtedness to his ideas appears clearly in the text. I am impressed by the extent to which the quality of one's thinking is influenced by the people whom one happens to know and like, and the books which they happen to induce one to read.

CHAPTER TWO

TOO LITTLE PRODUCTION

WHY does Britain's wealth grow so much more slowly than the wealth of countries on the continent of Europe? If we start at 1952, when world economic conditions returned to something like normal after the boom-and-bust following on the outbreak of the Korean War, and measure the increase in national output that has taken place since then in Britain and in the six countries who are forming the European Common Market, we get the following picture:[1]

	Per cent increase 1952–1956
Germany	38%
Netherlands	27%
Italy	26%
France	20%
Britain	15%
Belgium and Luxemburg	13%

A little under half of the national output in this country consists of services, rather than goods – e.g. transport, retail trade, medical care, education, and all the other services provided by the state. This high proportion of services is a mark of our high standard of living. But if we leave them out of account and concentrate on the actual output of goods by industry, the result looks rather better. Industrial output in this country expanded faster than the provision of services. The increase between 1952 and 1956 was 20 per cent – that is to say, there was one extra physical item produced in 1956 for every five items that were produced five years before. This might seem on the face of it quite a respectable increase in the national wealth – until we start looking at what has been happening to industrial production abroad. Once again Germany leads by a large distance: for every five items produced in Germany in 1952 there are an extra two-and-a-half coming out of the factories and mines in 1956. But it is not Germany alone which has been forging ahead at top speed. Industrial production in Italy and Holland has been advancing almost twice as fast as in this country. France comes next, with industrial output increasing at one-and-a-half times the speed of this country; and even Belgium is slightly ahead.

Looking at these figures, one can hardly be surprised that the problem of wages and prices has proved so intractable in Britain during recent years. It is not that British wages have been going up all that much faster than wages in other countries; the crucial fact is that the output of physical goods and services to match the increase in wages has been rising much more slowly. The inevitable consequence is that British prices have been tending to rise faster than elsewhere. It is the balance between the total amount of money being spent through the shops and so on and the total volume of goods and services available for sale which determines the price level. When the first rises more than the second, the only way to keep prices down is to pull in more imports from abroad to plug the money-goods gap. This happens with depressing regularity in post-war Britain and results each time in a balance-of-payments crisis. The usual next step after one of these crises is a policy of restriction of investment, which imposes a check on the rate of growth of industrial output. Thus the short-term remedy aggravates the long-term problem.

If the British wage earner in the 1950s has been more demanding than wage earners in other countries – and it is true that hourly earnings in this country have gone up rather faster than on the continent of Europe – the reason is not to be sought in the exceptional greed of the British working class character, but rather in the behaviour of the price level. Since Sir Stafford Cripps's bargaining experiment with the trade unions in 1948, when they agreed to hold the wage level stable so long as the Government held the price level, a mood of acute suspicion has settled upon British labour. The representatives of labour, who are perfectly responsible men, start with the determination, when they enter into any kind of wage bargaining, that they are 'not going to be had'. 'Being had' means that the bulk of any increase in wages – sometimes the whole – is wiped out by the subsequent increase in prices. After about a decade of this experience, they naturally try to insure themselves by keeping something in hand against the likelihood of a further rise in prices. It is no use telling them that in this way they merely aggravate the problem. So far as their own particular group of workers are concerned, what matters is that they have managed for a period of a few months to get a little way ahead of the rising wave of prices. These are the facts which explain the emergence of Mr Frank Cousins, the General Secretary of the Transport and General Workers Union in the mid-1950s, and of the new belligerent mood of labour, of which he is the natural leader.

Here is a vicious circle with a vengeance: Britain's slow rate of economic growth, which is not matched by any slowness on the part of anybody to demand a rising standard of living, causes the rise in prices; this rise carried on over a period of years results in higher and higher demands for money wages; and that in turn drives up the price level further. On the other side the remedies which are applied, with the intention of creating a psychology of restraint through the restriction of output, tend to impose a further check on the growth of British industry.

A variety of explanations have been advanced for the failure of British economic growth to keep up with the pace of the continent of Europe since the war. It has been suggested by some people that the main cause lies in the personality defects of the British working man – on the one hand his perpetual demands for ever higher wages, and on the other his alleged unwillingness to offer an honest day's work in return. The existence of this state of mind is sometimes blamed on to the trade union leadership, which occupies an unusually powerful political position in this country. An alternative view is that the trouble lies in the defects of British management: a lack of sheer professional expertise among the people who are responsible for running British industry, combined with a slowness to adopt new and useful techniques as they become available. It may be that there is something in the criticism that there is an insufficient intensity of work on the part of labour or management or both in particular firms and particular sectors of British industry. The criticism can only apply to the quality of the work, not to the quantity of hours spent at work, which are longer now than they were before the war. The average working week of adult men working in British industry is scarcely any shorter than the average in Germany, and it is about seven hours longer than in the United States. There is certainly a widespread impression that more firms tolerate slacking on the job and more men indulge in it in this country than in the other two. But such evidence as is available comes by way of example only, and it is impossible to say whether these examples are typical of the vast majority or merely a bare minority of British industry. There is no representative sample by which to judge. It is hard to believe, in any case, that this can be the whole explanation for the failure of British industry to expand as fast as that of its competitors in Western Europe – or if it is, that the attitude behind it is simply an odd temperamental defect of the British people, entirely unrelated to other factors of a less permanent character. After all, British industry has a long history – longer than that of any other industry in the world – of ingenuity and initiative in management and hard work at the factory bench. It would be strange, though of course it is not impossible, that these virtues should suddenly have disappeared without trace in the middle of the twentieth century.

As to the bargaining strength and political power of the trade unions, it is true that they are greater today than they were before the war. But if the comparison is made with contemporary unions in other countries, the differences do not appear to be very significant. The Swedish trade unions for instance are not noticeably less powerful than the British, nor are the German trade unions, to take another example, markedly more reticent about asserting their demands for ever higher wages. That is not to deny that these countries have obtained big benefits in the past from the moderation shown by their trade union leaders in the immediate postwar period. This was particularly true in Germany during the early phase of reconstruction. But it should be remembered that the British trade union leaders were not wanting in a spirit of moderation during the early post-war period, either. There has been little enough of this spirit in the 1950s. But if British workers have recently shown themselves more impatient or more greedy than workers on the continent of Europe, there is one contributory cause which should not be overlooked – their standard of living has also been rising more slowly than on the continent of Europe.

Must we then, as some writers have recently been suggesting, accept it as a fact of life in the middle of the twentieth century that Britain has become an 'undynamic society'? There is no doubt that once one starts to look around with this in view, one can find plenty of signs in contemporary Britain of a lack of dynamism. The sort of thing which catches the eye is the ferocious determination to stay put, expressed in the compacts that are made by certain groups of working men, for instance in the ship-building industry, that no member of the group will earn more than an agreed maximum sum in any week. In the conditions of today in the shipbuilding industry this cannot conceivably be aimed at protecting anybody from being worked out of a job. It is just an automatic gesture, derived from the past, which holds up progress. Right through the economy there are the endless demarcation lines between one job and another, dividing industry into rigid compartments, in each of which a determined effort goes on to maximize costs. And behind all this is the widespread feeling that none of it matters a damn, because whatever is done things are not going to change very much anyhow.

DEFECTIVE TRADE UNION STRUCTURE

The British trade unions attract some of the blame for fostering this undynamic way of life. Disputes about privileges, differentials, demarcation lines between trades, opposition to any redundancy resulting from improved equipment or organization, are not of course peculiar to Britain. But they do seem to be more effective in this country than elsewhere in putting a damper on technological initiative. That generalization must at once be qualified by reference to those industries where labour accepts changes readily and appears to have accepted fully the conjunction of high wages and high output, with the concomitant of technical change. Steel manufacture is an outstanding instance. But unfortunately such industries are still in a minority.

The forces of conservatism in organized labour in Britain are encouraged by certain features of the trade union structure. It is normal in the early days of the trade union struggle to find labour organized exclusively on a craft basis. The skilled men are the natural leaders at this stage, when the unskilled generally have neither the moral nor financial staying power for a serious fight with the employers. These leaders have left a deep mark on both the physical organization and on the distinctive class culture of British unionism. The craftsmen were, and often still are, pretty exclusive people. They tend to emphasize the differences between similar trades, to form themselves into small, rather than large groups, to insist on status and differentials. This kind of jealousy still leaves room for an overwhelming spirit of solidarity with their fellow workers in any struggle against the employers. But that is a matter of principle, a blind devotion to the workers' alliance, regardless of the rights or wrongs of any particular conflict in which another group of workers may be engaged.

The protection of special craft interests, combined with strong support for the claims of any part of the working class for higher wages or better conditions, was an effective formula in the early stages of industrial development for forcing employers to give up bit by bit an increasing share of the nation's income to the wage-earner. The skilled men made the running; the rest followed. It is however not a very helpful approach in the conditions of today, when there is little scope for improvement in workers' living standards through a further process of redistribution, and when an increase in output per man is the only way of obtaining a significant increase in real wages. Today the trade union leader who demands an increase in wages must also will the means of paying it. Now, craft workers have never had notions of this sort. In their tradition, the machine is an aid to human skill – a more or less refined implement, nothing more – and the level of output achieved is believed to be chiefly determined by the strength, the ingenuity, or some other personal attribute of the worker, or, alternatively, by the degree of intensity of his effort. There is no natural place in the ideology of craftsmen for the vision of an automatic annual increase in the output per man through more investment and better technology. These men are in many ways the inheritors of the medieval guild spirit: their concern is to assert the high value of skilled effort in general and of their skill, whatever it may be, in particular.

To appreciate the significance of this attitude, it is necessary to compare such a craft union with a modern 'industrial' union, like the United Automobile Workers or the United Steel Workers of America. The first point is that such unions start their negotiations with the explicit demand on the employers that they must do whatever is necessary – by way of investment or improvements in organization – to increase output per man by a substantial annual amount in the two or three years ahead during which the wage contract is to run. They now take the adjustments for *future* productivity just as much for granted as the automatic adjustments to current changes on the cost of living sliding scale. But of course, in making these technological demands on their employers, they have to be ready to accept radical alterations in plant and methods, and the dismissal of workers, if these become redundant as a result of improved methods of output. They try to screw as much money as they can out of the employers for the people who lose their jobs; but they do not insist on a process of dilution of labour which will keep them in work at their old jobs. They insist on the opposite. Here is something which it hurts the average militant trade unionist in Britain even to contemplate.

Yet these industrial unions in America show no lack of militancy when it comes to making demands on the employers. By European standards what they ask for is frequently outrageous; and their attitude towards any employer who is genuinely unable to pay up is ruthless – to a degree which only goes with ruthlessness as a matter of high principle. The American union leaders have explained in engagingly frank terms the merits of their technique of 'key bargaining' – that is, picking on a particular firm in an industry for the first round of negotiations, wringing the maximum concessions from it, and then forcing other employers to follow suit. 'The great advantage of key bargaining,' they say in a special article written jointly by a number of union officials in 1957,[2] 'is that in negotiating with the leading company in a particular industry, the union is dealing with the concern that is generally in the soundest economic position – i.e. most able to accede to the bargaining demands of the union. In multi-employer negotiations, on the other hand, the ability of the group to meet union demands is likely to be limited by the ability of the most marginal producer in the group to meet such demands.' Nat Weinberg, an official of the United Automobile Workers, goes on to enlarge on the economic principles which guide his union in the approach to such negotiations. 'To accept lower wages or less adequate benefits,' he writes, 'because a company is not as profitable or efficient as its competitors is, in effect, to subsidize managerial inefficiency out of the welfare of the workers and their families. If the inefficient companies could expect such a subsidy they would tend to perpetuate their inefficiency rather than to try to correct it.' And finally he explains how the wage standards (and therefore presumably the standards of productive efficiency) set by the big militant unions in motors and steel have an effect far beyond these industries: 'It is generally accepted . . . that any settlement made with a major corporation in the auto or steel industries in the United States will soon be reflected in varying degree throughout all organized industries and, to a lesser extent, even in unorganized companies and industries.'

But the method only works because these particular American unions are appropriately organized to fight their battles on a plant by plant basis. That means, first of all, that the workers in the plant are organized in a single union, which takes full charge of the negotiations. This is not by any means true of all American wage bargaining, but it works in the key manufacturing industries, where the wage pattern for the country as a whole is ultimately determined. The fact that a single plant is the basic unit of organization in these industrial unions, rather than a collection of men working in the same trade within a given geographical area, offers a considerable convenience to the employers, as well as to the trade union officials concerned. The employer is able to operate on a single contract for his whole works, and he can deal with one man on the union side, instead of a multiplicity of separate craft interests, in the event of a dispute. There was a striking illustration of the importance which American management attaches to this arrangement, when the Esso Petroleum Company built its big English refinery at Fawley a few years ago. The operation was a model of its kind, using the best U.S. techniques of organization, with Englishmen working under American

21

direction to reach unusually high standards of productivity.[3] The American in charge, Mr Cole, told an investigator afterwards that he would himself have refused to take on the task, if he had not been able to base his labour relations on a single contract for all the men. It had been possible to reach this arrangement with the local representative of the Confederation of Shipbuilding and Engineering Unions, an organization with forty unions affiliated to it. Mr Cole called liberally on the services of the local Confederation representative in dealing with disputes – a most unusual course – and, above all, refused to enter into any kind of bargaining with shop stewards on the spot. He regarded this as a vital issue of principle. Matters which affected the decisions of management had to be negotiated at a higher level than the man actually working on the job. The one serious piece of trouble which threatened during the building of the refinery came over the dismissal of an electrician shop steward, who had absented himself from work on union affairs.

The essential truth that lies behind this American management attitude is that a shop steward of a craft union is likely, in any matter involving changes in industrial methods, to be a reactionary force. He can hardly avoid being so on occasion, since his sole task, after all, is to seek the comfort and advantage of a particular group of men bound together by a fairly narrow interest. He is not supposed to look beyond this. The union official looking at the plant as a whole is more likely to accept the fact that a certain amount of change and discomfort at one spot may be unavoidable in the interests of the efficiency of the works as a whole, and therefore of its capacity to pay high wages. It is indeed the bane of British industrial relations that the initiative in so large an area of union affairs has passed to the shop steward. The official trade union leaders seem to spend half of their energy in avoiding being caught out by him or in placating him or in getting one move ahead of him. Judging by Mr Cole's experience in the building of the Esso Refinery, the union official is only too anxious to claw back some of the initiative, once the opportunity is offered him, and to make effective use of it.

The British system seems to give the union leaders the worst of both worlds. On the one hand, their concern with matters which have to be settled on a regional or industry-wide basis inevitably makes for remoteness from the man actually at the work bench. On the other hand, the technique of negotiating with hundreds, or even thousands, of employers at the same time means that they are not able to strike the best wage bargain for their members. Again, it is worth quoting the pointed comment of the American trade union leaders, taken from the same article which was mentioned earlier: 'Settlements made through the technique of key bargaining are geared to the capacity of the firm with the best ability to pay, while those concluded through industry-wide bargaining are apt to be limited by the ability of the firm least able to meet the union's demands.' When one considers that in the annual wage negotiations in Britain of the Confederation of Shipbuilding and Engineering Unions there are forty unions and some 4,500 employers involved at the same time, it is evident that the opportunities for marginal interests on either side to slow down the tempo of industrial change must be considerable. The forty unions have one overriding consideration to guide them: that nothing must be agreed which might put the job of any single one of their members in jeopardy. They are thus also the natural defenders of the interest of the marginal firm – in some instances more concerned about it than the employers' organization itself.

I do not wish to leave the impression that similar sectional interests in the American trade union movement have been completely swamped. There are plenty of demarcation troubles in American industry, more violent than in Britain, and labour is still capable of indulging in some pretty irrational and destructive activities. But the essential point is that there is a powerful vanguard of the trade union movement which has turned against such tactics. Those in the rear are bound in the end to be impressed by the sheer success of the vanguard in obtaining high wages. This situation has only come about since the establishment of the Congress of Industrial Organizations, as a body of militant 'industrial' unions, following a split in the U.S. labour movement during the 1930s. Before that, the American Federation of Labour provided leadership of a similar kind to that of the old craft unions in Britain. The establishment of the C.I.O. may be regarded as the revolution of the modern machine worker, creating for himself a new organization better adapted to the conditions of twentieth-century industry. Now the two organizations, A.F.L. and C.I.O., have come together again and made up their differences after many years of violent quarrelling. Today it is the C.I.O. techniques which set the tone for the American labour movement.

Unfortunately there has been no similar rebellion against the domination of craft union ideas in Britain. When the unskilled workers came forward and started to organize themselves, they were rapidly captured and integrated into the traditional trade union structure. The standard solution was to have a reliable union of skilled men standing at the centre of the new type of organization and holding an umbrella over a number of lesser trades formed into what was termed a 'general' union. The largest of these organizations today is the Transport and General Workers Union, which was originally formed by Mr Ernest Bevin around the dockers, a group which had been an organized and militant force since the earliest days of the labour movement. By now the 'general' workers of the union, employed in a great multitude of trades which have no connexion with one another, far outnumber the dockers or the groups employed in transport who are supposed to form the backbone of the organization. The dockers and the busmen are still its most militant sections. Similarly, the other big general union, the Municipal and General Workers, was originally formed around a nucleus of workers in the gas industry. The greater part of the trade union field is now divided between the older unions, still very much influenced by craft ideas, and the new general unions. The only industrial union on a really large scale, that is, one taking practically all the workers in a major industry regardless of the jobs that they do, is the National Union of Mineworkers. Apart from this, there are a few smaller unions organized on an industry-wide basis, notably in steel manufacture and in certain branches of textiles. But the possibilities of this form of organization have not apparently been grasped; in no case, except steel, does it operate in an industry where there is much scope for the new kind of militancy based on rising productivity. To be successful, the industrial union needs to operate on an ascending curve of demand for its products, combined with a steady technological advance, as the scale of production increases. In the big manufacturing industries, in metals and engineering, which provide the natural opening, the dominant voice is still that of the Amalgamated Engineering Union with its craft traditions. It is characteristic that in America the big compact unions of the steelworkers and the motorworkers make the running for the whole of the labour movement; while in Britain the motor-workers are not a coherent organization at all, and the steel-workers, although they present a model on a small scale of what a modern union ought to be, exercise no important influence on the level of wages outside.

It is possible to exaggerate the influence of trade union structure on the development of British and American industry. It will be pointed out, for example, that the American employers are by now getting wise to the technique of picking them off one by one, and finding the obvious answer to it. In 1956 the steel companies insisted on negotiating as a group with the trade union. No doubt, if this trend continues, the industrial unions will find themselves facing some of the problems that are familiar to their British colleagues. But the essential feature of modern American unionism – militancy based on genuine industrial understanding – remains. It is, for example, scarcely conceivable that an American union should refuse, as a matter of principle, to include in its wage negotiations a discussion of methods of increasing productivity, insisting that the wage demand was a separate issue – as our own Associated Society of Locomotive Engineers and Firemen did in the spring of 1957. It takes a craft union with its spiritual roots firmly embedded in the nineteenth century to stand pat on a position like that – and not even ask itself whether the formula, as a guide to working class action, does not make all wage increases perfectly pointless, since they would be swallowed forthwith by increases in prices.

One advantage which the British trade unions do possess over the American is the highly developed sense of political responsibility in the leadership here. Many of the senior people in the movement are used to thinking about the major issues of the day, and doing so in broad national terms. Unfortunately, their practice in dealing with such matters at the highest level, through the Trades Union Congress, seems to have remarkably little effect on the actual conduct of industrial relations at the level of the factory. When these men are speaking as the T.U.C., they often show a high degree of sophistication on economic, as well as political questions. They have admirably enlightened views on such matters as automation, they constantly stress the need for higher productivity, are concerned about restrictive practices, and talk sound sense on the subject of costs and prices. But, when it comes to it, the T.U.C. has no effective power whatever over its constituent unions. The men who talk so reasonably as members of the General Council revert at once to the role of violent watchdog of sectional interests, once they return to the fold of their own union executive. Thus there is no serious curb on the narrow parochial spirit of the shop stewards, who, as we saw earlier, dominate a large sector of trade union affairs. No one has the effective power to assert the larger interest of organized labour as a whole, against the blinkered vision of small groups of angry men acting independently on the shop floor.

Swedish experience shows what can be done by a responsible trade union leadership, with political traditions similar to our own, to rationalize industrial relations – once there is a constitutional structure which allows real authority to be exercised from the centre. The main point is that the Swedish Landesorganisation (the equivalent of the T.U.C.) is much richer than the individual unions belonging to it. It is, indeed, essential to secure its approval and financial backing in any industrial conflict. The individual trade unions are also exposed to financial pressure from the courts, which may impose considerable fines, in case of a breach of a labour contract. The central trade union organization provides its members with many useful services, economic, legal, and statistical. Swedish trade unionists are astonished to hear that in Britain, the T.U.C. does not calculate its own cost of living index, in spite of the fact that this is the usual point of departure for any wage negotiation, and that it does not carry out any kind of independent investigation into the state of unemployment, or of short-time and overtime working in individual industries. The Swedes themselves have in recent years gone further than this. Since their concern is with the level of real wages of their members, they recognize that they must be just as interested in price movements as in money-wage movements. Whether the benefit of successful wage claims will be wiped out by a subsequent rise in price depends chiefly on the amount of extra output that is going to be produced for people to spend their money on. A trade union movement which is trying to protect the real interests of its members must, therefore, equip itself to take an expert view on such matters as the trend of industrial output and the size of the national income. It must, according to current Swedish ideas, be prepared to negotiate on a national wages policy, unless it is ready to admit its indifference to the whole problem of prices and inflation. In recent years, the Landesorganisation has had to conduct a lengthy annual argument with the employers about detailed points of fact and interpretation in the figures for the national income, as a preliminary to fixing the maximum permissible wage increase, which will not be inflationary.

At one time, it looked as if the permanent executive section of the British T.U.C., the General Secretary's Department, might be strengthened to the point where it began to acquire some of the status and power which it has in Swedish practice. This was the period in the 1930s when Citrine, as General Secretary, having created a modern and efficient organization at the centre, went on to use it to bring a new coherence and initiative into the conduct of affairs by the T.U.C. One of the causes of the structural weakness in the British trade union movement since the war is that men of outstanding talent, like Citrine himself, and Sir James Bowman, the present Chairman of the National Coal Board, have been drawn away into the management of the new nationalized undertakings. Others have been diverted into the whole-time pursuit of national politics. Ernest Bevin, who spent the last decade of his life in ministerial positions of one kind and another, is the outstanding example of such a loss. The pull of a Labour Party, stronger than ever before, combined with a lot of interesting industrial jobs created by the party's nationalizing efforts, have withdrawn several useful people from the upper ranks of the trade union movement. The trade union problem, in the end, is one of men.

But is the lack of sufficient supply of able young men coming up into positions of power perhaps another aspect of the general trouble that goes under the heading of being 'undynamic'? It seems to me an extremely broad thesis to use in order to explain what is after all a fairly short-lived phenomenon, thus far, on a narrow front. It is highly probable that if the trade union movement faced up to the fact that it had to pay higher salaries and carry a larger full-time staff to contend with modern conditions in industry, it would get the men that it needs. What is more worrying is the absence of any reforming urgency in the face of the blatant inadequacy of the present trade union structure – and indeed, of many other inadequacies like it in other fields of economic life. It is the constant conspiracy to make-do-and-mend which distinguishes our society. It is part of the cultural atmosphere, as pervasive as damp weather. It appears in the exaggerated anxiety not to put a foot wrong; not to cause trouble. It also manifests itself in a certain lack of personal vigour in the business of making money, compared, for example, with people in the United States or even in some countries on the continent of Europe. There is certainly no popular myth here that the big opportunity of one's lifetime is probably just around the corner. People are not all that interested in opportunities, and scarcely believe in corners. The effect of this attitude of scepticism towards the whole subject of achievement makes itself felt at all levels. Here, as a sample, is the opinion of a British engineer, writing after a period of close study of American engineering production: 'Most important of the reasons for higher productivity in the U.S.A. is the general atmosphere there that nothing is impossible and most things are worth trying. In contrast, the attitude here seems to me to be that most things are impossible and not worth trying.'[4]

In spite of all this, I find the attempt to explain Britain's economic failure solely by reference to a peculiar and inherent trait of the national character not very plausible. After all, a society changes its moods. The cultural atmosphere which has just been described is not, according to the historical evidence available, a permanent feature of the island. Nor does it stick to Englishmen when they go to work abroad. Moreover, it is impossible to measure in any way the economic effects of this spiritual state; if one is personally irritated by it, one may be inclined to exaggerate the material consequences. But allowing that there is a certain lack of productive vigour more in evidence in this country than elsewhere at the moment, the cause may, I think, be found in the inhibiting psychological influence of British economic conditions for some time past. People's attitudes have certainly been affected by the feeling that if anyone thinks of something really new, useful or attractive, it is ten to one that the community will not be able to afford the cost of making it. There is still today in Britain an overwhelming sense of public penury. New ideas are not very highly prized, partly no doubt because it takes so long to translate the idea into some new thing actually on the ground. Everything takes so long because there is never a surplus of the necessary physical resources available to get on with a new job quickly.

THE MISSING SURPLUS

An economy without a surplus is like an army without a reserve: it cannot cope with the unforeseen situation. In consequence, the very thing on which the national myth is most emphatic, the capacity to 'muddle through' – a characteristic phrase of understatement to describe the flexibility which has allowed Englishmen to deal with the unexpected by brilliant improvisation – is absent from the story of British economic development in the later postwar years. During the first phase of the actual transition from war to peace there was still some of it. But later on, except in one or two special fields, like atomic energy and aircraft, where the state intervened directly to ensure that any resources required were made available for the men breaking through these particular technological frontiers, there has been little evidence of improvising, brilliant or otherwise, because the necessary physical means for improvisation have been lacking. And this in the end induces a habit of mind with a positive antipathy towards any kind of economic surplus. It is so comfortable to be without one; it means that everything has to be organized and planned well in advance, if it is to get done at all. There is not the endless chopping and changing, rushing after the foibles of this particular customer to-day and entirely different set of foibles of another customer to-morrow. Because there are so many delays, any industrial scheme, once formulated, tends to become fixed and sacrosanct; there is always the risk that if something is altered, everything will be held up still further, all along the line. When I describe this situation as 'comfortable', what I mean is that it allows a lot of people to dispense with the need for thought and initiative. A surplus means uncertainty; a shortage is secure. There has in fact been a curious reluctance in postwar Britain to change the psychological postures that went with wartime scarcities. Was it entirely accidental that we clung to all kinds of food rationing longer than anyone else? It is extraordinary, at any rate, how long the British people were willing to accept without demur the awkwardnesses of life, the petty shopkeeper tyrannies, which went with rationing. I do not think that it is fanciful to suspect that there was some other kind of satisfaction which provided, at least, a measure of psychological compensation for these evils.

Of course the very notion of an economic surplus is popularly associated with the horrors of the 1930s. A surplus of physical resources, it is believed, inevitably translates itself very quickly into mass unemployment. This is plainly true in a period of economic stagnation like the 1930s. But it is no accident that the two countries which had the biggest surplus, and also the biggest unemployment problem then – the United States and Germany – are also the countries which have benefited especially from the opportunities for economic growth in the postwar world.

The argument about the need for an economic surplus must not be equated with the familiar thesis of certain economists about the benefits of having a larger amount of unemployment. A big reserve of unemployed is only one of many possible kinds of surpluses, and certainly the most wasteful. Moreover, it will usually be found that those who assert the need for more unemployment are less concerned about the advantage of having some kind of reserve, which will allow the nation to take advantage of any new economic opportunity more rapidly, than about the psychological effect of the existence of a lot of employed on the balance of bargaining power between employers and wage earners. Unemployment is not seen as a means of speeding up economic development, but as a way of making the whole economic process more 'orderly' – above all by curbing the inflationary rise in prices which has been a feature of the postwar period.

There has also in recent years been a constant hankering after another kind of surplus – a surplus in the external balance of payments. Year after year Chancellors of the Exchequer have asked the people of this country to bend their energies towards this end – as if it was a self-evident truth that it is necessarily a good thing for any nation to earn a great deal more abroad than it spends. There are of course particular circumstances in which a surplus of foreign exchange could be very useful. No one would deny that Britain's economic affairs would be much easier to run if we had a bigger gold reserve; we could then afford to take risks in embarking on a policy of expansion, which governments shy away from at the moment. But that is not at all the same thing as saying that we ought to pinch and scrape at home, economize on our building plans, forgo machinery that we want ourselves so that it can be exported, hold back production here so as to keep down the size of our import bill – all in order to increase the surplus in our balance of payments. That kind of surplus, when it is shovelled straight into the gold reserve, is the least productive of all. For example the machine costing say £10,000, which was sent abroad, instead of being installed in a factory at home, might well have added £3,000 or more each year to the national output. The proceeds of this £10,000 sale of machinery abroad, which go into the reserve, produce nothing so long as they remain there. And if they are turned into dollars and invested in U.S. Government securities, they may produce £300–£400 of foreign exchange income for the country in a year in the form of interest at 3–4 per cent. The point is that a balance of payments surplus bought at the cost of retarding Britain's economic development is not worth having.

What is worth having is the kind of surplus which would help to cushion any sudden shock affecting the balance of payments – the sort of thing that happened in 1951 during the Korean boom, when the cost of our imports rocketed upwards, and again in 1955, when there was a boom at home which caused a lot more imports to come in. A bigger gold reserve would have been a great help then. But almost as useful would have been a reserve of productive capacity for making steel or machinery or ships or vehicles. The advantage of having a big gold reserve is that it is a surplus which covers a wide variety of contingencies, whereas it is always possible that the surplus of physical capacity may happen not to be in the right sector of the economy. After all, there has for some years been a growing surplus of cotton textile machinery in this country, which has been no help to anyone. However, in practice, it is clear that if Britain had concentrated since the war on establishing a handsome margin of extra capacity at a few critical points in the economy, for example in the steel industry and the machine tool industry, the balance of payments would have had a most effective safeguard.

One difficulty is, however, that although it may be good public policy to aim at the creation of reserve productive capacity – as a kind of national insurance in an age of expansion – it may not be good private business. The ideal situation for a private concern is when it can be guaranteed that every piece of equipment installed will be employed one hundred per cent throughout its lifetime. If that ideal could be achieved, the return on investment would be maximized. But, of course, there are all sorts of compensations that go with a more venturesome policy: the firm which has the extra capacity during a period when there is a shortage of the goods which it produces, can charge very high prices for its marginal output. It may well be able to finance even a risky investment out of these additional profits. There is no set of economic principles which meets this situation; it is impossible to judge in advance which would be the wiser course for a businessman to take. The actual choice is largely a matter of temperament, and is also influenced by whatever happens to be the public mood at the time. There is little doubt that over the whole of the postwar period, the chief aim of the people in charge of the British steel industry – and this applies also to the interlude of nationalization – has been to avoid a surplus of capacity at all costs. The likelihood that it would be necessary to import steel from abroad to supplement British supplies of certain products was accepted as a sound commercial calculation. On balance, it was believed, the British industry would lose less by having to import at high prices during good times than the foreigner would lose by having surplus capacity in bad times. In fact, over the whole of the postwar period the Belgians, who have had just such a surplus of steel-making capacity, have done a great deal better than the British. For in the event the good times have outnumbered the bad; and the British steel industry is now adjusting itself, belatedly and still rather hesitantly, to the probability that this will continue to be so. In this case, as in shipbuilding and several other of the heavy industries, it seems to have been unusually difficult for British management to rid itself of the depression mentality. The defensive attitude, operating constantly in the shadow of an imaginary slump, has not been by any means confined to labour. Indeed it could be argued that the reactionary views of certain sections of organized labour, springing from the basic disbelief in an expanding economy, have been much influenced by the views of the boss. He didn't believe that capitalism could be made depression-proof either.

However, the real significance of Britain's missing surplus is not the absence of an additional steelworks and some engineering factories on the ground. Even if these precious things were suddenly presented to us, the problem would not be solved. These assets would certainly help towards the desired end; but the kind of surplus which allows a country to grow very fast, on the one hand, and on the other hand provides it with a useful safeguard against an adverse movement in its balance of payments, is of a rather more complicated nature. It consists of the resources that remain over, after two things have been subtracted: (1) the goods and services that are bought to meet ordinary consumer needs, (2) the resources that are needed to keep the country's productive equipment in good shape. (The second of these two items is important, because a great deal of the fixed investment done annually in this country – rather more than half of it – is to replace assets that are being worn out in the course of work. The stock of productive equipment and buildings in an advanced industrial country is large, and a substantial part of the national resources produced in any one year has to be devoted to keeping it up to scratch.)

R—B 33

THE BIT OF INVESTMENT THAT COUNTS

It is of course only the bit that is left over after replacement needs have been met, that really adds anything to the stock of national wealth. Economists distinguish between these two things by calling the total 'gross investment', and the part of it that constitutes a genuine addition to the national wealth 'net investment'.[5] Net investment represents the surplus of national resources which an economy requires in order to grow in productive power. Other things being equal, the bigger the surplus the more rapid the rate of growth. There is one further slight complication about the constituents of the surplus. After you have deducted from the national product the things that people use for their ordinary consumption needs and the replacements of worn out capital equipment, the resources that remain may go either into building new factories, etc., or they may go into increasing stocks of raw materials and other goods. Stocks are in fact an important part of the national wealth: the existing accumulation is the equivalent of about half of the nation's annual output. So it is obvious that even a comparatively small movement of stocks in any one year, either up or down, could make a big difference to the amount of resources that are left over for spending or investment. But in the ordinary way, although the nation needs bigger stocks as production expands, the extra resources that are required in a normal year for this purpose are fairly small. 1951 was an exceptional year when the sudden rise in stocks precipitated a crisis. But in 1955 and 1956, for example, the increase in stocks absorbed something between one-sixth and one-eighth of net investment inside Britain. When these extra stocks are left out of account, the surplus that is actually devoted to the creation of new assets on the ground is called 'net fixed investment'. It is on this that attention has to be concentrated, since the movement in stocks from one year to another is a bit haphazard, depending on things like war scares or the anticipation of a rise in prices, which may make businessmen fill up their warehouses more than usual.

The crucial sum, which is likely to determine a country's rate of growth over a period of years, is the ratio of net fixed investment to the national product – or better still, for the sake of precision, its ratio to the national product *less* the amount that has to be devoted to the replacement of the country's capital assets. That is called the 'net national product', as opposed to the 'gross national product', which includes everything. The net national product is worth looking at in this context, because it is the sum that the community has available for spending in any one year, without running down its own capital. The ratio which we are considering is the nearest thing to a measure of the rate of accumulation of wealth. Ideally, in order to see how fast a given stock of wealth is increasing, one should start with a valuation of the stock and then calculate the percentage addition to it represented by net investment each year. But to try and put a value on all the items that make up a country's stock of wealth is pretty well an impossible task. In the end the valuer is always driven back to saying about some pieces of property that they are worth the figure that he names, because they produce a certain measurable amount of wealth each year. In other words, he does not derive his answer by some direct assessment of market value of the asset, but indirectly, by reference to what it contributes to the national product each year. The limitations of our instruments for economic measurement thus make it necessary to assess the rate of growth in relation to the national product, and to relate this at second hand to the national stock of wealth.

Once one looks at the ratio of capital accumulation during the 1950s in this way, there ceases to be any mystery about our poor productive record compared with the rest of Europe. Net fixed investment as a proportion of the net national product has been consistently lower here than in any of the other industrial countries. In 1950–1 it was about 5 per cent. Since then it has been rising, and the investment boom of 1955–6 has brought it up to something above 7 per cent. But this only means that we have now surpassed the rate of accumulation of Belgium, and are probably just about level with France. We are still well below Germany's 15 per cent or Italy's 12 per cent.[6] Norway heads the list with a rate of accumulation of 20–22 per cent, financed it is fair to say with the help of a good deal of foreign money, and Finland is only slightly behind. This also seems to be about the level of accumulation reached in Russia during the 1950s, though comparisons are especially difficult here, because of the different statistical treatment of net investment in the Soviet figures. The interesting point is the demonstration that it does not require a totalitarian régime, with a high degree of compulsory saving imposed by the state on a people who have no means of redress against it, in order to achieve a rate of accumulation which is up to Soviet standards.

What now appears so extraordinary in the light of these comparisons is the view that the belated rise in British investment from 1954 onwards was a kind of 'capital spending spree', and had to be curbed before it got out of hand. The final outcome of the investment boom, which was held chiefly responsible for the balance-of-payments crisis in 1955–6, was that something between 1 and 2 per cent more of the national product was shifted over to the creation of new capital assets in the form of factories, machinery, plant, and buildings. That extra 1–2 per cent is of course well worth having.

Because the level from which we started was so low, even a small increase looks spectacular. One has to examine the make-up of British investment more closely, the actual things which were being constructed out of the rather meagre surplus of capital resources, to see exactly why this is so. In 1954 this surplus amounted to about 6 per cent of the national income;[7] it was divided about half and half into 'productive' investment, i.e. in industry, agriculture, commerce, and public utilities, and 'unproductive', i.e. housing, social services, and other government expenditure. I do not call the latter 'unproductive' in any pejorative sense – much of this expenditure is in fact devoted to the most useful things that any community can buy – but to indicate that these things do not add in any direct way to the capacity of the community for producing more physical wealth. It is obvious that in an indirect way they may make a very important contribution. The extra houses which allow workers to move into areas where industry is being held up by labour shortages, or the extra schools and colleges which help to give the country more scientists and technicians are obviously important aids to the advance of production. This is therefore only a rough-and-ready division between the kind of investment which is predominantly an addition to the stock of productive capacity of the country and that which is not.

Now the whole of the increase in investment since 1954 has gone into the 'productive' sector of the economy. Housebuilding, which is much the biggest part of the 'unproductive' investment, has actually fallen off. Thus the extra 1 per cent of the national income that was shifted into investment represents an increase of no less than one third in the rate of installation of new industrial and other productive equipment. For in 1954 this investment absorbed 3 per cent of the national income, and it has since risen to something over 4 per cent. The increase was made possible by the deliberate policy of holding back housebuilding. During most of the period since the end of the war, it has only been the curb on residential construction which has saved Britain from the worst consequences of the very low level of investment maintained in this country. There is something in Mr Bevan's wry comment on the big Conservative building programme of 1952–3: 'Any fool can build houses'. He ought to have added in fairness, however, that it takes more than a housing shortage to get factories built; for the Labour Party's record in this matter is as bad as that of the Conservatives: there have always been at least as many good reasons produced on the Left as on the Right for cutting investment first in any emergency. The only point that is worth making is that matters would have been even worse if, given the limited amount of investment which either party appeared to be willing to regard with any favour, they had allowed housing to absorb a bigger share. Investment in projects required for the social services has also been comparatively small in this country. It is only in work connected with defence that capital expenditure financed by the public authorities in Britain has been markedly higher than anywhere else in Europe.

THE FECUND SACRIFICE

The arithmetic of the 1 per cent shift of the national resources into investment suggests an encouraging line of thought. In recent years the real output of the British economy, that is excluding the effect of the rise in prices, has risen by about 3 per cent each year.

That is the average rate from 1949, when industrial production returned to something like normal after the war, until 1955. (1956–7 is left out of account, because these were wholly abnormal years, when for the first time since the war industrial capacity was deliberately underemployed, as a result of the policy of the credit squeeze.) Assuming that 3 per cent per annum is the normal current rate of increase in the national product, then if a national agreement could be reached that for just one year there should be no rise whatever in consumption, that the standard of living of everyone should remain static, so that the whole of the extra output could go into developing our resources, the result would be to make it possible almost to double the level of 'productive' investment. This now represents about 4 per cent of the national income, and with the addition of the normal increment in the nation's resources over a period of twelve months, say about 3 per cent, the figure would go up to 7 per cent. Even if, after this short interlude, the whole community returned to a round of riotous living, its productive power would have been permanently strengthened. Of course if the moratorium on higher living standards could be extended for two or three years, the additional productive power created in the interval would put the British economy onto an entirely new plane where it could advance much faster; it would be able to make up for the lost years of static living standards very quickly, and thereafter secure a continuing and much more rapid rise, without any strain on the national resources.

The explanation for this apparent magic, flowing from a short period of restraint, is chiefly that modern industrial equipment is extremely productive. Also, since we are already so rich in this country, forgoing even the relatively small proportion of the normal increase in wealth from year to year produces a very considerable sum. An investment in new manufacturing capacity worth £100 will probably produce at least £33 of additional output each year.[8] On this ratio of capital to output of about 3 to 1, you would, if you could invest the *whole* of your output, be able to double your manufacturing capacity in less than three years.[9] This would then permit an increase of production by 100 per cent. Of course, nothing like this could ever happen in real life.

In any case, the problem of British investment can be met without an actual cut in the supply of ordinary consumer goods; all that is necessary is that the total of such goods consumed in this country should be the same for, say, three years running, and that the normal increase in manufacturing output should be devoted to the creation of new machinery and plant. Three years of investing the 3 per cent annual increment would create an additional stock of capital equipment with an output capacity equal to the original 3 per cent of the national income. Thus at the end of the period, there would be enough extra plant to double the annual *addition* to manufacturing output. The rate of growth would rise to 6 per cent.

In order to make this possible, however, a lot of ancillary services, like roads, railways, offices, would have to be enlarged too – or otherwise the whole manufacturing process would get seized up – and these things do not all produce the same fruitful yield on capital invested as ordinary equipment installed in a factory. £100 invested here would produce less – in some cases considerably less – than £33 of additional output. So the three-year plan could not be expected to double the rate of growth over the economy as a whole. We produce so much else besides manufactured goods; the latter represent rather less than half of the national output. But it would not be unreasonable to expect that at the end of three years, the country would be producing 5 per cent more each year, instead of the recent average of 3 per cent. Thereafter we could look to a more rapid rise in our living standards than anything we have had in the past, with our productive capacity continuing to grow at a satisfactory rate. It would not grow as fast as during the three-year hot-house period, but the rate ought to be up to the normal European standard. If we used our extra production capacity properly we could afford to consume quite a bit more, and still go on getting richer. This is the essential trick which the Soviet countries under Russian leadership have learned – that it takes comparatively few years of horrid privation, backed by a ruthless tyranny, to create the initial stock of productive wealth, which makes it possible thereafter for an economy to grow at a vastly accelerated pace.

The tendency of Britain to grow more slowly than its competitors on the continent of Europe is no new thing. It has been in evidence ever since the beginning of the century, and even for some years before that. At first people comforted themselves with the reflection that Britain was bound to lose some of the advantages which it had gained by being first in the field of industrialization, as other nations began to industrialize themselves. And later on, the British failure to sustain a rapid rate of economic growth was masked by the effects of two wars and a slump. Each of the two wars caused a bigger setback on the Continent than it did here. In Britain, war actually provided the missing stimulant to investment in manufacturing industry – a most powerful stimulant in some cases where expansion had previously been held back by cautious calculations of prospective profit. After the Second World War, in particular, Britain emerged with a considerably enhanced industrial capacity in the engineering industries. After both wars German industrial production fell sharply; but the rate of advance, once the recovery began, was much more rapid than in this country. Indeed, Britain's industrial record during the years of normal peacetime prosperity that we have had in this century is consistently poor. Both in 1900–14 and again in the 1920s, in the period of prosperity before the crash in 1929, British output grew at a slower pace than that of the other industrial countries in Northern and Western Europe. But Britain managed to make up for lost time in the years of the great depression in the 1930s, when the nations on the continent of Europe found the normal outlets for their exports of manufactured goods largely blocked, and entered on a period of stagnation. It was during this period, from 1929 to 1938, that British industrial output increased by one quarter.[10] Britain's political advantage as the centre of an empire of primary producing countries, which was used to foster the development of imperial trade at a time when world commerce was shrinking, went far to compensate for the failure of the British economy to expand at a satisfactory pace in normal times. Political successes of this kind and military victory in two wars have helped to save us from some of the worst consequences of our lack of economic vigour during the first half of the twentieth century.

The evidence as it stands seems to point to the dismal conclusion that British industry as a whole is content with a slower rate of progress than is regularly achieved by other nations similarly placed. This is a generalization covering a wide range of variegated economic activity; it does not touch the record of technical advance and the initiative in developing new products in several individual industries. A special factor is that during much of the twentieth century the cotton textile industry, which was the spearhead of Britain's industrial advance in the nineteenth century, has been in a state of continuous and sometimes rapid decline. This has undoubtedly been a big psychological depressive. The bursting vigour and optimism that Manchester supplied to English political and economic life during the Victorian era has been sorely missed. Neither Birmingham nor any other of the boom towns of the twentieth century have been able to replace it. Besides, industrialists, particularly those of the second and third generation, are perhaps even more inclined than other folk to go around the world observing calamity, and muttering to themselves: 'There but for the grace of God . . .' To many no doubt the decline of Lancashire provided a warning, above all, of the dangers of investment.

HOW THE BRITISH SHIPBUILDERS ALLOWED JAPAN TO OVERTAKE THEM

Unless one runs to these somewhat speculative historical and psychological explanations, it is very hard indeed to account for the extraordinary behaviour of certain British industries in recent years. Shipbuilding is perhaps the most remarkable case of all. Since the end of the Second World War there has been an almost continuous boom in the shipyards of the world. In no field did Britain have greater initial advantages when the transition was made from war to peace – a labour force in being, uniquely skilled, prosperous yards which had been operating at a high tempo for half a dozen years, and a worldwide reputation for making a high quality product. What happened? The answer is that in the post-war decade Britain achieved the longest shipbuilding order book in the history of man, increased actual output by a moderate amount, and lost the first place as the biggest shipbuilding country in the world to an ex-enemy nation, Japan, whose yards only restarted work seriously five years after the war was over. During the earlier post-war years in the 1940s, the failure of British shipbuilding can be wholly explained by the shortage of steel. But this particular excuse had worn very thin indeed by the middle of the 1950s. A vigorous shipbuilding industry with a determination to expand would have obtained its steel plate from somewhere, just as the motor industry managed to lay its hands on the sheet steel that it needed, in spite of the inadequacy of home-produced supplies.

The striking thing about the British ship industry that emerges, when one comes to look beyond the blanket excuse of steel shortage which has covered its activities ever since the war, is its stubborn refusal to invest in the creation of more productive capacity. Things may now be changing, but in most years during the 1950s the amount of money spent on plant and equipment can have been barely sufficient to cover normal wear and tear and obsolescence in the shipyards. During the four crucial years from 1951 to 1954, when first the German yards and later the Japanese were going ahead with large scale re-equipment, British shipbuilding firms spent £4m annually on their fixed assets. For an industry which was producing an average of £120m a year at this time and employing over 200,000 workers, this is a figure which is so low that it would suggest to the outside observer that someone was trying to get out of the business, and in the meantime was determined to spend as little as possible on it. In the normal course the cost of replacing worn-out plant and equipment in British industry is estimated to be around 5 per cent of the value of the output produced. This is an average covering a wide variety of different needs – it means that one-twentieth of production of the whole of British industry has to be set aside for replacement costs – but there is no reason to think that the needs of shipbuilding are significantly below the national average. The 5 per cent rule works out in their case at £6m which is half as much again as the shipbuilders of Britain actually spent. But even if, in spite of statistical appearances to the contrary, they were in fact managing to maintain the industry's capacity to produce at something like the level at which it emerged after the end of the war, this would have allowed nothing for development required by the new techniques in shipbuilding or for the changing needs of the shipowners themselves. The men responsible for the huge growth of tanker tonnage in the international oil trade since the war have been keenly receptive to any new ideas which would allow them to achieve lower costs of operation or quicker voyages. But none of these ideas have come from the country which, ever since the invention of modern shipbuilding, has been the largest shipbuilder in the world. Others have led in the new technique; Britain has followed. In view of the record of low investment year after year since the war, it scarcely comes as a surprise that when the Greek shipowners were developing the giant tanker, which is going to revolutionize the business of oil transportation, they had to go to the Germans and Japanese first.

The explanation given is that the British yards are always so full. But why are they, whatever the circumstances, always so much fuller than everyone else's? It is not only that the demand for the British product is exceptionally heavy – although it fortunately remains true that the skill of the British industry and its reputation for reliability still count very much in its favour. The reason why British yards are permanently choked up emerges clearly from a comparison of recent figures of output in Britain and in Japan, which in 1956 took the lead as the world's biggest builder of ships. In the middle of 1956 Britain had 2,028,000 tons of shipping under construction and Japan had 1,116,000 tons under construction. In the following twelve months Britain completed 1,417,000 tons, but Japan got through 1,993,000 tons. The answer is that it took Japanese shipbuilders nine months to build a vessel, while the same vessel took eighteen months to be completed in a British yard. Nor can this extraordinary discrepancy be dismissed simply as a reflection of the difference in quality of workmanship. Lloyd's Register of Shipping is worth quoting on this point. 'The quality of workmanship in Japanese shipyards is high,' it says in its 1957 annual report, 'and the speed of production, without complications of piecework or too troublesome trade demarcations, is impressive. Keen interest is shown in all new developments in engineering. . . .'

Whatever the special difficulties caused by the habits of labour in British shipyards – and there is no doubt that rules created long ago, dealing with who exactly shall not do what, hold up production – the under-equipment of this country's shipbuilding industry since the war must bear a large share of the blame for the fact that it has so rapidly lost first place to Japan. The industry still produces less than it did in 1913, when it launched 1,930,000 tons. In 1957 its order book rose to nearly 7,000,000 tons – a total that has only been exceeded once before, and that was in 1952 – and yet for some reason or other the rate of production of $1\frac{1}{2}$ million tons a year is thought to be a reasonable target. Meanwhile the Japanese, who before the war had a capacity of less than half a million tons, have managed to raise their rate of output to over 2 million tons a year. It would be wrong, moreover, to think of Japan as an isolated or exceptional case. There are several other countries which have invested heavily in shipbuilding since the war, and are now showing the benefits in higher productivity and a more rapid rate of construction than Britain. Germany and Sweden are outstanding: in 1956 they completed ships as rapidly as the Japanese, and about twice as fast as Britain. Germany has greatly expanded her capacity above pre-war, and now produces about one million tons of shipping a year. It is no coincidence that both in Germany and in Sweden the governments have given big tax reliefs to businesses which reinvest their profits in the shipbuilding industry. Indeed at one time during the period of German recovery in the early 1950s, businessmen were going around begging for the opportunity to invest their money in the shipyards at Hamburg and Kiel, in order to cut down their tax liability. Evidently many of them were successful.

NOTES

1. *Free Trade in Europe*, Stationery Office, 1957.
2. *Labour News from the U.S.*, published by the American Embassy, London.
3. A. P. Gray and Mark Abrams, *The Construction of the Esso Refinery, Fawley*, British Institute of Management.
4. *Target*, a monthly bulletin on productivity issued by the Treasury, March 1952.

5. The distinction between *gross* and *net* investment is not nearly as clearcut in practice as it appears in theory. When a businessman replaces a worn-out machine, he is usually able to put down something better because of technical improvements that have been made in the interval. The very act of replacement therefore usually results in a *net* increase in productive capacity on the ground. This can be important when a nation is engaged in a large-scale process of scrapping obsolete equipment: there are considerable technological windfalls, new ways of doing things, gains from improvements in factory layout, which no one was willing to consider while the old machines were in place. British industry has certainly obtained major benefits of this kind since the war, benefits which find no counterpart in the figures for net investment. In spite of all this, the conceptual difference between *gross* and *net* investment is a clear and important one, providing a measurement, however crude, of the process of economic growth.

6. These international comparisons (derived mainly from *Economic Survey of Europe in 1955*, Economic Commission for Europe, Geneva, 1956) cannot be treated as precise measures of the varying rate of accumulation in different countries. In making comparisons of this kind there are all sorts of difficulties. To name only one, there are very big differences in the cost of building and capital equipment in different countries. Thus, the cost of new machinery is especially high in Italy, compared with the prices of other consumer goods that go into the national product. As a result Italian fixed investment tends to show up as a bigger proportion of the national product than it would if the internal price structure were the same as in other countries. It is impossible to allow for all these special factors. The comparative figures can therefore be treated only as a rough guide to orders of magnitude, and not as precise measures of differences in the rate of growth in different countries.

7. The 'national income' is the true income of the nation, that is, what remains over from its output, after setting aside the sums required to replace worn-out capital assets. It is the same thing as the 'net national product'. Throughout this book, national income, gross national product, etc., are always taken – except when expressly stated otherwise – at market prices, i.e. including the value of indirect taxes on expenditure. This is the usual basis for international comparisons, but differs from standard British practice.

8. There is a good deal of uncertainty about this whole subject of how much capital it takes to produce a certain amount of output. It is rather surprising that on a matter which is of such close concern to

businesses, there is so little accurate information available. What is clear from the limited data that has been collected is that there are huge variations in the capital/output ratio between one industry and the next. Some industries produce as much as two-thirds of the value of their fixed assets in the course of a year; others produce only one-seventh. The arithmetic is also complicated by somewhat technical questions about what should be included within the definition of 'fixed assets'. The average, according to some calculations done by Mr T. Barna and published in the *Journal of the Royal Statistical Society*, volume 120, Part I, 1957, for British manufacturing industry as a whole is a capital/output ratio of 2·2. This means that £100 worth of equipment contributes on average about £45 to the gross national product. Other calculations suggest however that in manufacturing capital assets are considerably more productive than this. Much obviously depends on how you put a value on your capital assets. It is easy enough to deal with a new piece of equipment; but when you are still using a machine that you bought fifteen or twenty years ago, when the price level was quite different, and which you have written down in value as the years have gone by, the complications are considerable.

My argument, which is based on the hypothesis that it takes £100 of new fixed assets to produce £33 of additional wealth a year, probably understates the case. It is intended to allow something for the possibility that as the total stock of capital assets increases, any extra piece of equipment installed tends to produce a rather lower return than the average. My own view is that there is very little evidence as yet to support the economists' pet theory of the diminishing rate of return on capital. On the contrary, such evidence as is available suggests that in the United States at any rate a given amount of new capital assets installed in the 1950s produces considerably more additional output than capital of the same value produced back in the 1920s. (See Barna in *The Banker*, April 1957.) With automation immediately ahead, I cannot see any prospect of a serious decline in the productive power of new capital investment.

The more important point is that in a developed industrial society new additions to manufacturing capacity require more capital expenditure to support them, in a lot of ancillary fields, than in a less developed society. The roads, the cinemas, and the other amenities cost more. I am impressed, however, by the crude arithmetical fact that during the six years 1949–55, a net investment in all fixed assets in Britain of around 6 per cent was accompanied by a 3 per cent increase in the real national product each year. The British labour force was increasing by an average of 1 per cent per year during this period; making an allowance for the amount of production that would have resulted from the employment of this manpower alone, without the aid of any extra machines – rather less than 1 per cent – the remainder, 2 per cent plus, represents something over one-third of the value of the net fixed investment during this period. Of course, there were other factors – e.g. better organization of labour, elimination of bottlenecks in supplies – making for increased output; but it does appear that over the British economy as a whole the capital/output ratio for new investment was of the order of 3:1. For manufacturing alone it must have been considerably better than this.

9. The calculation allows for the amount that has to be set aside each year to keep the original assets up to scratch and to replace them as they are worn out.

10. *Industrial Statistics 1900–1955*, O.E.E.C.

CHAPTER THREE

WHERE THE MONEY GOES

THE case of shipbuilding which was analysed in some detail in the last chapter as an example of the consequences of low investment is by no means unique. I have singled it out not because it is the most important instance, but because it is in some ways the most depressing one: a British industry with the cards all stacked in its favour, which has strikingly failed to exploit its natural advantage. There are certain British industries – cotton textiles is one – which have suffered since the war because conditions in world trade have been against them. But the shipbuilders have never had it so good. Their experience also provides pretty clear proof that it is not any lack of good and profitable business openings which has held up investment in British industry. Rather, it seems, there is a climate of opinion which tends to make businessmen invest much or little. With a few honourable exceptions – notably chemicals and oil, together with the two major industries, atomic energy and aircraft, which have benefited from state subsidies in one form or another – it has for too long been too little. And the psychological accompaniment of this climate of low investment is a tendency to eschew innovation, to be slower than other people in adapting yourself to a changing trend in design, in technology, or simply in popular taste. Thus, to take a familiar example, British manufacturers were inordinately tardy in recognizing that the motor scooter had come into public favour, and they showed little interest for some years in the moped – the bicycle with a small motor attached – in spite of the indications from the Continent that a lot of post-war pedal cyclists would pay for a little extra horsepower. The consequences of this particular failure have now made themselves felt in the British balance of payments. In 1957 Britain became a net importer of motor-cycles – a dismal end for the country which pioneered the motorbike. It is equally noticeable – though this has not yet caused the same direct damage to the balance of payments – that British manufacturers failed to exploit the market for the new miniature cars, until they were shown how by their Continental competitors. In general, it is true that the innovations for which Britain has been responsible since the war, e.g. in the field of chemicals, in synthetic fibres, in aircraft design, all come from industries with a record of continuous high investment. The moral seems to be that where there is room to expand there is room for new ideas. It is not that the other industries are con-genitally incapable of novelty in thinking; it is that management has failed to provide the occasion for it.

To the question why British industry has not invested more in its plant and equipment, one simple answer is that the country as a whole did not have the necessary resources available for such investment. People blame the defence programme, the greedy consumer, the social services, according to personal choice. Now the first thing to be observed is that even if it were true that these things had absorbed an unduly large proportion of the nation's resources, that by itself would not explain why industrialists had so obligingly cut back investment. They were under no compul-sion to do so, at any rate in the 1950s. They could have insisted on investing more; they had money with which to do so. That would of course have overloaded the economy still further and added to inflation. But it was not the spontaneous fear of in-flation for the community at large that prevented the average industrialist from investing more in the re-equipment of his own works. He was responding to pressure from the Government. For the fact is that whenever the Government has faced an economic emergency since the war, it has reached out, like a blind man with a single automatic gesture at his command, and taken a smack at investment. In 1949, in 1951, and again in 1955, 1956, and 1957 the remedy chosen for the deficit in the balance of pay-ments has been to cut back expenditure on new plant and equip-ment. The latest series of cuts, from 1955 onwards, failed initially to achieve their object; the investment boom went on for several years, regardless. But the earlier efforts, in 1949 and 1951, particularly in their effect on some of the nationalized in-dustries directly subject to the Government's axe, were all too successful.

The truth is, then, that British investment has been held back since the war, first because the balance of payments has been weak – our foreign exchange income has barely covered our outgoings – and secondly, because the Government has chosen to regard industrial investment as the first expendable item in an emergency. It has been constantly tempted by the idea that the balance of payments should be strengthened by a deliberate policy of denying capital goods to British industry, so that more of them would be sent abroad. There has also been the more general notion that by reducing the pressure of demand at home, on critical materials like steel and on the skilled labour absorbed in investment projects, the balance of trade would tend to improve. This would follow, because imports of materials would fall as home demand slackened, while the export industries would be relieved from the strain caused by labour and material shortages. There is little doubt that the formula works pretty well as a short-term expedient. But as a piece of first aid too frequently repeated, it suffers from the same defect as a tourniquet so tightly bound that it paralyses the limb that it is intended to save.

The analysis of the causes of the failure of British investment since the war then resolves itself mainly into the question: Why is the British balance of payments weak? There is another subsidiary question about why British industrialists have been so ready to obey the wishes of their Government to cut down investment at the drop of a hat – in spite of ten years of almost uninterrupted post-war boom, which might have been expected to whet their appetites for more equipment. Why did they not scheme to make bigger profits by expanding their productive capacity, whether the Government liked it or not? Perhaps their mood of compliance is one of the psychological consequences of living too long in a low investment economy. A long period of low investment in a particular industry seems to consolidate a low investment mentality there, and equally high investment produces its own psychological momentum. It is remarkable to what an extent economic growth is a matter of habit. Particularly in the U.S., in the industries which form the spearhead of technological advance, where long-range planning is necessary, the large corporations seem to get into something like an arithmetical groove, and year by year new investment bears a pretty constant relationship to the value of their output. As their output expands, so does their investment in future expansion.

However, the central problem for Britain is the weakness in the balance of payments, which has in one way or another inhibited the growth of a high investment mentality in this country since the war. There are three reasons commonly given, either as alternatives or in combination, for this weakness. They are: (1) that we are consuming too much; (2) that we go in for too many social services; (3) that we carry too big a defence burden. I shall consider each of these in turn.

DO WE CONSUME TOO MUCH?

Taking the whole of the postwar period, the rise in living standards in this country is by no means precipitous. People only got back to the prewar level of consumption round about 1949. Then in the 1950s there was a continuing and moderate rise. Between 1950 and 1956 personal consumption in the aggregate increased by around 12 per cent. That was markedly less than the increase in the output of goods and services produced in Britain over the same period. The improvement in the standard of living was also rather erratic. In 1953 and in 1954 there was quite a big jump; but then the level from which the jump took off was rather depressed. Consumers saw no improvement whatever between 1950 and 1951, and in 1952 there was a slight fall. Again, after the boom years 1953–5, the consumer had to mark time in 1956. There is certainly no evidence here that the British consumer has been greedier than consumers in other countries. The only criticism that might be made is that the increases, when they did come in the years 1953 and 1954, were too sudden and sharp: the economy was jolted out of gear by this eruption of consumer demand. Still, it should be remembered that these were the years in which the belated task of dismantling the wartime system of food rationing was completed. The British would have been less than human if they had failed to evince some ebullience at that late stage of the peace.

However, to show that the demands of consumers on the *extra* wealth that has been produced since the war have on the whole been moderate does not entirely dispose of the problem. It is possible that the starting point was itself too high, that the British consumer was already absorbing too large a proportion of the national income. There is, in fact, some evidence that private consumption absorbs a somewhat higher proportion of the national income in Britain than in other industrial countries of Western Europe. That was true before the war as well as after it. It is probably connected with another feature of the distribution of income in this country: the comparatively large share taken by wage and salary earners. It is markedly higher here than in other West European countries, and was so before the war. Such evidence as is available on this contentious subject suggests that Britain has throughout had a more even distribution of income than these other countries. It is extremely hard to arrive at any kind of satisfactory measure of the degree of inequality in different countries. But an interesting study recently made by the Economic Commission for Europe[1] suggests that after deducting income taxes, there was less inequality in the distribution of income in Britain, before the war as well as after it, than in such traditionally egalitarian societies as Denmark and Sweden. In other West European countries like Holland and Germany there has always been much more inequality.

Now although too much must not be made of these figures, they do point to one factor which may make it more difficult for Britain to accumulate capital. For it is reasonable to suppose that at any given level of income, the rich will tend to save a bigger proportion of any extra that comes in than the poor. It may not always have been so; indeed, there have been periods of history when the rich were wholly absorbed in a cult of lavish display, which absorbed any increase in their substance, while some of the poorer classes were so concerned about the terrors of economic insecurity resulting from war, from bad trade or simply from sickness and old age, that they were much more inclined to save. Characteristically, it is this situation which gives rise to a thrifty bourgeois class, who eventually take over the leadership of society from the aristocracy with its high propensity to consume. In the history of modern societies this stage marks the beginning of the process of accelerated accumulation of capital, and with it of much more rapid economic growth.

Some people would argue that the main economic function of communism is to step up this acceleration by using the uniquely powerful apparatus of a modern despotic state to enforce a still higher rate of saving on the people. There is no doubt that without this despotism, the introduction of a more even distribution of wealth, particularly in a poor society like Russia, would have resulted in less saving, more difficulty in accumulating productive capital assets, and so to a slower rate of economic growth than in an ordinary capitalist society. If Soviet Russia has had a rate of economic growth unmatched in any capitalist countries, with the possible exception of Japan and post-war Germany, the achievement is due in large measure to the political tyranny which Stalin successfully clamped onto the Russian people. Socialism by itself tends to reduce the rate of economic growth. There may, of course, be all sorts of other social advantages, resulting, for example, from the mitigation of class conflict, which ultimately help forward the process of economic growth. But none of this has been demonstrated so far. What has been shown is that emphasis on greater equality in the distribution of wealth, on social security, and on the other desirable objectives of a civilized society tend, in the short run at any rate, to weaken the urge to save.

I am not suggesting that in Britain the urge to save has in fact been weakened catastrophically. Far from it. I am only concerned to point out that because of the more even distribution of incomes in this country and the high proportion of the total which is absorbed by wage earners, Britain has an initial handicap in the race for economic growth compared with a country like Germany. The larger proportion of wages and salaries in the national income here is partly the result of the decay of farming, which in other countries carries a considerable number of small enterprises working on their own account with very little hired labour. In general, self-employed persons play a smaller part in the British economy than elsewhere. In this sense Britain is the most advanced capitalist country in the world. But the self-employed person on the make in a growing society does tend to provide a useful source of savings. This is perhaps another way of saying that proletarian virtues are much closer to aristocratic vices than bourgeois virtues are to either.

To some extent, however, postwar Britain has benefited from a built-in protective mechanism against some of the economic pressures of egalitarianism. While wages and salaries have advanced, so that they absorb a larger proportion of the national resources than before the war, profits have advanced significantly too. Here is the main source of savings. Economic conditions in the past decade or so have been kind to the entrepreneur, as well as to the wage earner. The group that has been squeezed in the middle between these two consists of the people who neither make profits nor earn wages or salaries – broadly the rentier class, who live on the proceeds of past investments in stocks and shares and land. Particularly in the early postwar years the proportion of the national product taken in rent, interest, and dividends was cut very sharply indeed. It is interesting to observe that the new policies which have been gradually introduced by the Conservatives in the 1950s have gone some of the way towards reversing this process. The first step was the ending of dividend limitation, which had been imposed in the last year of Labour rule in 1951. This formal limitation had, however, only reinforced the moral pressures which had kept dividends fairly effectively in check under Labour. When the reaction came with the revival of business activity from 1953 onwards, dividends made up rapidly for a great deal of their lost ground. The second factor was the raising of interest rates as part of the Conservative policy of monetary control. Plainly, the benefit accruing to people lending their money at a fixed rate of interest or investing it in more attractive forms of gilt-edged stock was only an incidental outcome of the new measures. But whatever the intention, the effect was to increase rentier incomes. Finally, the Rent Act of 1957 furthers the process on an even larger scale. It may well be that the rewards offered to the owners of property under the old system of rent control were insufficient to induce them to keep the existing stock of houses in a satisfactory condition; certainly, it is plain that a low rate of interest during a period of rising prices and rapid economic growth is bound to drive money away from government loans or anything else offering a fixed return into other more attractive forms of investment. If the community had to depend on private initiative for the provision of loan capital to the nationalized industries or other government undertakings and for the upkeep of houses, it would have been extremely difficult in the long run, whichever party had been in power, to avoid some increase in rates of interest and in house rents. On the principle that these increases will add to the incomes of the more well-to-do and of the big financial organizations, like insurance companies, while at the same time positively reducing the available spending power of the ordinary citizen by making him pay more in rent, this second post-war redistribution of wealth ought to do something to assist the process of capital accumulation. It is impossible to say how much.

THE COST OF DEFENCE

The greatly enlarged defence programme, which was set in motion after the outbreak of the Korean war in 1950, effectively shackled the British economy for a couple of years. Between 1950 and 1952 the size of the defence burden that had to be carried by the economy increased by over 50 per cent. Moreover, the weight was mainly concentrated on a fairly narrow and critical sector of the economy: defence production pressed hardest on the resources of the engineering industries. Thus the demands of British industrial investment, which also fell on the engineering industries, found themselves pushed two places down in the queue, with defence orders, as well as the export orders for capital goods, way up in front. In these two years, which straddled the 1951 economic crisis and the recession of 1952, the national product increased in real terms by only some 4 per cent. At the same time, the proportion of the national product taken by the defence programme rose from 6 per cent to 9–10 per cent. That meant that all but a tiny fraction of the increase in Britain's wealth over this period was absorbed by the nation's military requirements. The standard of living fell slightly and industrial investment was depressed.

The reaction, when it came to 1953 after this period of suppression, almost inevitably took the form of a spending spree. If the crisis which followed in 1955 can be fairly blamed onto the official policy of giving free rein to the desires of the consumer, regardless of the fact that the country's productive machine had not yet been built up to meet his wants, it should also be remembered that the consumer was, in fact, only trying to make up for two years of enforced abstinence in rather a hurry. He was moreover, as I pointed out earlier, taking the edge off some of the rediscovered pleasures lost in the long era of food rationing. However that may be, the final count for the first half of the 1950s in Britain shows the following sad record: two years, 1951–2, in which the natural increase of the country's wealth went into defence; another two years, 1953–4, in which it was absorbed mainly in the satisfaction of immediate consumer needs, while investment began to recover and got back to its pre-war level; then a final year, 1955, in which industrial investment achieved some real momentum, and the economic expansion was halted by a balance-of-payments crisis. It was in these five years that Germany, investing at home up to the very hilt of its resources, refurbished the whole of its industrial machine.

Thus Britain's uncalculated act of sacrifice during the crisis at the start of the Korean war, in embarking on a defence programme which used up all the resources in sight and more, continued to exercise an unfavourable influence on economic development long after the event. In fact the share of the national resources devoted to defence has been declining ever since 1953. The new defence policy formulated by the Government in 1957 should carry this decline further. However, it would be misleading to leave the impression that the heavy defence programme of the 1950s has produced only damage for the British economy. There have been some economic benefits from it too. Even the country's external trade has something to show for it, in the form of foreign exchange earnings, particularly dollar earnings, from the large-scale export of British armaments.[2] This was of course only a minor consolation prize for the serious loss to the balance of payments caused by the rearmament programme – though it is worth observing that we are still obtaining a useful income of Deutschemarks through the export of arms required by the German forces.

Far more important than this is the fillip that was given to scientific and technical research in industrial fields related to defence. In recent years private enterprise has put up only the smaller part of the funds spent on scientific research in this country. The bulk has been supplied by the Government; and without the defence programme the total would certainly have been less. Of course it is a pity that the effort in research and development supported from public funds has been concentrated on such a narrow front, mainly the aircraft industry and nuclear energy. From the purely economic point of view, it would have been better if this effort had been spread more evenly over a number of less glamorous industries. But in the meanwhile, quite apart from the direct value of the civilian by-products of the work done on aeroplanes and atoms, there is some evidence that the high standard of achievement in these two fields does exercise an influence on other sections of British industry, which are in direct contact with them. Even in the field of cost accountancy the standard of accuracy established by the Atomic Energy Authority in its forward estimates of the cost of its programme tends to make for tighter discipline in the financial departments of the firms with which it has dealings. The value of a centre of high efficiency and initiative of this kind in industry, imposing its demands on those around, can scarcely be overstated. It is usual in a competitive society to rely on such organizations to establish a dominant position for themselves through their ability to undercut, destroy, or swallow their weaker rivals. But in Britain this process has been much inhibited for a long time past. The nearest that we seem to approach to it is by way of an occasional take-over bid. Here in a new industry a substitute appears to have been found for some of the pressures that are exerted by the thrusting and exceptionally efficient firm under conditions of unrestricted competition. At any rate, it is worth marking the fact that the highest technical performance of postwar British industry has come from a nationalized undertaking endowed with a lavish supply of capital and a high propensity to invest. Competition is not the only spur to industrial achievement.

A NAMBY-PAMBY STATE?

This is the most common accusation levelled against Britain abroad – that the substance of the country has been dissipated since the war in a proliferation of social services, which take the individual citizen by the hand, alternately guiding him and patting him, from the cradle to the grave. One is occasionally startled by the ferocity with which this view is held. I once sat next to a young American soldier in a train travelling from Atlanta City to Birmingham, Alabama. Discovering that I was an Englishman, this man, whom I found subsequently to be a gentle and diffident person, thought it reasonable to open the conversation thus: 'Say, why are you British such a lot of deadbeats?' He had a clear picture, it later emerged, of the fifty million inhabitants of this country floating through life on a kind of giant mattress provided by the state, consisting of a combination of cottonwool and old-fashioned down. In fact, he himself had already received benefits from his own public services, in his capacity as a soldier, and was going to receive more of them on a scale that few Englishmen dream of. But of course nothing would shake his certainty that his own government was stimulating the virtues of self-reliance in its citizens, while the British, after their moment of eccentric splendour at Dunkirk – he kept telling me about this – had entirely destroyed theirs.

What chiefly impresses Americans and others is the British health service. The truth is that this is in advance of anything provided by any other country; only Sweden has a system giving comparable benefits. The Americans are especially backward in their public arrangements for looking after the sick. However, in the other fields, outside health, the British social services are no better than those provided in several other West European countries. In their new scheme for old-age pensions the Germans, for instance, have now moved well ahead of us; and the French spend a great deal more on family allowances and maternity benefits of all kinds. Moreover, the British social services, after the great burst of development immediately following the war, have been static or declining for a number of years.

A study made by the International Labour Organization of the social security services of various countries in 1951 showed Britain with an outlay of 11 per cent of the national income occupying a middle position, at about the same level as Holland and Switzerland, but below France and Germany. Such international comparisons cannot possibly be exact. It is impossible to eliminate special factors like the high level of German unemployment at that time, which meant that a great deal of social expenditure was being incurred simply in keeping a lot of people above the subsistence line. Moreover, the national insurance benefits in Britain have been increased by over 50 per cent since 1951. However, the proportion of the national income absorbed by the social services as a whole has certainly not increased during the 1950s. Certain of the welfare activities of the state, such as the provision of subsidized food and cheap school meals, have been sharply cut down.

It is indeed wrong to regard Britain as a country which is particularly prone to pamper its citizens with lavish welfare services. The great reforms which were introduced after the war only brought Britain into line with established practices in several of the advanced industrial countries. The outstanding exception was the health service, where Britain did genuinely take the lead. And it is still a model which is looked upon with envy – and sometimes with hatred – abroad. But the pioneering in the other social services since the war has not come from Britain. The new German system of old-age pensions, introduced in 1957, makes a bold attempt to safeguard the standard of living of people when they are past the age at which they can supplement their incomes by going out and earning more. First of all, the pension rates are related to the wages that were being earned by the person concerned while he or she was still in work, in order to avoid the violent bump that occurs in this country for instance, when a well-paid wage earner, who has not accumulated a substantial reserve of savings of his own, reaches the age of 65 and stops work. This is the problem which the Labour Party is only now trying to tackle in its new pensions plan. The second novel aspect of the German scheme is its attempt to grapple with the misery which is caused by inflation to old people living on fixed incomes. It is generally agreed that the old are the chief victims of the financial mechanics of full employment, as they appear to work today. The means of defence now offered them in Germany is an automatic review of the value of pensions each year in the light of changes in prices, wages, and the general economic situation. The principle has been established that pensioners – and this applies to recipients of widows' and orphans' pensions as well – are to be compensated for any drop in the purchasing power of their incomes resulting from a rise in prices.

Of course a scheme like this cannot be had on the cheap. But the Germans do not appear to blench at the thought of spending the equivalent of £2,500m a year on all forms of social security; nor do they beat their breasts and accuse themselves of living recklessly beyond their means in the manner of the British, who spend a considerably smaller sum on the same objectives. The comparable British figure, taken from the Budget estimates for the financial year 1956–7, is just short of £1,700m.[3] The German social security schemes also represent a larger proportionate burden on the resources available, since the size of the national product is somewhat less than the British. To make the comparison as fair as possible, account should be taken of the remaining British subsidies on welfare foods, which are not included in social security expenditure on this definition. Even after the cuts in the milk subsidy and in the subsidies on school meals, the total cost of these nutrition services provided for mothers and children in Britain amounts to about £80m. On the other hand, Germany has a more extensive education system run by the state, and also continues to provide considerable subsidies for low cost housing, mainly in the form of cheap loans.

One important difference between British and German social security lies in the method of finance. It is sometimes argued that only the British type of arrangement can be regarded as being a social service in the true sense, because the cost is borne directly on the central budget here, with the richer classes paying the greater part through income tax. In Germany, by contrast, the wage earner meets about half of the cost of his social security directly out of his own earnings. Most of the Continental countries follow the German system, with Sweden and Switzerland as notable exceptions. Since the improved German pension scheme was introduced, the proportion of weekly wages deducted to finance all forms of social insurance has gone up to about 14 per cent. The other half of the cost of social security in Germany is borne by the employers. Again, it is sometimes argued that since the employer automatically adds the cost of such charges to the price of his product, and so reimburses himself at the expense of the consumer, the well-to-do manage in the end to avoid most of the burden of social security.

There probably is something in the idea that businessmen tend to treat direct additions to their wages costs, in the form of contributions to national insurance, differently from their income tax and profits tax payments. When income tax goes up, they do not say that their production costs have gone up by a corresponding amount and automatically adjust their prices accordingly. This is the grain of truth in the contention that is sometimes made by such unlikely votaries of the social services as Italian industrialists that British competition is 'unfair', because, they aver, our production costs are not burdened by the large sums which Italian employers have to pay in contributions to social security. When it is seen that an Italian employer has to reckon on an average addition of 53 per cent to the wages of every one of his workers as his contribution, the complaint does not appear to be entirely without foundation. At any rate it removes a large part of the advantage that Italian industry would otherwise gain from the low level of wages that it pays its workers. Hourly wages in Italy are on average only a little more than half of those paid in this country. But when the social charges that have to be met by the employer for every employee working for him are added in, as well as the cost of fairly extensive holidays with pay, the total labour cost per worker employed in Italy comes up to over 80 per cent of the corresponding amount in this country.

On the other hand, of course, Italian employers, and other members of the Italian middle classes, are much less heavily – and certainly less effectively – taxed than in Britain. The British businessman, when he embarks on a venture and puts his capital into it, usually thinks of the reward that this may bring him in terms of the ultimate profit that will be left over *after* he has paid tax on it. In other words, the rate of return that he looks for is higher than it would be if taxes were as low as they are in Italy. It has been claimed that the high level of company taxation in Britain is one of the factors which has held back investment in this country, since businessmen have only been willing to put their capital into ventures which yielded a very large return indeed.[4] Thus a number of useful investment projects get passed by, the urge to invest is diminished, and so the tempo of expansion slackens off. This may not be the whole story – there are so many other and varied motives which influence the conduct of businessmen, and some of the most important of them are non-economic – but there is enough here to establish the point that businessmen on the make are not prepared to alter their notions of what kind of return must find its way back into their pockets in order to make a venture worth while, simply because taxes have been raised in order to pay for social services. What gets adjusted to the new situation is the level of business activity. And that in turn must ultimately affect the level of prices. However, the influence of direct taxes on prices is slow and attenuated. Moreover, the whole argument applies only to taxes on businesses, not on people. The contribution made to the finance of the social services by the millions of income-tax payers out of their wages and salaries does not affect production costs and prices.

To this extent the British system of financing the social services is an arrangement for social redistribution in a sense that the Italian, the German, and most of the other Continental systems are not. But of course the redistribution only works fully if the tax system as a whole is so graded that the burden on the individual diminishes progressively with the movement down the scale from riches to poverty. What the extreme protagonists of the British system sometimes forget is that a very considerable proportion of tax revenue in this country, over 40 per cent, is derived from indirect taxes, which are no respecters of persons, rich or poor. Take the main heads of indirect taxation for the financial year 1957–8: tobacco (nearly £700m), alcohol (£425m), purchase tax (£460m), petrol and oil (£340m) – together they come to substantially more than the total cost of social security expenditure borne on the Budget. Roughly the dimensions are as follows: indirect taxes on consumers amount to a little over £2,000m, while all social security expenditure (pensions, national assistance, health service and national insurance) which is financed out of taxes, comes to nearly £1,100m. It is by no means certain that if the £1,100m for social security were taken right out of the Budget, and put into a contributory scheme, on the Continental model, with employers and wage earners paying equal shares, the wage earners would in fact be worse off. After all, they pay the great bulk of the indirect taxes at the moment, and if these were reduced by the appropriate amount – a little over half – they would be the main beneficiaries.

However, I believe that the decisive argument in favour of a reform of the British system and the introduction of more contributory schemes is a political one. The fact is that if each advance in the social services is to be weighed down by the political objections to increasing taxes on people who already feel themselves to be overtaxed, progress will be slowed down. There are signs that, after the postwar spurt, this country is now falling behind the standards of rising social welfare being achieved abroad, precisely for these reasons. It is clear, at any rate, that the recent German advance towards a more civilized system for the protection of the living standards of the aged would not have been achieved easily, if the ordinary citizen had been asked to accept higher taxes in order to meet the cost.

ARE WE TAXED TOO MUCH? – AND GOVERNED TOO MUCH?

It is true that taxes in Britain take a higher proportion of the national product than in most other European countries. Not in all, however: Finland and Norway, both of which deliberately aim at a big government revenue surplus as a matter of policy, have carried a similar weight of tax burden in the 1950s. And this, it is worth observing in parentheses, has not prevented either of them from achieving an unusually high rate of capital accumulation and investment. On the contrary, it is the compulsory saving imposed on the community by these governments which has helped to support their exceptional investment effort. But so far as Britain is concerned, taxes have been kept high mainly because of the cost of defence. Then in addition there is the British preference for a method of finance which keeps the main cost of social security in the taxpayer's budget, rather than in contributory schemes. This is purely redistributive taxation – though, as we have just seen, of somewhat doubtful benefit to the ordinary working class consumer who buys goods carrying purchase tax and spends even a moderate amount on beer and tobacco.

But the main point is that in this instance the state is not spending the money itself, but shifting it, however misguidedly, from the pocket of one citizen to another. In fact, the expenditure incurred in the actual process of civil government – that is, on such things as police, education, and all forms of administration – in this country is by no means high by international standards. It is around 9 per cent of the national product. In Germany the comparable figure is nearer 11 per cent.

In popular polemics on this subject there is a standard bit of folklore about how the British middle class taxpayer is the victim of a combination of miserable inefficiency on the part of the Government and a conspiracy of redistribution intent on his complete impoverishment. In fact, the bulk of the middle class – say, all those with incomes up to £2,000 a year – are not worse treated here than in several other countries, including Germany. It is when it gets to the higher reaches of income – which very few members of the middle class are lucky enough to enjoy – that the British income tax system becomes really fierce. The very rich man in Germany is much better off than he is here. But the British rich are in practice not quite so depressed a class as the Inland Revenue statistics would appear to suggest. If the realities of income tax in Britain corresponded to the theory, then one might have thought that it would be quite noticeably easier for a rich man living on earned income to crawl through the eye of a needle than to do most of the pleasant and expensive things that he seems to manage to pay for in the course of an ordinary day's pleasure. The trouble is that the method of getting by under the British system is to arrange to spend money legitimately in ways which the Inland Revenue will not quarrel with; whereas in Germany the big tax reliefs, given quite explicitly to the rich, go to those who can demonstrate to the tax authorities that they are saving in certain recognized ways. No one seems to worry about the fact that this saving is bound to give the rich a still bigger income in a few years' time. Here, once again, the whole German system is frankly oriented towards the objective of capital accumulation, and not towards any ideal of social justice.

NOTES

1. *Economic Survey of Europe in 1956*, Economic Commission for Europe, Geneva.
2. The Americans introduced a scheme under which Britain was paid in dollars for arms and military equipment exported to other countries of the North Atlantic Treaty Organization. Several hundred million dollars have been earned in this way.
3. Comprising old age and war pensions, family allowances, the health service, 'national assistance', unemployment, sickness, and other national insurance schemes. I am obliged to Mr I. Gilbert of the Ministry of Pensions for his help in the interpretation of the complicated arithmetic of British and foreign social service expenditure.
4. Nicholas Kaldor: *An Expenditure Tax*, Allen & Unwin, 1955.

CHAPTER FOUR

THE BALANCE OF PAYMENTS

THUS far we have been able to identify two factors which have helped to inhibit Britain's economic development since the war. The first is specific – the exceptionally heavy burden of military expenditure; the second more general – the fact that the whole slant of the social and political set-up in Britain is not oriented towards the task of capital accumulation. As regards this second factor, however, we have observed that, contrary to popular myth, the chief villain of the piece is not a spendthrift state. Rather it is the British penchant for social justice, or alternatively what the critics of this country regard as the national bent for keeping down with the Joneses. Nevertheless, it might have been expected that the pursuit of economic policies in keeping with these demands of the national character would have produced some purely economic benefits as a by-product. But in fact the more equal distribution of incomes has not produced an atmosphere in which labour is noticeably more willing to collaborate with management. The old divisions remain, and industrial conflict has been more widespread and damaging in Britain, at any rate in recent years, than in many other countries in Western Europe. Where the conflict has been sharper on the continent of Europe it is usually possible to identify a purely political cause – a powerful communist leadership within the trade unions. The obvious instances are France and Italy.

Britain thus appears to have had the worst of both worlds – a lack of incentive for private capital accumulation and an absence of any obvious popular satisfaction on this account. Still, too much should not be made of this egalitarian bias of the British economy. It is no more than an initial handicap; intelligently directed public policy can readily ensure that the process of capital accumulation is safeguarded none the less. This has been done in the Scandinavian countries. The Swedes in particular have gone out of their way to use the high rates of taxation as a positive instrument for stimulating investment – by the simple expedient of offering large-scale tax reliefs to businesses that plough their profits back into expanding or improving their productive equipment. At one time after the war the arrangements were so lavish that Swedish businesses could, if they wished, deduct the whole cost of any amount of new machinery installed in any one year from that year's taxable income. Even now, after the reforms to the taxation system, which were bitterly contested by Swedish industry as a blow to productive investment, the rule is that businesses may deduct 20 per cent of the cost of any new machinery or plant from their tax bill in each of the five years from the date of installation. In other words, all machinery can be written off, for tax purposes, within five years, regardless of the fact that the actual working life of industrial machinery is almost always a great deal longer. In this country, where the tax relief on new investment is related to the estimated real life of the particular plant or machine, the installation of a piece of steel manufacturing equipment – to take one example from an industry where investment has constantly lagged behind the community's needs – entitles a business to a deduction from its taxable income of no more than 4 per cent per annum over a period of twenty-five years.

Of course, over the whole of the twenty-five years the British steel firm will obtain as much tax relief as a Swedish steel firm, for during the last twenty years of the life of the equipment the Swede gets nothing. Taking the period as a whole, they pay exactly equal amounts of tax; and an accountant would argue that the only advantage to the Swede is that he receives a loan from his tax authorities which allows him to defer his commitments. A doubtful benefit, some accountants would add, since it may help to obscure the essential calculation of profit and loss. But that is, of course, the whole point. Businessmen are not, on the whole, cold, rational, and prescient supermen looking ahead twenty-five years – like accountants. In real life the Swedish firm, once it has run through its five years of big tax reliefs, immediately sets about buying another piece of equipment, rather than pay the much bigger tax bill which it would have to face without it. This technique of accelerated write-off of new industrial plant has been used with striking effect in several countries since the

war, notably in Germany and the United States, to stimulate expansion in particular branches of industry. But successive British governments, both Labour and Conservative, have set their faces stubbornly against this device. The main objection to it, it seems, is that it offends against the principle of fair play between different industries. It is an interesting sidelight on the character of the British Socialists that for a long time they rejected, as a piece of arbitrary intervention by the state in the working of private enterprise, a device that was used, with a gusto entirely free from such doctrinaire qualms, by the Christian Democrats in Germany and the Democrats in the U.S. More recently, while in opposition, the Labour Party has changed its mind and committed itself to discrimination in this matter. But so far only British shipping has been able to break through to a favoured position; there is a big tax allowance for the buyer of any new vessel. This seems to be regarded by the authorities as an entirely exceptional case.

However, the first problem for this country is not the choice between one kind of instrument for stimulating investment and another, but the fact that any successful encouragement of industrial investment on a large scale has the effect, as we saw earlier, of landing the country in a balance-of-payments crisis. In explaining why the natural bias against capital accumulation in Britain is not corrected by deliberate state action, as it is in other countries sharing the same social predilections as ourselves, we are driven back once again to the primary fact of the weakness in the British balance of payments. It is time to examine this more closely.

BRITAIN'S EARNING POWER ABROAD

It is necessary first of all to make a clear-cut distinction between what Britain spends on its own account – the actual goods and services which are bought and consumed by the people of this country – and the things which the country has to pay for whether it consumes them or not. Britain's foreign exchange earnings are in fact spent on a variety of objects which bring no *current* benefit to this country. It is on the current earnings and spendings that I want to focus attention. The capital items – the money spent on the repayment of foreign debt incurred in the past and the investment funds sent out from Britain, not in order to buy anything abroad which is then imported here, but to build up foreign assets in the ownership of British citizens – are a separate issue. When these are excluded, what remains is called 'the balance of payments on current account'. The other is called 'the capital account'.

It is, of course, the balance of payments as a whole, current and capital together, which determines what happens to the nation's foreign exchange reserves, whether we are in the red or the black, losing or gaining gold and dollars. But the current account tells one whether a country is succeeding in its primary task of earning enough abroad to keep itself going with the supplies of goods and services that it actually consumes.

Britain has been doing this for some years past, with a handsome margin to spare. Over the five years from the beginning of 1952 to the end of 1956 there was an average current surplus each year of £160m. This makes up a big sum when added together; if it had all been tucked away it would have been enough to double the size of the British gold and dollar reserve by the end of those five years. This is exactly what Germany has been doing with its current account surplus. And the reason why Britain's position has appeared weak and precarious by comparison with the German is not simply that our current surplus is smaller than theirs. If the situation had been reversed and the Germans had had a surplus only the size of the British, they would still have looked strong. The British look so weak because the special requirements of their capital account eat up the whole of the current surplus – and more. Judging by the experience of the last five or six years, Britain has no difficulty in 'paying her way'. What causes the trouble is living in a style which necessitates paying other people's way besides.

I shall return in the next chapter to a more detailed discussion of the special factors, political as well as economic, which impose an exceptional burden on the British balance of payments. I want to consider now the constituents of the position of strength which Britain has attained in its current balance of payments with the rest of the world. What is especially encouraging is the underlying evidence of a progressive improvement over the years in Britain's earning power. Ignoring the boom-and-bust period of the Korean war in 1951, and starting the story in the cold dawn of 1952, Britain has year by year been relying less and less on American aid. In 1952 U.S. 'Defence Aid' – as the funds supplied to the British economy to assist it in making dollar purchases of essential commodities came to be called, in line with the more bellicose post-Korean mood – amounted to £121m. By 1954 this figure had been halved; and in the following two years halved again. In 1956 U.S. aid was down to £23m. But in that year, in spite of the Suez affair, the current surplus in the British balance of payments rose to £233m – the highest it had been since 1952. The odds are that, without Suez, it would have been at or near the postwar record of £300m achieved in 1950. However, the 1950 success was gained by the unbusinesslike method of selling goods without replenishing stocks. The atmosphere was like a closing-down sale; and when the country had to face the problem of putting back stocks on its empty shelves in 1951, prices were a great deal higher, businessmen were panicky about the danger of shortages, they bought in a rush, and the result was that the current balance of payments ran into a tremendous deficit – much bigger in size than the surplus of the year before.

There were no artificial factors of this kind in the improvement in the balance of payments registered in 1956. In that year business stocks went on increasing steadily, despite the fact that economic activity had sagged under the pressure of the credit squeeze. This condition of affairs was evidently seen by business as a strictly temporary phenomenon, and they were getting ready for the expected revival, which in fact came in the first half of 1957. No doubt, there were certain windfall gains in 1956; it was possible to make some economies in the import bill because industrial demand for imported materials tapered off when production stopped rising. But when the rise was resumed in 1957, the current balance of payments continued to run a substantial surplus, in spite of the growth of industry's import requirements. For the moderate increase in imports which occurred was in line with the expansion of export earnings that was going forward at the same time. The one paid for the other.

Here is the crux of the matter. For the first time in many decades, certainly in this century, Britain's visible exports and imports had been brought roughly in balance. There was still, to be sure, a small gap. Actual export earnings were sufficient to pay for 98 per cent of the import bill. But the new fact was this – that when imports and exports were expanding at about the same pace, as they did in 1957, the balance of payments did not immediately and automatically come under strain. In the past this consequence did follow. For the total value of British imports was considerably more than the value of exports, so that the same percentage increase applied to each resulted in a bigger absolute rise in imports. In normal times the difference between exports and imports – the 'visible trade' gap – was covered by the income derived from investments abroad, from shipping and other British services, that is, by earnings from our 'invisible trade'. But given a good trading year, with both exports and imports expanding, say, at the recent rate of about 5 to 6 per cent, there was an automatic increase in the visible trade gap; and unless Britain's invisible earnings happened to be expanding at the same speed, which by no means always happened, there was trouble.

The revolutionary nature of the change which has taken place in the balance of payments emerges more clearly if one compares the visible trade account in the mid-1950s with the pre-war figures. In 1938 imports cost £835m, and exports of £533m covered 64 per cent of their cost. The visible gap was just over £300m. In 1956 imports cost a little more than four times as much as pre-war, £3,462m. Now, if British exports had just risen in the same proportion as imports between 1938 and 1956, the visible trade gap would have increased to no less than £1,250m. This is equivalent to rather more than one-quarter of all British earnings from all sources abroad at the moment. In fact, the visible trade gap in 1956 was £60m. The situation has been saved because, while British imports have increased four-fold compared with pre-war, British exports have increased six-fold.

The problems caused by the loss of Britain's overseas investment income are familiar ground for the economic commentators who have reflected gloomily on the state of our balance of payments ever since the war. What is insufficiently celebrated is the rapid and complete adjustment that has been made by Britain to the new situation. My own view is that some extra security has also been gained for Britain in the process; the economy is more firmly based, now that it is less dependent on the solvency of foreign nations to whom British investors have lent money in the past. It is not always recognized that the real value of British investment income from overseas would have suffered in any case as a result of the postwar inflation, even if none of the investments themselves had been liquidated to pay for the war. The point is that quite a lot of the nineteenth-century investments were fixed interest bearing securities; the value of what they produce today is, in real terms, only about one-third of what it was before the war.

Indeed, the whole process of paying for the war does not quite conform to the popular picture of Britain putting up one valuable piece of property abroad after another to auction at knock-down prices, in order to meet pressing debts for munitions. A large part of the foreign exchange that Britain received came from the redemption of low-yielding debts owed by governments abroad to lenders in this country. The proportionate reduction of British income, as a result of the sale of foreign investments during the war, was much less than the proportionate reduction in the nominal value of British capital assets abroad. The Bank of England in its analysis of these war-time sales points out that 'apart from investments in the U.S.A. . . . investments disposed of were, in general, fixed interest loans of good quality and therefore paying relatively low interest rates'.[1] The main loss has not come through pawning the family inheritance; we lost some, but we have added to it again on a large scale since the war. Our position as investors has deteriorated, chiefly because we have to pay so much interest on the loans obtained from foreign countries who have 'invested' in us. Before the war, the income from British property abroad amounted to £250m, and the payments to foreign owners of property in Britain to £60m. What was left over, £190m, paid for almost 20 per cent of all imports of goods and services bought by this country at that time. In 1956 investment income was £667m, and outgoings were £489m. The net investment income of £178m paid for 4 per cent of Britain's imports of goods and services.

One of the important elements in the additional payments that Britain now has to make abroad is the interest on the American and Canadian postwar loans, amounting to about £40m a year. But a much larger amount goes in servicing the huge total of £3,400m of sterling debt, owed chiefly to countries in the sterling area. As rates of interest have risen, partly as a result of the increases in bank rate introduced by the British authorities themselves, so the cost of servicing these sterling balances has gone up. In spite of the very substantial foreign investments that have been financed by Britain during the 1950s, the country's net income from this source has not increased. Any extra dividends that have been brought in from abroad have been swallowed up in meeting the cost of higher rates of interest on our own debts.

The British official attitude towards this whole question of interest rates, at the time when monetary policy was put up in 1955 as the instrument for dealing unaided with the new balance-of-payments crisis, is a striking example of the power of historical thinking, of the ability of people in authority to wrap themselves in a kind of cocoon made up of the nation's past experience, where they remain wonderfully impervious to the real fluctuations of temperature outside. The past in which officials were living when they framed the 1955 policy was the era when Britain was the world's greatest creditor and also its sole effective money market. When the bank rate was raised in London during the nineteenth century, the aim was temporarily to adjust the flow of foreign lending and borrowing, so that more came in and less went out. It was the British money kept at home by the pull of higher interest rates that played a large part in the operation, and for the rest the extra payments to foreigners were on comparatively small amounts of capital deposited here for a few months at a time. But when you have over £3,000m of sterling debt outstanding, raising the rate of interest puts a sizeable extra load onto your balance of payments.

Some of the sterling held by Britain's creditors is invested in long-term securities, which are not adjusted to changes in bank rate. But a considerable part is held in the form of short-term loans to the British Government, with the shortest, the three months' Treasury bill, as a popular medium. Naturally the foreigners, who have seen the benefits obtained by the holders of Treasury bills during the period of rising interest rates after 1955, have thought again about the wisdom of holding their sterling balances in the form of long-term government securities. The British Government seems positively to have gone out of its way to encourage them to hold their sterling in as liquid a form as possible, whereas it would have appeared a course of elementary self-interest to offer the big and attractive prizes to anyone who was willing to hang on to his sterling as a solid reserve, not to be disturbed except in case of an emergency, over a period of years. The holders of the sterling balances have now been made to realize that this was a mug's game.

Meanwhile, those who were fortunate enough to be holding their sterling in a fairly liquid form when the change came in 1955, have been able to add a considerable burden to the British balance of payments. The rise of 4 percentage points in bank rate, from 3 per cent at the beginning of 1955 to 7 per cent in 1957, means an additional payment of foreign exchange by Britain of not much less than £100m a year. In order to meet this cost alone, British manufacturers must export an additional £2m worth of goods a week. None of this was apparently visualized by those responsible for British monetary policy in 1955; or perhaps they imagined that the effect of the shock treatment on the world markets would be so startling that it would be unnecessary to keep British interest rates up for long. There is some evidence that they both exaggerated the likely international effects of a change in the British bank rate and also ignored the fact that its impact on the British balance of payments, now heavily loaded with foreign debt, was bound to be totally different from anything that had been experienced in the past. At any rate, when the bank rate was reduced by half a percentage point in early 1957 – from $5\frac{1}{2}$ per cent to 5 per cent – for no obvious reason except that the Government judged the interest rate to be inconveniently high for its purposes, it was explained to economic journalists eager for some doctrinal lead from the Treasury, that this really represented a windfall gain to the balance of payments. The fact that Britain was no longer a creditor, but instead a large-scale debtor on loans whose cost went up and down with changes in the short-term rate of interest, was treated by the pundits as a brand-new discovery. It did not stop them from adding another 2 per cent to bank rate in the emergency of the autumn, seven months later.

Because of the grave problems caused by the loss of net income from British overseas investment, particularly during the early postwar period, there has been a tendency to regard the creation of new and bigger foreign investments as a first charge on the country's economic resources. But analysis shows that the real problem is not the loss of a lot of highly profitable assets overseas, but rather the servicing of the new debts owed to overseas countries. The moral, if there is one, is that we should try to reduce these debts to more manageable proportions; it is by no means clear that the best way of doing this is by increasing other people's debts to us. In fact, as we have seen, the main problem of the British balance of payments since the war has been met and solved by other means – by expanding the productive power of British export industries and selling more of their products abroad. The conclusion would seem to be that investment in the expansion of these industries, and of others which would help us to economize on imports, should be a first charge on the nation's economic resources, rather than foreign investment.

I shall return to this problem, which lies at the heart of Britain's postwar difficulties, in a later chapter. For the moment it is sufficient to insist once again that the main object is the extinction of a large amount of troublesome debt that we owe to others, rather than the creation of new debts which others will owe to us. The two issues are entirely distinct, and clear thinking on economic policy has been hampered by the constant tendency to treat them as if they were one and the same thing.

CHEAP IMPORTS – DEAR EXPORTS

Somehow, British economic thinking has continued to be overshadowed long after the event by the short and quite exceptional experience of 1951. That year certainly had a traumatic quality, at any rate for economists. Its feature was that the balance of payments, which had been brought back with a great heave to solvency in 1950, was suddenly knocked sideways by a world-wide rise in the prices of the essential commodities which Britain has to obtain abroad. The rocketing prices were triggered off by the shortages following the outbreak of the Korean war. So far as Britain was concerned, there was a feeling of bitterness and disillusion that the great achievement of the export drive in the five years after the Second World War had been brought to nothing by forces right outside this country's control. I do not think it is fanciful to regard the lax and unwilling mood of the 1950s as being, in part at any rate, the consequences of this traumatic experience. Certainly, in political terms, the Labour Party's failure to consolidate the gains which seemed so securely within reach in 1950 left the party in a kind of dazed condition, from which it has been slow to recover. The impression was in 1951 that the Labour leaders did not know what had hit them; all they knew was that it was something pretty big.

That fact itself has had an influence in shaping subsequent economic thinking. For the main protagonist on the Labour side who presided over the débâcle of 1951, Mr Gaitskell, was himself a distinguished economist, a teacher who was able and willing to guide the thinking of other economists. The myth which emerged on the Left and held its own for a number of years was that 1951 really represented a foretaste of a secular trend, which would put the industrial countries at a permanent disadvantage against the primary producing countries. In this, Mr Harold Wilson, another economist on the Labour side, played as large a part as anybody. The new doctrine was based on a theory of shortages for ever. The principle was quite simple: the demands of the expanding industrial countries for food and raw materials would constantly tend to outrun the limited world supplies, and so their prices would rise faster than the prices of manufactured goods. In other words, the 'terms of trade' – that is the actual quantity of imports that can be obtained in exchange for a given volume of exports – would move steadily against the industrial countries. The record of the first six postwar years certainly seemed to bear out this thesis pretty well. This was the period in which the primary producers had it all their own way. The characteristic phenomenon of the time was the Peron régime in Argentina – a nation sustained by a series of windfall gains in world commodity markets, mainly at the expense of the industrial countries of Western Europe. But that was only the extreme manifestation of the spirit of the age. It was an established doctrine of the time that the erstwhile exploiters of colonial and quasi-colonial territories could now in their turn be exploited with impunity by their previous victims. The terms of trade were going to be the instrument for completing the impoverishment of Britain and the rest of Western Europe – finishing the job half-done by two world wars.

The image that emerged from the experience of 1951 showed Britain with a huge load on its back puffing away up a moving staircase, which was moving steadily downwards. While we were pushing up the volume of our exports, the ground was slipping away from under our feet, as a result of the movement of prices; after a back-breaking effort we would find that we were able to buy hardly any more for our pains. Indeed, some economists suggested that our very effort to sell a bigger volume of exports abroad had the effect of turning the terms of trade against us still more. They reasoned that if we tried to sell more of manufactured goods, while the primary producing countries had only the same amount of food and raw materials to offer in exchange, then the bargain struck to clear the total available surpluses on both sides would be less favourable to the industrial countries. Either the prices charged by the primary producers would go up, so that in fact they were able to buy more manufactured goods for a given volume of their output, or the manufacturers would find it necessary to cut their prices, in order to get rid of their extra production. Either way, on this simplified economists' model, the industrial countries were bound to lose.

Subsequent events showed that the only defect of this model was that it was utterly remote from the facts of life in the 1950s. It turned out to be about as helpful as a fruit machine in solving a problem of gunnery prediction. What it omitted altogether was the important element in world trade which consists of exchanges between the industrial countries themselves. As technology advances, the range of specialized manufactured products which industrial countries can usefully exchange among themselves constantly grows. In fact, it is these exchanges which have been the main dynamic force in the continuous and rapid growth of world trade from 1952 onwards. The idea that the advance in living standards in the industrial countries would be held back by unfavourable terms of trade, reflected in the increasing cost of imported raw materials, has been shown to have no substance whatsoever. Not only is our trade less dependent than the economists thought on the purchasing power of the primary producing countries, but our own demand for imported raw materials has not been as big as had been expected. Again, the advance in technology – the growing application of synthetic materials – has kept the primary producer in his place. The industrial countries have not been forced to bid up the prices of his raw materials, in order to obtain supplies that they needed to keep their factories going. This was another factor which was expected to turn the terms of trade against us. What has happened in practice is that world prices of the main manufactured goods have risen pretty steadily from 1952 onwards – that is after the end of the post-Korean boom – whereas the index of world commodity prices has remained well below the level of 1952.

There is some substance in the complaint of the backward countries in Asia and Latin America that their economic development is being impeded by inflationary forces in the industrial countries, which seem to affect everything but primary products. But to the extent that life has been made more difficult for them, owing to their unfavourable terms of trade, it has been made easier for us. In fact, the 1950s have been an era of unprecedented prosperity for the industrial peoples of the West – unprecedented in the sense that it has affected so many people and for so long, without interruption. It has been possible to devote more and more resources to the satisfaction of the demands of consumers with rising standards of living, and at the same time to find the wherewithal for an extremely high rate of investment. This is the picture for Western Europe as a whole; Britain, as I pointed out earlier, forms something of an exception to it.

GROWING MARKETS IN THE INDUSTRIAL COUNTRIES

To obtain a proper impression of this economic landscape of the 1950s, so favourable to the great trading nations of the world, one has to go up to a really high vantage point – the top of the Korean boom, which everyone regarded at the time as wholly temporary and artificial – and look at subsequent events from there. The adjective most commonly applied at the time to the sudden rise in world trade to a new peak in 1951 was 'unhealthy'. So it was, in a sense; it was too dependent on the precarious structure of high prices paid to the producers of raw materials – a prop which soon gave way. But before that, the value of world trade had expanded by no less than 40 per cent in one year. The vantage point certainly seemed high enough; and many people in the recession which followed in 1952 doubted whether it would ever be reached again. However, that recession turned out to be a very minor affair. In the industrial countries of the West it was no more than a short pause before production took another leap forward.

And so did world trade. One obtains a clearer picture of the essential trend, as it affected a highly industrialized country like Britain, if attention is concentrated on world trade in manufactured goods only. Between the 1951 peak and 1956 it increased by 38 per cent. It is true that Britain was under a certain handicap in participating in this bonanza, because so much of its exports of manufactures go to the primary producing countries of the sterling area. These have throughout this period been feeling the effects of depressed commodity prices. Purchases of manufactures by the rest of the sterling area rose by only 13 per cent between 1951 and 1956 – that is, by about one-third of the world average. The markets which showed the greatest absorptive capacity for imported manufactured goods were the industrial countries themselves; Western Europe and North America each registered an increase of around 60 per cent in these five years.

Moreover, this unusually rapid growth of trade took place in the context of a vigorous expansion of industrial output in nearly all the countries of Western Europe and North America. Rising industrial production here has had the effect of making nations not more, but less self-sufficient in manufactured products. In many of them foreign trade, both exports and imports, have grown at a faster rate than domestic industrial production. There is, of course, nothing inherently strange about this. It is precisely in the new and expanding industries that one would expect to find the greatest benefits of international specialization in advanced or expensive technology. With the increasing cost of research and development on the frontiers of science, the compulsion to trade, rather than to try and make everything yourself, grows. Since the new industries based on advanced technology are precisely those which are expanding fastest, it is natural that international trade in manufactured goods should benefit accordingly.

But however natural this may be in theory, it is unusual in practice. It requires, among other things, a state of mind among governments which deliberately goes out to foster international trade by making it easier for imports to enter their own territories. The truth is that everyone is always in favour of more international trade; but most of the time, at any rate in this century, governments have been reluctant to translate this into the proposition that it would be a good thing to have some more imports. It is the smaller countries of Western Europe, Belgium, Sweden, Switzerland, and so on, who have led the way in a deliberate policy of importing the things which they believe they will not be able to manufacture as cheaply themselves. They have shown how this policy can be used as an instrument for raising the general level of efficiency in their own domestic industries.

This is of course anathema to the crude type of socialist planner, who believes that he sins against his principles by taking any notice of world market forces in determining what goods his country should produce. Swedish or Dutch socialists would at once dismiss such a notion as belonging to a kind of pre-Marxian stone age of socialism, but it still seems to be widely held in the leadership of the British Labour Party, and has been given forcible expression by Mr Aneurin Bevan in particular.[2] It is easy to see how it leads to an outlook which, for all its protestations of internationalism, is basically opposed to an international approach to day-to-day economic problems. Its ideology is national sovereignty run riot. And in this it bears a marked similarity to the economic ideology current in the underdeveloped countries. Their notion, too, is to concentrate industrial planning on the task of import-saving, on making themselves less dependent on international trade. The tempo of expansion of output is designed to be much faster than the growth of foreign trade. These countries have, of course, special reasons for acute anxiety about the forces of the market place, which constantly produce violent fluctuations in the world prices of the one or two staple commodities on which they depend for their export earnings. They are much more vulnerable and exposed, apart from being poorer, than a developed industrial country; and the only way in which they can hope to create new industries is by carving out for them a protected slice of the home market. Without this they would expire through lack of competitive power. But leaving aside motives and having regard only to the practical results, what all this means is that nations which are dominated by doctrines of old-fashioned socialism and those which are simply underdeveloped make rather unpromising import markets. Both have been much in evidence in the sterling area during the 1950s, sometimes in combination.

This is one of the reasons frequently advanced for Britain's failure to maintain her share of world trade in manufactures during a period of rapid expansion. The British proportion of the total fell from 21·3 per cent in 1951 to 19 per cent in 1956. Two-and-a-half percentage points may not seem very much, but it is in fact equivalent to $1,000m worth of export earnings. Another factor which has hampered Britain more than most other industrial countries during the 1950s is the fact that traditionally Britain has depended much on textile exports, so that the contraction in world trade in textiles has been felt especially keenly here. So has the competition from the newer textile industries in Asia, operating at much lower wage levels.

However, analysis of the evidence available suggests that these two special circumstances – the dependence on trade in textiles and on the markets of primary producing countries in the sterling area – do not fully account by themselves for Britain's failure to retain its share of world trade. In an official study of the export record from 1951 to 1955 conducted jointly by a number of government departments, an attempt was made to calculate roughly what sort of effect these two factors have had on British export earnings.[3] The conclusion reached was that the combined result of the geographical distribution of Britain's exports, with its heavy dependence on markets expanding less than the average, and of the composition of the exports themselves, with their emphasis on textiles, might have been to lose for Britain 0·6 per cent of world export trade and divert it to others. This is only about one-quarter of the actual reduction in Britain's share of world exports of manufactures which occurred between 1951 and 1955. What accounts for the rest? Even in the enormously buoyant market on the continent of Europe at Britain's very doorstep, British exporters did not manage to retain their share of the total trade. This is a market which absorbs about one-quarter of our exports, as against rather less than half going to the sterling area.

In the United States, on the other hand, British exports have done well. This in itself is sufficient demonstration that the comparative failure of British sales elsewhere is not due to our inability to produce goods at competitive prices or of competitive quality and design. The United States has the reputation, at any rate, of being the most competitive market in the world, where customers are awkward and salesmen have got to like it. By the end of 1956 British salesmen had done so well there that the U.S. had become Britain's biggest single export outlet, bigger than any one of the Commonwealth countries. This was something which would have been regarded as a pipe dream when Sir Stafford Cripps launched the dollar export drive in the late 1940s. At that time it was thought a bold objective to try to make British exports to U.S. approach the somewhat meagre total then being sent to Canada. It was considered an extremely difficult task to make headway in the former, without the aid of the imperial tariff preference which British exporters enjoyed in Canada. But it turns out that imperial preference is not so powerful a selling device, at any rate where markets are expanding, as was imagined. Perhaps the common language with customers in the United States is a more important factor in explaining the British export success there. What is undoubtedly true is that the firms which were attracted by the challenge of the dollar export drive, and were determined to stay the pace because of the profitable business offered as a reward for their patriotic endeavours, were by and large the pushing and adventurous enterprises – the top end of British industry. The big electrical equipment makers, who periodically cause trouble by tendering for contracts at prices so much below those of their American competitors, are a familiar example. These are also the firms which have been investing heavily in new plant and equipment and whose output has in consequence been growing faster than the average.

The moral in fact seems to lie here. It is the same story all over again: where there is investment, output can respond to changing demand in export markets or at home. Where investment is low and order books are constantly at or nearly at 'saturation point', because output fails to expand, the response is sluggish. Businessmen do not keep chasing their customers or looking for new ones unless they think they are going to need the extra custom in order to keep their plant going at a profitable rate. The combination of fat order books and static productive capacity is a wonderful formula for making a salesman lackadaisical. Some of ours – foreign importers will tell you – do not even bother to answer letters. However, the solution is not to aim at a change of heart by means of patriotic exhortation; it lies in a change in business conditions which will give the salesmen more and more goods that they have to sell, if they are not to fall down on their job. The prospect of a surplus is a great cleanser of the businessman's spirit. There is, in my view, no substitute for it.

This is not to deny that it is possible, in the short term, to get results in export markets, in spite of a check to production at home. In 1956 that is precisely what happened: industrial output remained static while exports increased by a substantial amount. But the causal connexion between these two events has generally been overstated by economic commentators of the orthodox put-them-through-the-mangle school. The underlying rise in exports from one year to another, calculated after such fortuitous factors as the temporary interruption of shipments through dock strikes are eliminated, has not varied significantly, during the period 1955–7. The annual rate of increase was some 5–6 per cent during the boom in 1955 and after the end of it, when the credit squeeze made itself felt in 1956. And the subsequent recovery of home demand in 1957 seems to have left exports expanding – at least in the earlier part of the year, before the U.S. recession – at something fairly close to this rate. Where the credit squeeze made its effect felt was in putting a curb on imports. The check to production at home did mean that industry imported fewer materials, and this helped to bridge the period while British productive capacity for making things like sheet steel was being built up sufficiently to meet a higher level of demand. But plainly this expedient of checking production in order to reduce the demand for imports cannot be turned into a long-term policy, without damaging the country's ability to grow and thus export more.

AIMING TOO HIGH?

But the crucial fact remains that in spite of Britain's failure to maintain its share of world trade during the 1950s, it has emerged with its balance of payments on current account stronger than at any time since the war. Of course, the diminishing proportion of world exports captured by British traders is a cause for worry none the less. While world trade is extremely prosperous and expanding, a diminishing share can still mean a sizeable slice of the cake. But it suggests a weakness in Britain's export effort, which might result in a serious loss of earnings, if world trading conditions became less favourable. The truth is that the 1950s have been a period in which any moderately efficient industrial country had golden opportunities. This explains why, in spite of the comparatively slow rate of industrial growth in this country, it has, so to say, fallen on its feet. The radical adjustment necessitated by the loss of our net income from overseas investment, which made such a big contribution to the balance of payments before the war, has been achieved remarkably painlessly.

Britain's falling share of world export trade in manufactures is to be regretted for another reason. If the proportion had been maintained, there could have been a bigger surplus in the balance of payments which would have been used to finance a number of desirable objectives, like giving more loans to the Commonwealth or aiding the underdeveloped countries of Asia and Africa. Our ability merely to pay our way year by year in the 1950s with a margin of £160m a year to spare was not enough to do all the things that many people in this country would have liked to have done to help other nations, less fortunately placed. But that should not obscure the essential fact that by any ordinary commercial standard Britain in the 1950s had been thoroughly solvent. Leaving aside the wholly exceptional year of 1951, when ordinary commercial considerations were overlaid by a military emergency, the only time when there has been a current deficit in the balance of payments is the year 1955. The amount was trifling, some £80m – a fraction of the surplus earned over the other years – and it should have been perfectly possible to finance it by drawing temporarily on the gold reserve. That is after all what reserves are for: they are not a thing of beauty to be contemplated or to be waved proudly as an emblem in the face of other nations, but something to be used when, as in 1955, a comparatively small miscalculation of the growth of home demand results in a rather higher import bill than had been expected.

Anyone having regard to the succession of crises which have shaken the British economy and the desperate struggle to defend the pound sterling which has been going on right through the middle 1950s can hardly fail to suspect that the description of Britain's apparent commercial strength in the preceding paragraph must have a catch in it somewhere. Have all the crises then been a kind of optical illusion? Or if they are a natural accompaniment of such a position of strength in the middle of the twentieth century, couldn't we try a bit of weakness for a change? Of course the crises are real enough: the balance of payments is too often on the brink of disaster; but it is important to recognize that this is *not* because current spendings are grossly in excess of current earnings. On the contrary. The trouble lies in the country's capital account. There are old debts to be paid off – the £1,000m postwar loan from America is supposed to be extinguished in fifty annual instalments by the year 2,000 – and meanwhile the holders of the huge sterling debts accumulated by Britain during the war are able to draw on their balances in London at will. When you owe over £3,000m and there is no restriction on your creditors demanding payment of any amount that they may need, you can easily lose a couple of hundred million pounds in a year, in this way. Then there is the outflow of new capital from Britain, mainly to the Commonwealth, which has amounted to £150m – £200m a year. It is no wonder that the Government, after adding all these prospective capital commitments together, came to the conclusion that Britain would need to achieve an *average* surplus in the balance of payments of £300m to £350m a year in order to break even. 'Breaking even' in this context means having enough net earnings to spare to add a little each year to the gold reserve instead of drawing on it.

This was the target set by the Conservative Government shortly after it entered on its first term of office at the end of 1951. It was by no means an overstatement of the long-term demands that were likely to be made by foreign countries on the British balance of payments, if no special effort was made to hold them in check. And it was the declared policy of the Conservatives not to check them in any way. Subsequent experience has, if anything, suggested that the target figure ought to be revised upwards. The propensity to export capital from the United Kingdom by investors, either seeking a high rate of return or simply a more comfortable haven for their savings, seems to be very strong indeed. At the same time, the new members of the Commonwealth, as they pass from colonial to dominion status, are going to make heavier calls on their sterling balances than in the past. Indeed, the vigorous and admirable thrust of the whole Commonwealth towards a more rapid rate of economic development, particularly for its poorer members, is bound to increase the strain on Britain's capital account. It is to be observed, moreover, that the new dominions in Malaya and West Africa are among the largest holders of sterling balances, acquired mainly when the prices of their commodities were high during the years following the war. In spite of their poverty, these countries continued for some time to run a surplus in their balance of payments – they earned more than they spent abroad – not due to any volition on their part, but rather because it takes a little time before a country learns how to make use of large-scale imports of foreign capital equipment efficiently, in order to speed up the development of its resources at home. It is totally abnormal for a backward country, at any rate one which is concerned to raise its productive power, to run a balance-of-payments surplus. If it is really getting on with the job, it will be constantly running into deficits. This is the pattern in all the rapidly developing countries – the United States in the nineteenth century, Australia and Canada since the war, and latterly India. (If the deficit does not show, it is only because some of these countries, notably Canada, are able to borrow the funds that they need to meet their needs from eager investors abroad.) The conclusion is that we must now expect West Africa and Malaya to draw on their sterling balances instead of adding to them, as they have done since the war.

At the very least, then, the surplus required on the British balance of payments must be adjusted to the upper figure of £350m, in the original target set by the Conservative Government, if the prospective commitments now in sight are to be met. In no single year so far has this sum been reached. As an objective for an average surplus to be achieved year in year out, it must surely be regarded as a piece of fancy. Those who think it perfectly normal for a nation to indulge in a backbreaking economic exercise at the drop of an official hat in Whitehall will produce the usual calculation showing that the figure of £350m represents well under 1 per cent of the gross national product. The relevant fact, however, is that it represents over 10 per cent of Britain's export earnings; these are supposed to be set aside and our people are to forgo using them on goods and services, like travel, that they want to buy abroad.

To obtain a proper perspective on the problem, it helps to visualize it in terms of the balance of payments of some other nation: the equivalent proportionate burden on the U.S. national product of a surplus of this kind would be 8 billion dollars. When the Americans actually had a current surplus of this size in the 1940s, the whole world rose up and shouted 'crisis'. It was thought to be utterly abnormal for any country to export so much and import so little in return. The odd thing is that no one, either on the Left or on the Right of British politics, has ever seriously protested against an objective of similar dimensions here. Apparently the spirit of austerity dies hard, and it is assumed without question that the British can stand any burden that would be intolerable to lesser nations. The explanation offered in every one of the succession of economic crises is that Britain does not export enough and ought to do more. We tend to bow our heads before this complaint all too readily, and the minds of our politicians run at once to cuts of one kind or another. But before we accept the doctrine of necessary chastisement, whose first victim is almost inevitably the investment programme – because it is much the easiest thing to crush – we ought surely to reflect on our objectives. Do we really wish to cripple our long-term productive power by investment cuts, in order to meet a series of special commitments which are quite outside the normal commercial aims of any ordinary nation?

NOTES

1. *U.K. Investments Overseas 1938 to 1948*, Bank of England, 1950.
2. *Tribune*, 25 August 1957.
3. *Board of Trade Journal*, March 1957.

CHAPTER FIVE

THE SOURCE OF THE STRAIN

LOOKING back over the decade following the war, one of the strangest aspects of British politics now appears to be the mood of insouciance in which a whole series of political decisions were taken, regardless of their effect in adding to the existing overload of economic burdens on the country. The politicians, and even more the officials responsible, just assumed grandly that 'a way would be found' of paying for the decisions that were being taken in the interest of the nation. It was all very much like the wartime mood, extended without any sense of inappropriateness into peacetime conditions. It lasted right into the middle 1950s. The first clear signs of a change came after the Suez incident in 1956. Before this the calculation of costs tended to be the last thing which was considered in approaching an important political decision. The slogan was always: 'Of course we can afford it; it means so little, if only everyone will make the effort.' And it is by no means outmoded yet. Propagandists, particularly on the Left of British politics, are especially prone to use it as a device for making some desirable proposal – like more aid to the underdeveloped countries – appear financially painless.

This flag-day type of approach – *only* 1 per cent of the national income required, *only* the cost of a packet of fags to be forgone – is an insidious instrument of political self-deception. For the truth is, as even the propagandists know, that the millions of British smokers are not going to give up twenty cigarettes each week and set the money aside for the purpose that they have in mind. In any case, if the smokers had really been willing, they would have indulged in this piece of self-denial so often since the war, that there would have been no tobacco left long ago for them to give up. What happens in reality is that the commitments are taken on carelessly, because it seems they cost so little, more and more of them; no equivalent saving of foreign exchange is made on anything else; and ultimately they add up to the difference between economic solvency and a balance-of-payments crisis. After all, that difference is not very great either, at any rate in the global arithmetical terms used by the flag-day specialists – a mere matter of 1 per cent of the national income. The average annual surplus of £160m in the current balance of payments since 1952 works out at just about that figure.

But to be fair about this, it is not the philanthropists, in spite of their efforts, who have been chiefly responsible for the overloading of the British economy since the war. Nor, it is worth insisting again, can the result be blamed onto an extravagant government throwing foreign exchange away in order to finance things like the British Council, the diplomatic service, or an occasional overseas trade fair. On these matters Britain spends a good deal less proportionately than any other nation of comparable wealth. Indeed, the constant cheese-paring of these activities has been both purposeless and irritating: small sums were saved at great effort, and attention was diverted from the main issue. The real problem cannot be evaded by saving candle-ends. It is something much more fundamental – a national attitude based on a historic view of Britain's role in the world, which leads to a succession of political decisions of an extremely costly character. This is not extravagance, but a deliberate decision to live beyond one's means.

This attitude appears at its most vigorous and intransigent in the field of military strategy. We have already seen that the huge rearmament programme set in motion after the Korean war broke out was the main source of the burden which overloaded the British economy and interfered with its growth in the 1950s. However, my argument is not that the decision taken in 1950 was necessarily wrong on that account. Indeed, I believe that in the circumstances of 1950, with most of the countries of Western Europe still punch-drunk after the war and the Russians waiting on the borderland to take the maximum advantage of the first sign of weakness, it was profoundly right for Britain to give a clear military lead. Britain was far stronger than any other nation in this critical region: it was outstanding, after the successful social revolution of the previous decade, as a coherent and disciplined society with an efficient economic system in full working order. Germany, it should be remembered, was at this time still on its knees, and looked as if it might be overcome by a combination of misery, unemployment, and the constant inflow of ragged and starving refugees from the East. France and Italy meanwhile were under the constant threat of a communist putsch, abetted by militant trade union movements entirely subservient to communist leadership. In both countries, the Communist Party or its allies had the support of around 30 per cent of the electorate. I do not think it is an exaggeration to say that without the prompt evidence of British military determination, the position in Western Europe might well have been lost. Certainly, it would not have been possible to build up the North Atlantic Treaty Organization into some kind of effective deterrent force, without British leadership and, yes, British economic sacrifice.

But that is not at all the same thing as saying that the vast long-term rearmament programme on which the British Government embarked in 1950–1 was well conceived. Subsequent events, in the military as well as the economic sphere, showed that it was thoroughly badly conceived. In fact, the story of the inception of this programme has never, so far as I know, been properly told. There is much that requires explanation.

I happened at the time to be following events fairly closely from day to day, at the periphery of public affairs, because of the work that I was doing as a journalist. It was towards the end of 1950, and the newspapers had been given to understand that a decision about the new defence programme was about to emerge from the Prime Minister's office at 10 Downing Street. Finally, a press conference was called at Number 10, and in order to assist the journalists concerned, a confidential document was sent out in advance giving the broad outline of the programme. The amount that it was proposed to spend was substantially less than the £1,500m a year that eventually formed the basis of the enlarged British defence budget. But the plan set out in this document was never discussed in Parliament or even referred to in public. The document was hastily withdrawn and the press conference which had been called for the evening was cancelled, after the American ambassador had been to see Mr Attlee, the Prime Minister, during the afternoon. I have no means of knowing for certain whether the withdrawal of the plan and the American ambassador's *démarche* were in any way connected. I can only report that they had every appearance of being so.

The incident had a slightly bizarre sequel, in the course of which officials were desperately trying to get the cancelled document back, without letting it be known to those who were not on the distribution list that they had been left out. They were chiefly worried, it seemed, about the *Daily Worker*. If they put out a general message to the press in the usual way via the news agency teleprinter machines, the *Daily Worker*, like other newspapers, would receive it, and so the communists would know that something was up. They would soon find out what had been cancelled. The alternative method of writing a private letter to each of the named recipients of the document presented complications, because somehow or other someone had failed to keep a complete list of those who had received it. I do not know exactly how the story was brought to a happy ending. But evidently the piece of dynamite that had been inadvertently put out was safely retrieved, and the *Daily Worker* never showed any sign of having got wind of its existence.

The incident is interesting because it seems to suggest the enormous importance which the U.S. Government attached at the time to a really massive British gesture. It may have been right in its view, and the British Government may have been wise to accept it. The important point, however, as regards British economic policy, is that the Government here was in a position of overwhelming bargaining strength to secure a major American contribution towards the cost of the programme. In the event, despite its apparent doubts at the time about the size of the effort required from it, it did not press the Americans to specific promises. There was a great deal of airy talk about 'burden-sharing', but nothing came of it.

The moral is not that the Americans were insufficiently generous, but that the British were not insistent enough. This kind of reticence has admittedly a certain nobility; it is how one would like to behave oneself in one's own personal life. It may even have had the practical effect of increasing the weight of this country's international influence, when it came to crucial strategic and political decisions. This last consideration was certainly very much in the mind of the Labour Government at the time. But the Government never seemed to ponder seriously whether the aim of exercising a bigger influence on American strategic policy for a short while was worth the sacrifice involved in overloading the British economy with commitments that were bound to stunt its long-term growth. The truth is, of course, that the problem was never visualized in this way at all. It was always treated ultimately on the ethical plane – the nation would just have to afford it, our leaders would say, without stopping to consider what 'affording it' meant in terms of the long-term economic and social life of the British community. They solved the problem by imagining a personal austerity, accepted by the ordinary Englishman, sufficient to provide the savings required for the new effort. Hence the argument, which followed the introduction of the enlarged defence programme in 1951, between Mr Bevan and Mr Gaitskell, then Chancellor of the Exchequer, about the Budget proposal for reducing part of the service provided free under the National Health scheme, and making people pay for it. It split the Labour Government. As a serious means of attack on the economic problem caused by rearmament, Mr Gaitskell's proposal was barely relevant. Its main importance was in the gesture. It indicated the need for enforced savings of a kind that would be felt, not just by the rich, but by the ordinary person. And it was precisely on this principle as applied to the Health Service that Mr Bevan opposed it.

The real kick in Mr Gaitskell's 1951 Budget was in its frontal assault on the productive investment of British industry. Characteristically, this never figured in the Bevan-Gaitskell dispute. The device used was simple, direct, and completely effective. It was to suspend the tax concession that had been given to businesses installing new plant and equipment – the so-called 'initial allowance'. This worked in the following way. Normally, a firm is allowed to deduct as a business expense from its taxable income each year an allowance for the depreciation suffered in that year by its plant and equipment. Thus, if a machine costs £10,000, and its working life is assessed by the Inland Revenue at ten years, then the firm gets tax relief on £1,000 a year. The initial allowance is designed to give a business more tax relief of this kind in the year when it actually buys a new piece of equipment. The allowance for depreciation in that year is fixed at 20 per cent (40 per cent from 1949 to 1951) of the purchase price of the machine or installation, regardless of the actual length of its working life.

Plainly this was, and is once again since its reinstatement, a concession which is particularly valuable to an expanding business that is adding to its productive equipment year by year. So long as it goes on adding £10,000 worth of machinery each year it will get tax relief on £2,000, in addition to the normal depreciation on the rest of its plant. This is, in fact, a major inducement to companies to plough more money back into the business. The static company of course gets very little out of it. Over the assumed ten-year life of the piece of machinery in our example, the tax relief would be the same whether there was an initial allowance or not. The effect of the decision of 1951 to suspend the initial allowances was therefore deliberately aimed at the expanding business, the business with a will to invest. Its purpose was simply, by reducing the flow of orders for new machinery and plant, to free more resources for making armaments, and secondly, to divert a higher proportion of such capital goods as went on being made from British customers to export markets.

BRITISH MILITARY POLICY

Was it really necessary to adopt quite such a wrecking policy as this? It is when the actual content of the big rearmament programme of 1950–1 is examined more closely that the doubts begin to assert themselves with some force. One of the reasons why the burden on the British engineering industry was so heavy was the insistence of the Government on the need to manufacture itself, according to its own specifications, practically the whole range of arms and equipment required by the British services. It is, of course, natural for any great power to want to do precisely this. If it has to rely on another country for the supply of an essential piece of armament, it is no longer completely free to manoeuvre in a crisis. It has lost some part of its sovereign power.

In the mood of the early postwar period, which lasted into the 1950s, no economic considerations that anyone could have put forward would have persuaded a British Government, Labour or Conservative, to accept such a loss. It was, after all, the Labour Government which set off on the expensive business of making its own atomic bomb; and it had no qualms about hiding away the money being spent on this project in various obscure corners of the official estimates, so that there was no accountability to Parliament for the venture that had been undertaken. No one could seriously grumble at that, given the assumptions on which British policy was based; such clandestine activity was among the necessary amenities of a great power determined to keep ahead in the arms race.

The general principle of military self-sufficiency which guided British policy also had the effect of denying to Britain some of the military aid which the U.S. Government was offering to its allies. This aid was given in the form of military equipment, made in the United States, and so it was only of use to a nation that was prepared to forgo its sovereign desire to manufacture all its own armaments. In fact, Britain did take a certain amount of American military aid in the form of equipment, either as a temporary stopgap or to supplement its own supplies. But there was never until recently any question of a real division of labour, with Britain concentrating its energies on certain items of equipment and relying on American supplies for others. This would have been the simplest and most direct way of easing the intolerable load placed on the British engineering industry by the rearmament programme in the early 1950s.

The Americans, although they would have been willing to supply more arms to Britain if they had been asked for them, were, however, very content to see a second centre of arms production situated closer to a possible theatre of war in Western Europe. They even provided a certain amount of money to foster the effort. They were also quite glad to have another centre of research and development, particularly in military aircraft, where British designers and engineers had shown outstanding talent. Thus there was a happy marriage of British national pride and American military convenience.

I am not suggesting that this national pride was reprehensible or stupid. It would be asking an enormous lot from any nation which had just emerged victorious from the greatest war in history to understand straightaway, and accept the fact without a struggle, that since the emergence of the two colossi, Russia and the United States, the ideal of military self-sufficiency for any lesser power had become an illusion. Certainly, it was inconceivable from the beginning that Britain would engage on an atomic war on its own. Yet the delusion of grandeur led Britain not only to manufacture the bomb independently, but also to spend huge sums of money on developing the 'V' bombers capable of delivering it on a Russian target. The only serious argument that I have heard used to justify these endeavours is that the weapons provide something to brandish at the Americans, when they are not taking sufficient notice of the British views. Having the bomb would in the last resort make it possible for Britain to commit the Americans to fighting a war which they would otherwise be reluctant to undertake. The alternative for them would be to stand by and see their most powerful ally ruined. Even if there were something to be gained in this way – which I doubt – it could hardly be enough to justify an economic policy which is in the long run suicidal for Britain.

Here is the real argument for a smaller defence budget. It has been making some headway of late, though its reflection in British policy-making is still hesitant and uncertain. It is not yet clear at the time of writing, while the details of the new defence programme announced in 1957 are still being worked out, how far the Minister of Defence and his advisers are really guided by a sober estimate of economic considerations – or whether they have not really altered their views but now think it possible, because of changed conditions in the nuclear age, to be a first-class military power again on the cheap.

So far I have been concentrating on major issues of long-term military policy. An examination of the record of the 1950s shows that although the greatly enlarged defence programme was undertaken by Britain after the outbreak of the Korean war in a spirit of high international responsibility, there were special elements in the military problem which had very little to do with this country's commitments to the Western alliance. With the same loyalty to the alliance and the same readiness to make sacrifices for it, we could have got through the required military effort with a great deal less economic dislocation.

The basic attitude of mind which is intensely unwilling, when it comes to a military or strategic issue, to take a serious interest in economic implications and to weigh these carefully in the balance, has affected a whole range of decisions about policy since the war. It is not just that the big decisions have been taken with a deliberate disregard of their economic cost. The attitude goes much deeper than this: it is temperamental rather than philosophical. That is why I called it 'insouciance' earlier on. It is the sort of mood which does not bother to count the cost when, for example, a decision is being made to build a huge new Middle East base in Cyprus, after the evacuation of the Suez Canal Zone. It was argued at the time by some military experts that the best place for a Middle East base serving the Western alliance would probably be in Turkey. Certainly, the obvious choice was not an island, with a population fiercely divided, on which another member of the Western alliance, Greece, had staked a territorial claim. But even if such political considerations had not been present, the calculation of cost alone might have induced Britain to seek the means of sharing the burden of establishing a Middle East base. In other words, the sensible course would have been to try to find a home for it somewhere outside British colonial territory.

But this is plainly not an argument that could be expected to appeal spontaneously to generals and admirals, imbued with the traditional idea that the only way of making your lines of communication secure is to have a piece of land under the British Crown. It is in fact by no means certain, in an age when colonial territories are being emancipated with great rapidity, that a base built on such a piece of land is more secure than one established on the territory of an ally with a fair record of loyalty. But my main point in the present context is not that the political choice in Cyprus was wrongly made, but that the economic cost of the choice was never considered in making it. When it came to the point, those responsible saw only that the Middle East was a

British sphere of influence, and that in order to maintain British prestige in the area it was desirable to have a British base on British territory. They have since discovered, after several years of effort and many millions of pounds spent in preparing the base, that the island is no use for the purpose, after all – partly because of the impediments that can be placed in the way of aeroplanes flying from here to any trouble spot in the Middle East by the Arab countries *en route*. Aden has now replaced it as the main Middle East base. Somewhat surprisingly, the existence of this obvious geographical disability was not taken into account by the planners, until the difficulties of shifting British troops to the Persian Gulf during the civil war in Oman in 1957 brought the point home. But then the planners were at least as concerned with the establishment of a prestige position in the Eastern Mediterranean as with anything else; and there are no known principles of costing prestige.

Allowing for the fact that at least an equally convenient air base against the Russians for use by the Western Alliance might have been found on the territory of one of the allies, the special importance of remaining in Cyprus lies in its status as one of the series of stations on the route across the world that Britain has been able to maintain for more than a hundred years past. Malta, Aden, and Singapore are other points along it. And at present the Maldives Islands are being prepared to replace the air stations that are to be closed down in Ceylon. Nobody apparently stops to ask whether all these stations are really necessary – whether there is anyone left at the other end of the lifeline in the Antipodes or the Far East whose life depends on rapid aid from Britain, and what aid Britain would be able to give in an emergency. Perhaps the truth is that a military power on the wane tends to be more concerned than ever to show the flag at the various points round the world where its sovereign authority can still be asserted. There is nothing essentially evil about this desire to show the flag. It may even do some good on odd occasions, in the few places where a gesture of the traditional sort still makes people sit up. But carried on in the unrestrained way in which it has been pursued since the war, it can be abominably expensive.

A COSTLY DIPLOMATIC VICTORY

It would be wrong, however, to imagine that this large-handed approach to military expenditure is confined to the imperial domain or to traditional zones of influence. It keeps cropping up in less expected places. And it is not always an active policy, a conscious pursuit of prestige; it sometimes wears an air of sheer forgetfulness – an impression that British statesmen are too concerned with the major issues of world politics and strategy to bother overmuch about the minutiae of cost accountancy. So in a sense they are – or, at any rate, have been until recently. They have had the habits of rich men, exercising their sense of responsibility around the world in the grand manner.

This may be thought to be an exaggerated and fanciful description of a lot of sober and hard-headed people. That such sober men behave very peculiarly at times can be demonstrated only by a detailed examination of particular cases. The one that appears to me most striking in recent years is the handling of the crisis over European defence and German rearmament in 1954 by Sir Anthony Eden, who was then Foreign Secretary. From a purely diplomatic point of view, there is no doubt that on this occasion he managed a most difficult situation with great brilliance and address. The whole structure of the Western military alliance was suddenly in danger of breaking down, with the rejection of the European Defence Community by the French Parliament. This had been regarded up till then as the linchpin of the whole scheme for a strengthened NATO with a revived German army inside it. The Americans, in particular, took the rejection of the European Defence Community by the French Government, under the premiership of M. Mendès-France, as a direct body blow.

What Sir Anthony Eden did in a few weeks of agile negotiation that summer was to conjure out of practically nothing an entirely new scheme – Western European Union – which was acceptable to the Germans and gave the French the guarantees that they required to permit German rearmament. The full weight of British prestige and diplomatic skill was brought to bear on the problem most effectively. And to achieve the final result, Britain made an important concession of principle to the feelings of the French. A firm promise was given that a substantial British force, consisting of four divisions and a supporting air force, would remain stationed on the Continent for at least fifty years.

Certainly, this was a big and generous gesture on Britain's part. Once again British statesmen showed themselves capable of acting with a characteristically high sense of international responsibility, and in doing so to overcome a lot of powerful traditional prejudices against a long-term Continental involvement in peacetime. This was long-term involvement with a vengeance. However, it was freely argued in Whitehall at the time that the concession did not in practice represent a major sacrifice on Britain's part. After all, it did not matter very much, so far as their military effectiveness was concerned, if the troops forming the strategic reserve were kept stationed in Germany rather than in Britain. With modern means of transport they could be moved quickly to any place where they were wanted; and the Western European Union treaty left Britain with the freedom to move them as it saw fit in response to a military emergency. As regards the principle of a formal Continental commitment, this might seem to be a new departure to some people, but in fact any major war on the Continent was bound in future to involve British forces. So why not admit it in advance?

The only thing that was left out of account in this argument was that maintaining a force of this size in Germany would cost Britain several hundred million Deutschemarks, which would have to be earned or obtained somehow. It was true that the British taxpayer would have to meet the ordinary budgetary cost of clothing, feeding, and arming these soldiers, whether they were stationed in Germany or in Britain. But the burden on the British balance of payments would be very different. There is no doubt in my mind that Britain's allies in Western European Union, who had much to be grateful for, as well as the Americans, would have recognized this point promptly. But they were never asked. So far as I know the point was not so much as raised. The new British commitment was presented as an unconditional free gift of military aid for half a century.

Now, it is easy to understand the desire of the British diplomatists concerned to avoid raising awkward questions of payment in a delicate issue like this. But one might at least have expected that they would have considered, however briefly, the economic consequences for Britain of the exercise of such restraint. They are quite fearsome. At the time when the British undertaking was given, in 1954, the Germans were meeting all local expenditure of the British garrison in Deutschemarks out of their standing budget for occupation costs. But since the Germans got back their full sovereign status in 1955, they have made it clear that they do not regard themselves as being bound to provide any contribution whatever towards the Deutschemark expenditure of the British garrison. In other words, British exporters will have to earn the money required to maintain 50–60,000 troops on German soil. These men might as well be 50–60,000 permanent British tourists with expensive tastes in transport and no restriction on their travel allowances. For even after the considerable economies made by the British Rhine army, the annual cost of the force in foreign exchange has recently been running at about £50m a year. What this means in commercial terms is that we need to sell an extra £1m of exports a week for the rest of this century in order to meet the undertaking to Western Europe.

It is, therefore, no wonder that when the British Government got down seriously to the business of cutting the defence budget at the end of 1956, it started by taking a sour look at this commitment. But even then there was a strange reluctance to go to the other members of the Western European Alliance and explain frankly that the whole thing represented an excessive burden on the British balance of payments. In all the arguments about how many troops Britain should maintain on the Continent, this was the one thing which was not suggested from the British side. All sorts of reasons were given to justify the reduction of the British garrison in Germany. None of them convinced either our allies on the Continent or the American commander of NATO. Behind the arguments on the British side there was a marked propensity for self-deception about a new sense of comfort that was supposed to have arrived in Western Europe as a result of having an independent British-owned nuclear deterrent on its flank. Indeed, the insistence on Britain's special military contribution as the possessor of a nuclear weapon that could now be wielded, independently of America, produced considerable strains within the Western alliance. It was only at the end of 1957, after complaints about Britain's troop withdrawals from the Continent had become the subject of sharp dispute in the Council of NATO, that the Government was at last ready to admit that the military decision was motivated by the fact that we were hard up.

REAPPRAISAL OF DEFENCE COMMITMENTS

It is as if British statesmen had an enormous reluctance to face the truth on this issue – which is that although there is still the old military prowess, the same national readiness for sacrifice in an emergency, the inventiveness, the doggedness, and all the rest, there are no longer the material resources required to sustain Britain in the same kind of international role that it has successfully fulfilled in the past. It is emphatically not that the country is failing to match up nowadays to tasks which it has managed successfully in the past. The tasks themselves are different, and they are beyond our means. The true measure of British vulnerability in the new conditions surely became evident during the Suez crisis at the end of 1956, when a few days of fighting on the scale of a minor colonial war were sufficient to rock the pound sterling to its foundations. That fact played a large, though unacknowledged, part in the decision to call the whole thing off. At any rate, the pacific role of Mr Harold Macmillan, then Chancellor of the Exchequer, in the final stage, after his earlier belligerence in support of military measures against Egypt, was, it appears, prompted in large measure by the sudden evidence of their financial consequences. Indeed, although this aspect of the matter was pushed aside in the violence of public discussion on the major moral and strategic issues at stake, it was here perhaps that the most important historic lesson of Suez lay – at least so far as it affects the future conduct of the British nation in international affairs. The economic hazards of fighting even quite a small war, in which Britain does not have the immediate and visible support of the United States, are now overwhelming. Put in another way, what this means is that such a war could only be fought at the cost of sacrificing the pound sterling, and with it the international responsibilities that go with the headship of the sterling area. Paradoxically, Britain might regain some of its freedom of manoeuvre by losing its position of international leadership in the economic sphere. However, even that would still not solve the military problem.

What is urgently required is a more careful examination of the financial arithmetic in the new British defence programme. There are two distinct sides of the problem: the saving on military production and manpower at home on the one hand, and the reduction of foreign exchange expenditure incurred by British garrisons overseas on the other. So far, attention has almost exclusively been concentrated on the former; except for the attempt to cut down the Rhine Army, very little has been heard about the latter. Yet the truth is that while the economies on the production side, for example in the aircraft programme and in the closing down of a number of Royal Ordnance factories, will be considerable, they will take some time to produce any major benefit for the economy as a whole. It cannot be expected that resources released by the aircraft industry, in skilled designers and establishments for research and development, will be turned over immediately and usefully to other purposes. Releasing such highly specialized resources as these means inevitably releasing them for a temporary period of unemployment. Indeed, there is a danger that unless the Government does something positive to keep the existing teams of research workers together, the main value of this human and technical asset will be dissipated. A team of this kind is often as much an integral unit as a piece of capital equipment: it has to be put together laboriously, and then run in over quite a lengthy period. As to the leaders, that is the small number of original scientists who initiate and guide research, releasing them from their existing occupation and doing nothing more about it may simply mean transferring them out of the country altogether – into some better paid job in the same field in the United States or elsewhere.

This is another way of saying that reducing the burden on the Budget does not automatically mean adding an equivalent amount to the country's economic potential. Not all resources are transferable. The market in human beings, especially the talented ones, is very imperfect, and sometimes it does not work at all. Nevertheless, there should be considerable savings of materials and industrial productive capacity generally as a result of the cuts in the output of conventional military equipment. The unanswered question is how much of this will be swallowed up in the expensive business of research and development in nuclear weapons.

The balance of payments has been affected by the heavy defence programme during the 1950s in three ways. First, it has directly lost the country certain overseas business, which could not be fulfilled because the productive resources of the engineering industries were stretched to the limit. Secondly, it has had the indirect effect of holding back investment, and therefore the expansion of industrial capacity, which would among other things have produced more exports. The third way in which the balance of payments has been burdened is simply by the expenditure on British garrisons overseas. Any foreign currency which is spent on maintaining British forces outside the United Kingdom has to be bought by the Government, and this means that it has to be paid for ultimately by British exports of goods or services. This is true whether the military costs are incurred in a country that is inside the sterling area or outside it – in Aden, as much as in Germany. The only difference is that sterling countries are more inclined to let Britain have the money temporarily on tick. The Germans will usually want to turn any pounds they get from us into cash at once, whereas a sterling area country may be content just to hold the pounds in its bank balance in London. But the distinction between the two is a distinction of time rather than of kind: it is a matter of taking a little longer before we have to meet the bill. Eventually the money will be spent.

Total military expenditure abroad came to £158m in 1955 and £178m in 1956. The figure for 1956 included the cost of the Suez operation; something around £160m is probably nearer to the normal amount. This is just about equal to the average annual surplus on Britain's current balance of payments in recent years – after allowing for all expenditure on goods and services overseas, including military expenditure. In other words, if we had not had this military commitment, if for instance we had been in the position of Germany and thus prevented from maintaining any troops overseas, then our average balance-of-payments surplus on current account would have been doubled to reach over £300m. This is, in fact, more than the German average for this period.

Even that, however, is not the whole story. There are a number of other foreign expenses of a strictly political character, which Britain has undertaken. Thus there is no German equivalent of the annual subsidy which Britain pays to the Government of Libya in return for certain military favours. Nor has there been anything comparable to the payments to Jordan which have swallowed up several tens of millions of pounds since the war. All told, these grants and subsidies of various kinds added up to £19m in 1956. In addition, there are the direct grants of money which the British Government makes to various colonies whose budgets are in the red. These grants are quite separate from the aid provided for colonial economic development. The latter, being a form of investment, naturally come into the capital account of the balance of payments. This will be considered separately later. For the moment I am concerned to find the sum of the special expenditures of a political and military character burdening the current account. Money handed over to a colony in order to help it balance its budget, so that it can carry on its day-to-day administration without financial strain, comes into this category. These colonial grants amounted to £27m in 1956.

Adding together all these special expenditures – military costs overseas, colonial grants, and subsidies to foreign countries – the total in foreign exchange came to £224m in 1956. There was an exceptional £20m or so in it during that year, because of the Suez operation; but even in a normal year the figure is probably around £200m. It has been growing fairly steadily. Here is a comparison with the cost of the main items in 1950:

	1950 £ million	1956 £ million
Military expenditure abroad	100	178
Colonial grants	20	27
Other foreign subsidies	15	19
Total	135	224

An obvious course for a British government seeking a rapid way of strengthening the country's balance of payments would be to review the whole of this military spending abroad, the subsidies to foreign governments as well as the cost of actual British garrisons, with a determination to make a drastic cut. If it set itself the objective of bringing the total back to the 1950 level, that would be a useful initial target. But it should be possible to do better than that. Perhaps the best way to set about it would be to have a Royal Commission on the future of Britain's island bases – a Royal Commission with a brief to recommend the extinction of any one of these costly enterprises, unless it could be shown to be serving a major strategic purpose. Hong Kong would perhaps be the first candidate. Gibraltar would not be far behind. But there are a number of other spots, including Malta, which are of doubtful strategic value to Britain, in view of the diminished role of the navy and the gradual surrender of British pretensions to act independently as arbiter in certain of the smaller kinds of international conflict.

If the bases are useful, their usefulness will almost certainly be shown to be collective, that is, for the Western military alliance as a whole. In that case, the other members of the alliance and particularly its leader, the United States, should be pressed to share the responsibility for them and to contribute to the cost of their upkeep. This applies to such places as Aden and the Persian Gulf Stations as much as to anywhere else. It means, of course, that Britain would have to give up any notion of an exclusive and dominant role in the Middle East area. It is high time this happened anyway. For if it is true that our interest in the Middle East is an interest in securing the safety of the flow of oil to the West, then this is something which is shared with all the countries of Western Europe and ought to be paid for by them. If, on the other hand, the British military strategic interest in the area is regarded as being primarily the protection of very valuable oil investments there, then the calculation of profit and loss – treating the whole military cost as a loss to be set off against the net earnings of foreign exchange by the oil companies – ought to be brought out into the open.

At the moment the prestige factor plays altogether too large a part in British thinking about the Middle East – even about its oil. Each American concession gained is regarded somehow as an intrusion into a domain which is British as of natural right. Curiously enough, the oil companies appear to be those who are least concerned about the Anglo-American rivalry over Middle East oil, which produces so much fever in the popular press. They are perfectly content with a friendly division of the spoils. There is, of course, a tendency for companies to gain certain benefits if they have the backing of the most powerful government in the world. To that extent, the sterling oil companies are at a disadvantage against the Americans. They have, for instance, had to make way for their participation in what had previously been a British monopoly in Persia. But the strong do not necessarily always have it their own way – as witness the recent concession to the Italians in Persia and the Japanese in Saudi Arabia.

U.K. INVESTMENT OVERSEAS

History once again is the greatest impediment to clear thinking on the subject of British investment overseas. The words themselves have a subtly pleasing and adventurous sound. One way or another it has gone pretty deep into the folk myth that British greatness and wealth have depended on pouring out our treasure abroad, rather than hoarding it at home. And ordinary people go on believing that this kind of investment in underdeveloped countries is a most profitable form of exploitation, giving Britain economic benefits which are not open to nations that do not have access to such virgin territories. Thus has Marx triumphed. The popular attitude is a combination of shame at making such large profits out of black men and of a desire to make some more – so long as this can be done without being morally embarrassing. The instinctive reaction of most Englishmen to the thesis which I am going to put forward here – that the British economy is robbed of necessary nourishment, that its growth is stunted, as a result of this too vigorous pursuit of overseas investment – would almost certainly be to dismiss it as hopelessly eccentric. It is taken for granted that this kind of activity is, at the very least, an important, and probably an indispensable adjunct to British overseas trade.

This is where history is so important. There is no doubt that in the nineteenth century, British overseas investment was an enormously fecund force in the expansion of world trade; and since so high a proportion of world trade came from Britain or was conducted with Britain, the benefit to this country was considerable. The building of the Argentine railways and the subsequent development of the trade in cheap imported meat for Britain is the typical example. It is repeated in other places many times over. Railways were the favourite instrument of investment overseas; it is estimated that at the high tide of British capital exports just before the First World War, investors here put up £600m in the seven years 1907–14 for railway construction alone in countries supplying Britain with food.[1] With the greatly increased dependence of this country on imports of primary produce from the 1860s onwards, the search for cheaper sources of supply, with the aid of British investment funds in Australia, in Canada, in India, and the United States, was an important factor in the British standard of living. Transport was usually the key.

But all this presupposed first, an absolutely dominant position in world export trade – ensuring that the extra purchasing power in the new countries was spent on buying goods from Britain – and secondly, a willingness, indeed a positive urge, to import more and more cheap food and materials in the place of costlier home supplies. Neither of these conditions exist today. A modern example of the nineteenth-century conception, in socialist dress, was the East African groundnuts scheme which came to grief after the war. The national purpose was in this instance not to obtain a high financial return on an overseas investment, but to secure for British consumers a cheap and reliable source of food.

In all other cases, however, a simple arithmetical test of whether the overseas investment is worth while has to be applied: Is the return in the form of profits repatriated to Britain greater than the return that could have been obtained from an investment of this size at home? The first point to notice is that this is not just a matter of comparing the dividends paid out on home and on overseas investment. That is, of course, the investor's personal criterion. But the national interest does not always correspond with it. For example, a British-owned enterprise overseas may pay low dividends or no dividends at all, and yet contribute generously to the foreign exchange income of the country by bringing back the profits which it has earned and depositing them in Britain. What matters for the balance of payments is the net profit earned after all expenses overseas have been met, which is brought back to this country, rather than the amount actually distributed to shareholders.

But in assessing the national value of investment at home, a totally different criterion applies. What matters here is the value of the additional physical output, i.e. the contribution to the national income obtained from the new machinery or plant installed. This is the *net* value added, after deducting the cost of materials that have to be put into the machine and of the wear and tear on the machine itself. Now, we saw earlier that a given amount of fixed investment in British manufacturing industry might be expected to give rise to a net output each year equal to about one-third of the value of the original investment.* How much of the value of an overseas investment would it be reasonable to expect to repatriate to Britain as net profit each year? Certainly a lot less than one-third. Views on what constitutes a normal profit vary widely from one industry to another and even from one businessman to the next. Over the whole field of British industry and commerce, the net profit earned by all companies on their operations inside this country amounted to some £2,300m in 1956.[2] (This figure is *net* in the sense that it allows for the cost of the replacement of machinery and other assets used up in the course of producing the output which created the profit.) The net output behind this profit amounted to £9,600m. So that it took rather more than £4 worth of output to produce £1 of profit. It is true that 1956 was a relatively poor year for business, in which profit margins were squeezed. But the experience of earlier, more prosperous, years suggests that there is a fairly constant ratio of around 4:1 between the output produced by private enterprise in this country and the profit that it makes on

* See Chapter 2.

it. The profit margins in manufacturing industry appear to be about in line with the national average, perhaps slightly less.

Now, if we take the annual output in the average manufacturing industry as being equal to roughly one-third of the capital invested, and the profit on it is one-quarter of the value of this output, then the average rate of profit on an investment here works out at 8 per cent. The profit margin on many overseas business ventures may be rather higher than this; it has to be, in order to compete for capital against what are judged to be safer investments at home. But there is another category of foreign investment on which the normal rate of return is considerably lower. This consists of the fixed interest-bearing securities issued by Commonwealth, colonial, and foreign governments and municipalities. The latest Bank of England survey for the year 1955 shows the total of overseas government and municipal loans held by British residents at a nominal value of £768m. The rate of return on this money was of the order of 3 per cent.

Unfortunately, the Bank of England's survey covers only part of the field of company investment overseas. But so far as the figures go – and they include a fairly large sample of the total – they show a return in the form of dividends to British investors of around 14 per cent of the *nominal* value of the capital invested. The actual value of the British capital employed in most of these enterprises overseas may be assumed to be considerably more than their nominal share capital – twice as much would not be exceptional – and the dividends therefore represent a proportionately smaller percentage rate. It is impossible to make even an approximate estimate of the actual figure; but it would be surprising if it were not less than 10 per cent.[2]

The total amount of earnings actually sent back to the United Kingdom each year from investments overseas is more than just the sum needed to cover the payment of dividends. Apart from office management expenses here, which will in most cases be a comparatively small item, there are the undistributed profits earned by British companies which may be repatriated because they are needed for some purpose at home, or they may simply be held in reserve in a British bank. However, since the concession to Overseas Trading Corporations introduced in the 1957 Budget, these enterprises are no longer compelled to bring back anything for the payment of British taxes. They have now been exempted from British taxation on all profits which they retain in the business. The idea, the Government explained at the time, was to remove the handicap to the British firm operating overseas, caused by the high level of British taxation; the result is a policy whose general effect is once again to discriminate in favour of overseas investment at the expense of home investment. The Overseas Trading Corporation, which is no longer under an obligation to send back to Britain a part of its profits to meet its taxes, may of course elect to repatriate the same amount and use it for investment here. Or it may not. There is now a very strong tax incentive to plough the money back again into the overseas enterprise.

An annual return of around 10 per cent, in the form of dividends and undistributed profits sent back home, looks like a reasonable guess at the amount of foreign exchange that Britain obtains from a fairly successful overseas investment. That, together with the money required to pay British management expenses, represents the contribution which it makes to the British national income. It has to be compared with the addition to the national income, in the form of increased physical output, created by an equivalent investment at home. In British manufacturing industry this contribution is around 33 per cent. Unless the net profit repatriated to Britain out of the earnings of an overseas investment matches this very high figure, there is a prima facie case against it.

This is a clear principle, which usually gets hopelessly obscured in the aura of history and national emotion which tends to surround the whole subject of overseas investment. The first question that ought to be asked, in deciding whether to put down a motor manufacturing plant in Australia, or an aeroplane factory in Canada, or any one of the dozens of projects which are constantly being presented as bargains that the British investor must not miss for the sake of our national future, is whether the enterprise overseas is going to pour out profits to be brought home to Britain so enormously faster – at least three or four times faster

– than an expanding manufacturing enterprise now looking for funds at home. There are in fact very, very few ventures in overseas investment which fulfil this condition.

OIL—AN EXCEPTIONALLY PROFITABLE BUSINESS

Middle East oil is the one outstanding case. Here the foreign exchange earnings, on the fifty-fifty profit-sharing arrangement with the kings and sheiks of the area, provide an extremely high rate of return on British investment. This could not be bettered by diverting the money into most branches of British manufacturing industry. On the other hand, an allowance ought to be made for the big political risks of business investment in the Middle East. The chief question is how long the present principle of fifty-fifty profit sharing will last. Operations could still be reasonably profitable, even if the cut taken by the company holding the concession were somewhat reduced. This is undoubtedly the way things will go, and it is in this sense, rather than because of any risk of outright expropriation, that the British stake in Middle East oil must be regarded as an asset which will yield a diminishing return over the years.

But the return at the moment is still very large indeed. There seems to be a certain coyness about admitting quite how large it is. At any rate, there is no official figure of British oil investment income from overseas, although this represents much the biggest single source of revenue from any foreign investment. It is buried away in the official statistics on the balance of payments in a ragbag residual, which also includes such things as earnings from films, insurance, civil aviation, royalties and commissions. Ingenuity is required in order to winkle out an estimate of oil earnings from this welter. Someone seems to be extremely anxious to cover his tracks. When they are uncovered, what emerges is that oil accounts for over half of the net income from British overseas investment.[4] This is a source of foreign exchange which has grown up rapidly since the war with the development of the Middle East oilfields. It is still growing; and providing there is no interruption in the flow of Middle East oil, the British balance of payments should benefit accordingly.

British or combined British and Dutch companies (Shell Petroleum) occupy a commanding position in three out of the four main sources of Middle East oil. They own 40 to 50 per cent of the concessions in Iraq, Kuwait, and Persia. The only place where they are not represented is in Saudi Arabia. The concessions in which British interests are concerned will probably account for anything between two-thirds and three-quarters of total Middle East oil output during the next few years; and it is already clear that production in the Middle East will have to double and treble by the late 1960s, if the world demand for oil continues to grow at anything like the recent rate. Production costs in this area are extraordinarily low, and the fifty-fifty profit-sharing arrangement provides a return that businessmen in other industries only dream about. Aramco, the U.S. company which holds the Saudi Arabian concession, earns an estimated average rate of profit, after the deduction of all expenses, of 70 U.S. cents a barrel of oil. I remember once asking an American oil man with considerable earnestness why it was that his countrymen did not stand up a little more vigorously to some of the impertinences put upon them by the Saudi Arabian Government. Was it, I said, the airfield at Dahran, the only one held by the American forces in the Middle East, which made them so pliable? 'Look,' he said briefly, 'for three-quarter million dollars a day free of tax you'd be bringing them women too.'

Oil, however, provides no sort of guide to the economics of overseas investment at large. It is a totally exceptional case. To begin with, it is the one natural resource for which the demand increases in geometric progression from one year to another. Rubber and tin producers, and latterly, even the great copper mining companies of Rhodesia, will tell a very different story. Secondly, Middle East oil is exceptionally cheap to produce, compared either with U.S. or Venezuelan oil. Thirdly, there is a highly favourable profit-sharing arrangement with the governments of the somewhat primitive societies in the area. This is another way of saying that local taxes are very low – and justifiably so, the oil companies would no doubt insist, since they provide most of the local amenities out of their own pockets. Fourthly, the dominant position of the few big international oil companies in the area is consolidated by their world-wide grip on the marketing outlets. The experience of Persia, after it tried to abrogate its concession to the British Petroleum Company in 1951, demonstrated what an organized boycott by a few British, American, and French companies, supported by their governments, could do to make the whole of a country's natural wealth entirely valueless to it. In 1951, moreover, Persia was much the biggest oil producer in the Middle East; ever since its abortive attempt to throw out the foreign oil company, it has been struggling to move forward from the last place in the queue of other producers. In retrospect, the Persian affair emerges as a unique incident in modern times – a sovereign state effectually blockaded by less than a dozen foreign companies. The reason why the companies were able to do it was primarily that they were so big and powerful in the world oil trade that it was hard to find anyone operating in the same business who was ready to defy them, and also because they presented an absolutely solid front to Persia, as a recalcitrant Middle East oil country which was trying to break the fifty-fifty profit-sharing rule. For this was ultimately the real point at issue. It is no accident that the eight companies who first held the Persians at bay, and then joined together to form a consortium which now runs the Persian oil industry, between them own practically all the oil concessions worth having in the Middle East.

I must make it clear that I am not complaining about the set-up of the Western oil companies in the Middle East. It seems to me, on the contrary, that given the special political difficulties of operating at all in the region, a powerful corporate organization working on the side of the consumers of the oil is an elementary piece of self-defence. My only purpose is to emphasize once again that the situation of the foreign investor here is quite unlike anything to be found elsewhere. Outside the Middle East, there is another form of pressure by governments on foreign capitalists, which is encountered increasingly nowadays, and which, if successful, will whittle away still further the value of overseas investment as a source of foreign exchange for the British balance of payments. The leaders of the underdeveloped countries feel – and they make their feelings felt as soon as they emerge from colonial status into full independence – that foreigners exploiting a natural resource in their country ought to keep a higher proportion of their profits in the place where they originate than has been the practice in the past, and reinvest the money there. This feeling is much in evidence today in Malaya, for example, about the rubber and tin companies. It was also behind the pressure exerted by the North Rhodesian Government a few years ago on the two great copper combines, Sir Harry Oppenheimer's outfit, the Rhodesian Anglo-American Corporation, and the Rhodesian Selection Trust under the chairmanship of Sir Donald Prain, to cancel the registration of their companies in London and transfer the headquarters to Northern Rhodesia. Both groups eventually complied. This kind of pressure does not necessarily express itself in a demand that lower dividends should be paid to foreign shareholders. It is concerned with the fate of the undistributed profits, if these happen to be substantial and are being repatriated to the United Kingdom. Once again, although the individual investor may not feel the effect, the British balance of payments does. From the British point of view these undistributed profits are particularly important, since, when they are repatriated, they add directly to the pool of savings in this country, which can be used for productive purposes here.

The political pressures on the foreign investor exploiting some natural resource do not seem to be exerted with quite the same force when he is making money out of an ordinary manufacturing industry. Investment in manufacturing, particularly in the countries which have made a start and are beginning to move forward successfully on the road of industrialization, has attractions for other reasons. It is towards these countries that the argument for a big British effort to foster overseas investment is nowadays especially directed. The typical case is where a country, which has provided a long standing export market for some British product, decides to manufacture the product itself behind a high tariff wall. Unless the British firm gets in first with a big investment in the new manufacturing industry being established overseas, so the argument runs, the market will be lost for ever. The truth is that the market, as an export market for the British product that has been sold there up till now, is lost anyhow. One might just as well argue that there was a special urgency for the British firms concerned to adapt their productive capacity at home, and invest more *here*, in order to be able to meet the situation caused by the loss of their export trade. If each time we lose an export market because of local competition, our answer is to devote more British capital to investment in the up and coming industry abroad, we shall end up with a lot of very rich individual British investors and our productive capacity enfeebled to the point where we are incapable of selling anything of our own anywhere in the world against foreign competition. No doubt the investors will then decide to emigrate, because this country has no future.

IT PAYS TO IMPORT CAPITAL

A more plausible argument advanced in favour of foreign investment is that while its contribution to the national income is not as great as an equivalent amount of capital invested at home, the contribution is more important qualitatively, because it is directed to a critical sector of the economy. The income from the overseas investment may be comparatively small, but it is all pure foreign exchange. The great bulk of investment at home produces no foreign exchange whatever. In fact, some 30 per cent of all British manufacturing output was exported in 1956. In other words, it would be reasonable to expect that something less than one-third of the net product of investment in British manufacturing industry will be converted into foreign exchange earnings.[5] Now, take £100 worth of investment in manufacturing; on a capital/output ratio of 3 to 1, this would give rise to an annual product of £33; and if slightly less than one-third of this output went into exports, the total amount of foreign exchange generated at the end of the operation would be around £10. So that from the point of view of the British balance of payments, it looks as though an overseas investment, which gives a return of 10 per cent in repatriated profits, is just as useful as the ordinary investment in British manufacturing industry.

But this conclusion depends on ignoring altogether the benefit of the other £23 of home manufacturing output in our example, which produces no foreign exchange. After all, man – even

English man – does not live by external payments alone. His sole object in life is not the amassing of foreign exchange. Indeed, most of the foreign exchange that he requires is used to buy food and raw materials abroad, which enter in one way or another into consumption at home. If the sole object were to improve the balance of payments, then the simplest way of doing it would be to cut down these imports and let the standard of living drop. It is some measure of the intellectual distortion that has resulted from the pressure of national legend surrounding this whole subject that one has to bother to assert the truth that a strong balance of payments is needed in order to serve the standard of living, and not the other way about.

But even for those government officials who make it a point of professional pride to keep their eyes blinkered against all considerations other than the balance of payments, the argument for overseas against home investment is not really as strong as appears at first sight. To begin with, there is a lot of domestic investment which, although it produces no export earnings, saves foreign exchange by replacing imported goods that would otherwise have to be bought abroad. Secondly, there is the more fundamental point that all production of saleable goods and services at home does eventually impinge on the balance of payments. Even the investment in a greyhound track produces something which people pay for, and so mops up purchasing power. If the greyhound track were not there, something else would have to be provided in its place – or there would be an increase of inflationary pressure: the same amount of money chasing fewer things to spend it on. That in turn would tend to push up the price level; the pull of the home market would grow stronger and production would be diverted away from the export trades; finally, a part of the home demand that was not being met by home production would probably satisfy itself at the expense of increased imports. The moral is that although investment in, say, a uranium mine in Canada may appear so much more important in the national interest than a greyhound track or a pub or a new road for pleasure motoring, a policy which makes it a point of virtue to ignore the frivolous, but real, desires of the population carries its economic perils – thank goodness.

What seems to be constantly overlooked is the enormous advantage of being invested in, rather than investing. It is wrong to think that this advantage applies only to undeveloped economies; it often applies with special force to a highly developed country. Here the foreign businessman will, in general, only venture his capital if he has some decisive new technique or an exceptional contribution of some other kind at his disposal, which fills a gap that has been left open by the industrialists on the spot. The development of the British office machinery industry with the aid of American capital and know-how since the war is an obvious case in point. Indeed, there are several American subsidiaries or associates of American companies which have added to the technological strength of British industry. Many of the names that come to mind are British household words – Hoover, Thomas A. Hedley (the manufacturers of detergents), Ford, Vauxhall. In the motor industry the two American companies are respectively the second and third largest in the country; they are responsible for a high proportion of total British output, and, significantly, for an even higher proportion of British exports.

The truth is that the Americans have traditionally regarded Britain as the best available outlet for direct industrial investment outside the western hemisphere. That is because they have recognized that this country has exceptional advantages as a terrain for new manufacturing industry, not least in the facilities which it offers for the development of a useful export trade. And what is important is that the foreign exchange derived from these exports accrues to Britain, whether the companies earning it are American subsidiaries or British owned. The Ford Motor Company, when it exports cars to the United States or anywhere else, has to surrender the foreign currencies that it earns to the Bank of England, like any other British firm. The benefit to the British balance of payments is only offset to the extent that British Ford hands over a part of its profits – after British tax has been paid on them – to the parent company in the United States. In this particular case, the total foreign exchange earnings of the company are several times larger than the amount that goes back to the United States. Moreover, the company is able, when it turns its hand to exporting to the U.S., as it has done recently, to make use of a huge marketing organization on the spot, which could only be created at prohibitive cost by a British exporting firm.

Ford is an outstanding, though not a unique, example of the benefits that Britain obtains from foreign investment here. Another dozen similar enterprises with the same interest and success in developing export markets, and the British balance of payments would be a great deal stronger than it is now. It is interesting to find that the Germans, too, have benefited on a large scale from foreign investment in their manufacturing industry. And it is not only American investment: French, British, Swedish, and Dutch capital have all played their part. All told, some 10 per cent of the capital of German public companies, whose shares are quoted, is owned by foreigners.

It may be asked why, in the light of these facts about foreign investment, any country finds it worth while to invest in another. The answer is partly that it is not the country, but its private citizens or corporate enterprises which do the job; and they, as we have seen, find plenty of profit in it. The second point is that governments may wish to foster foreign investment in particular countries for non-commercial reasons. Or there may be a combination of political and other reasons in which the maintenance of commercial goodwill plays a part. The foreign investment in two of the big integrated steelworks that are now being built in India, one with British capital and the other with Russian, appears to have been prompted by such a mixture of motives with the element of prestige thrown in. Finally, there are circumstances in which a genuine surplus of capital exists; and unless this is invested abroad, it is not invested at all. Thus, a country like the United States with a natural tendency to run a big balance-of-payments surplus with the rest of the world, has a problem which can be most easily met by a decision to export capital. If it does not invest abroad, and so fails to provide the dollar funds required to pay for the surplus of its exports, then the rest of the world will be compelled to buy less of its goods. It is most unlikely that the resources which previously went into these exports would then be diverted into additional U.S. investment at home. Indeed, in so far as the export industries suffered a contraction of business, as a result of the loss of their overseas sales, they would probably tend to invest less.

This was also the situation in Britain during part of the nineteenth century. It is probable that even then too little was being devoted to investment in the productive equipment of British industry and too much to development of resources abroad. But we have already seen that this development abroad did bring other important indirect benefits to Britain by lowering the cost of its imports of food and raw materials. No similar commercial principle operates nowadays. In the middle of the twentieth century it is a straight choice for Britain between home investment and foreign investment. Home investment is constantly curbed in the interests of the balance of payments. And it is the capital element in the British balance of payments, of which foreign investment is the most important, which changes a handsome surplus on current account into a deficit on our external accounts as a whole, eating away at our gold and dollar reserves and bringing with it an atmosphere of constant anxiety and crisis. At the least, this is bound to produce a mood of national niggardliness – and guilt. We find ourselves constantly compelled to put up our interest rates and restrict credit, in order to fend off would-be borrowers of sterling, or to induce nervous foreigners to keep their money here – and we succeed in inhibiting the growth of our own industries. In the end we come to feel that we can afford as a nation none of the little things that we want, and so we become ashamed of wanting them.

NOTES

1. Professor A. K. Cairncross, 'Did Foreign Investment Pay?', *Review of Economic Studies*, October, 1935.
2. *National Income and Expenditure, 1957*, Blue Book.
3. It is interesting to find that the calculation of yields on British overseas investment in the late nineteenth century by A. K. Cairncross puts the average at 5–6 per cent (*Home and Foreign Investment*). But there were more fixed interest loans and less high-yielding company investments then than now. Sir Donald MacDougall suggests (*The World Dollar Problem*) that the yield on U.S. foreign capital in the period since the war is perhaps 8 per cent of market value. The yield would be even lower as a proportion of *replacement value*,

which is the relevant concept for the comparison between new investment at home and overseas made in the text.

4. In 1954 the proportion of oil income was nearer two-thirds of the total. But in 1955 and 1956 there were special circumstances which reduced the flow of Middle East oil profits – first the heavy expenses involved in starting up production in Persia again, when the dispute which had interrupted operations for over three years was finally settled, and then in 1956 the Suez crisis. The effects of the latter continued in the early months of 1957. Profits were especially affected by the cutting of the Iraq Petroleum Company's pipeline through Syria.

The approximate amount of oil investment income can be derived from the National Income Blue Book (table 7), which gives the total of property income paid and received abroad, by deducting the figures of 'interest, profits, and dividends' in the Balance of Payments White Paper (items 3 and 10) from it. The latter include all overseas investment income, except from oil. The picture that emerges in 1956 is that oil accounted for £323m out of the total of £667m gross income from overseas investments, and, when outgoings are deducted, for £95m out of a total net overseas income of £178m.

5. This cannot be proved. The only statistics available are of the value of *gross* manufacturing output exported, i.e. including that portion of the cost of the final product which consists of the raw materials, fuel, etc. – the things brought into the factory from outside. In 1956 this amounted to £2,055m out of a total gross manufacturing output of £6,720m (both figures measured at constant 1948 prices). There is no reason to suppose that the ratio between total *net* manufacturing output and that portion of it which is exported would be much different from this. It would only be so if the import content of manufactured goods consumed here were markedly higher or lower than that of goods destined for export markets.

CHAPTER SIX

THE PROBLEM OF STERLING

AT the root of Britain's economic troubles are the political objectives of a great power. So far, we have examined two of the great power maladies, which are together responsible for converting a thoroughly healthy balance of payments into a kind of national anxiety neurosis – the overloaded military budget abroad and the excessive foreign investment. No doubt, it will now be pointed out that Britain does not go into this business of foreign investment on a narrow calculation of profit and loss. It has to be viewed in the wider context of foreign economic policy as a whole. Britain is, after all, the leader of the sterling area, a group of countries which together account for close on one-quarter of all the world's trade. Moreover, Britain is the guardian of the pound sterling, the most widely used medium of exchange both inside and outside the sterling area.

It is plainly time to look more closely at this aspect of the matter. Is it indeed the truth that British foreign investment is some kind of necessary ransom that has to be paid in order to keep the sterling area going, and that without the sterling area, Britain could not survive? If this is so, then much of the argument in the last chapter falls to the ground. In that case, our position is a rather depressing variant of that of Ethelred the Unready, with the difference that we are paying out our Danegeld to our friends rather than our enemies, in an effort to persuade them not to desert us.

It is quite true – and this should be the starting-point for any analysis of the sterling area – that the system does depend on the ever-open door for capital movements out of London. The basic principle is that the British authorities do not impose any exchange controls whatever on the transfer of money from Britain to any country in the sterling area. It is partly because of this arrangement that the Treasury, rather surprisingly, has no figures of its own on the volume of investment in the sterling area financed by this country. It has to rely for its computations on statistics put together by the recipient countries, who, incidentally, have no similar inhibitions about imposing exchange controls on the movement of sterling funds.

The free movement of British capital into the sterling area has had some rather awkward consequences since the war. There was the rush of British 'funk money' into South Africa during the early days of the Labour Government. More recently, there has been the problem of the drain of dollars through the 'Kuwait gap'. Kuwait is a part of the sterling area – a very valuable part, since with the aid of its oil it earns a great deal more than it spends – but it operates no legal controls over transactions between Kuwaiti businesses or banks and the dollar area. Thus, an Englishman who wants to change his pounds into dollars can do so by moving his money first of all into a Kuwait account. The same sort of thing can be done through Hong Kong. Of course, he would in the end be doing something illegal by holding dollars in his private ownership, and not surrendering them to the British Treasury.

But until the regulations were tightened up in 1957, there was a much easier way of moving from pounds into dollars with the help of the Kuwait gap. The Kuwaiti pounds were simply used to buy American shares in New York, and the shares were then shifted from Kuwait to London into British ownership. For there is a perfectly legal market in the London Stock Exchange in a number of American shares. These are part of the fairly considerable pool of dollar securities which have been in British ownership for many years past, and which Englishmen are allowed to buy and sell freely among themselves. But the theory is that the stock of such securities remains constant; whereas in fact a flood of new dollar securities was coming into London through the Kuwait gap. Indeed, by 1957, this buying of American and Canadian securities was imposing a serious strain on the gold and dollar reserves; much of the speculation which helped to weaken the pound sterling in the early part of the year came from this source, not from foreign speculators at all. Finally, in the middle of the year, when the flow of dollar securities into London began to reach menacing dimensions, the authorities introduced a new control over the transfer of dollar securities from Kuwait or any other part of the overseas sterling area to Britain.

This was the first important departure from the principle of complete freedom for the movement of capital in the sterling area. However, it is, when all is said and done, not a very onerous form of interference. It applies only to the movement of dollar securities into London, and does not impede in any way the outflow of British funds for long-term investment. Thus, it really leaves untouched the hard bargain between Britain and the rest, which lies at the heart of the sterling area. This bargain has two parts. Neither has been given formal expression in a written agreement, and in ordinary times, when things appear to be going reasonably well, they are not often talked about. Like so much else in the sterling area, they operate as a tacit understanding; everyone rather pointedly avoids inquiring too closely into what precisely is involved, so long as the arrangements appear to be giving moderate satisfaction. The whole show is, in fact, run in an enormously British spirit; and it is interesting to observe that the most fervent protagonists of this spirit are the bankers and officials who have acquired it by adoption rather than by birth – the members of the sterling area outside the British Isles.

But the hard bargain is there just the same, even though the spirit that has been established in the sterling system allows a good deal of latitude and generosity in its interpretation. First, the members of the area, who agree to hold their reserves in sterling and to sell to Britain any surplus of foreign exchange that they may have in exchange for sterling, must be assured that Britain will supply them with any foreign currency that they need, including dollars, in reasonable amounts in exchange for sterling. In other words, there is a substantial measure of convertibility for members of the sterling area. Everyone within the club is, however, extremely well trained in the limits of the possible, and so there is in practice a great deal of restraint in exercising a right on which absolutely no formal restrictions are placed. The second part of the bargain is even less precise. It is that Britain will give reasonable assistance to investment in sterling area countries, first by providing facilities for the export of private capital to them, second by giving them an official preference over other foreign claimants on British funds. The basic assumption here is that Britain is by nature an exporter of capital on a large scale, so that it only remains to ensure that an existing flow is directed mainly to the privileged group of countries. This is done partly by granting to their governments the right, which is denied to the governments of countries outside the sterling area, of borrowing in the London capital market.

BRITAIN'S ROLE AS A BANKER

Thus the old relationship of banker to client, on which the original idea of the sterling area was founded, is preserved first of all, by offering the client payment on demand in any kind of currency he wants, and secondly, by giving him something in lieu of overdraft facilities – the right to borrow – which he can use if he offers the right kind of security. There is nothing automatic about the overdraft; the sterling area is quite unlike the European Payments Union, for instance, where a nation that runs into trouble in its balance of payments automatically gets a certain amount of credit to cover part of its deficit. Nevertheless, the opportunity offered for obtaining funds in London through the market is an integral part of the system. So is the freedom for investment funds to move out of Britain into the rest of the sterling area, without passing through the market. This flow of funds, from British companies mainly but also from individuals, nowadays accounts for much the greater part of the money being invested from Britain in sterling area countries.

Total private investment in the sterling Commonwealth – that is, excluding the Middle East countries, like Iraq and the Persian Gulf states, which are members of the sterling area but not part of the Commonwealth – is officially estimated at an average of £100m a year from 1952 to 1956. Government loans to the sterling Commonwealth over the same period have averaged about £25m a year. Finally, there are the grants of money for colonial development and welfare amounting to some £30m a year. All told then, the capital cost of keeping the sterling area together may be put at something over £150m a year. To complete the picture so far as the Commonwealth is concerned, a further £30m a year should be added for British investment in Canada. This is an activity which imposes a special strain on the gold and dollar reserves. Since 1952, Canada has absorbed about £200m of direct British investment. But that is not the whole story. There have been considerable purchases of Canadian, as well as U.S. securities, by British nationals through the 'Kuwait gap'. In two and a half years, until the middle of 1957 when the regulations were tightened, the 'gap' swallowed £160m. Thus well over $1,000m has been spent by Britain in North American investment, open and clandestine, in the past few years. If that had been saved, the gold and dollar reserve would have been 50 per cent larger to meet the crisis that came in the autumn of 1957. We might have avoided 7 per cent bank rate.

It is worth labouring these comparisons of the order of magnitude of British investment, because there is a familiar myth about an alleged British failure to invest in Canada since the war, which has become firmly embedded in the national consciousness. Of course, we have not invested nearly as much as the United States; but then look at how much investment the United States had already put into its own industries, public utilities, and its ordinary amenities of life. For the United States, investment in Canada is a genuine overspill: it allows Canada, which has a large deficit on its trade with the U.S., to buy American manufactures which it could not otherwise afford. Like Britain in the nineteenth century, the U.S. keeps certain of its export industries going by providing favoured customers with the wherewithal, in the form of investment funds, to buy their goods. But Britain in the twentieth century has itself a large trade deficit with Canada; British investment there only adds to the strain on our balance of payments. This is not to deny that the British stake in a rich pioneering country like Canada is a good deal less than the ideal. But it is a great deal more than Britain can afford. It is surely absurd that Britain should be pinching and scraping, starving its own industries, in order to put money into another country where investment is already extremely high and where the general standard of living is well above the British level.

The only possible justification for such a policy would be that British industries were so decrepit that the extra money could not be usefully devoted to making them more productive. In that case there would be something to be said for a plan for pouring this country's capital surplus into more productive enterprises overseas, on condition that these enterprises would absorb British workers displaced from their comparatively unproductive activities at home. But this argument would imply such a state of desperate economic weakness at the centre of the Commonwealth that the game would be up anyhow. It is strange how British policy goes on being guided by the view that we generate a natural surplus both of population and of capital for export, whereas the truth which has been plain for the last fifteen years is that the country suffers from an acute shortage of both. Only people – and this includes economists – who were so corrupted by history as to be incapable of looking at facts could have failed to notice what has happened.

However, leaving aside the ideology that has built up around this issue, it still remains true that so far as the sterling area is concerned, the promise of the ever open door to the London capital market is, as we have seen, an important factor in keeping the system together. The argument is sometimes taken one stage further, in order to show that Britain has in reality no alternative but to continue to export capital in this way, if it is to avoid being overwhelmed by the demands of its creditors. The point is that since Britain already owes so much money to the sterling area countries, they will, if they do not receive a sufficient flow of normal investment funds from Britain, draw on their sterling balances in order to meet their needs. After all, they only keep their assets in London because they continue to treat Britain as a banker and as a source of capital. £150m a year is cheap at the price, it is claimed, if it stops a run on the bank, whose liabilities to its customers exceed its available assets by two or three billion pounds.

On this showing, the whole thing is a huge confidence trick. Britain, a gentleman banker much reduced in circumstances, with clients who continue to deposit their money with the firm largely because of tradition and habit, has to keep up appearances by handing out a certain amount of largesse each year. Meanwhile, because of this expense which the banker cannot any longer afford, there is no money to pay the bill for repairs on his own house, which is now in danger of falling down. Then unfortunately his clients really will notice that something is wrong.

The problem has now become more urgent because of the rapidly growing needs of the sterling area for external capital. It will no longer be possible to get by with largesse on the traditional scale. There was a time when one lot of sterling countries in deficit was offset by another lot in surplus. The identity of the countries concerned changed from year to year; but in ordinary times we could usually rely on there being some of each. Now they have all been infected by the investment virus. This is a direct tribute to Western ideology in its modern form: they all see themselves developing into high consumption economies in the image of America; and they now believe that this can be done fairly quickly after a period of intense capital incubation. Britain meanwhile does what it can to moderate the investment fever in the sterling area. But the truth is that by now all of its members tend to see themselves as having a God-given right to run a balance-of-payments deficit in the interests of a high investment programme.

The essential fact is that the sterling area has changed its character. It has ceased to be an old-fashioned bank; its members now regard it as an investment fund. They feel no incentive to make fresh deposits in London, to aim at a surplus which will allow them to set something aside for a rainy day; they all want to borrow. Yet Britain goes on acting as if the business had not changed in any way – treating it indeed as if it was still a nineteenth-century family concern, taking down the shutters each morning, making much of the personal relationship with customers, and reminding them periodically of the need to live within their means. Of late these reminders have become more and more insistent. Hardly a meeting of Commonwealth finance ministers goes by, without the point being reiterated. It is the constant theme of British Chancellors of the Exchequer when they make statements about the future of the sterling area. If only, they say, if only all countries would just *try* to keep their expenditure down to the level of their incomes, then the pound would be able to look the dollar in the face. Of course, there would be some who would fail to make it every now and then. But they could be taken care of, so long as the majority balanced their accounts over a period, taking one year with another.

This is very much a banker's notion of how the world ought to be run. If he is a merchant banker, in the traditional British style, he is prepared to lend some of his own money as well as that of his depositors. But if the flow of new deposits dries up and at the same time all the bank's customers decide that they need borrowed money on a much greater scale than ever before, then in order to continue with his business, the merchant banker must, first of all, be enormously rich himself, and secondly, be willing to devote the whole of his personal fortune to the job of being a banker. Few bankers have found banking quite as attractive as that.

British politicians have only recently begun to think seriously about the size of the problem that they have taken on in the postwar version of the sterling area. It may seem strange that they have not done so before; even now the new thinking on the subject is confined to a very few of our political leaders, and it is still highly tentative and uncertain. For it has to proceed against the determined legend of the Government's advisers, both in the Bank of England and in the Treasury, that the sterling area is still, after all, a bank, and that what Britain really has to do is to play it like a hard-faced banker. Playing it that way means chiefly refusing sterling credits to countries which run themselves into trouble, as a result of 'extravagant' investment policies. What these bankers and would-be bankers stubbornly refuse to grasp is that all the sterling area countries nowadays have such extravagant investment aims, and that they regard it as one of the main functions of the institution of the sterling area to provide help in fulfilling them.

GROWING NEEDS OF THE COMMONWEALTH

The sterling area countries seem to be less and less impressed, as time goes on, by the alleged advantages of a cautious and conservative policy in budgeting for their future. The difference between the first Indian Five Year Plan of 1951, conceived with a large amount of British guidance, and the second Five Year Plan of 1956–61, formulated by the Indian planners independently, with the model of the Soviet Union and other high investment economies in the front of their minds, tells the story. During the first Five Year Plan the Indians fairly consistently underspent the foreign exchange at their disposal. They were regarded as an ideal client by the banker in London. But they came out of the experience with the conviction that the original plan had been too modestly conceived, that they could run a good deal faster than their erstwhile tutors thought, and that in any case they ought to be bolder and take more risks with their foreign exchange budget, in order to get a move on. Their approach to the second Five Year Plan was characteristic of the new mood of the underdeveloped countries. They decided first on the minimum amount of investment that they regarded as necessary for the country, and then went ahead with their plan *before* they had made any arrangements to obtain the foreign exchange that they needed to buy the planned amounts of capital equipment from abroad.

Thus from having been the banker's ideal client, the Indians became in 1956 and 1957 the banker's nightmare. Their idea, it became clear, was to use their sterling holdings in London as a kind of buffer stock of cash, while they looked around the world for fresh sources of money. Then, at the end of the first year of the new quinquennium, after they had run through a considerable part of their sterling holdings in London, they turned to Britain in 1957 and asked for a loan of some £200m. The Indians, at any rate, regarded this as a natural request. They were trying to avoid reducing their sterling holdings below the minimum which they had laid down, in agreement with Britain, as the reserve cover for their currency. When Britain refused to give them the loan, they simply continued to draw on their sterling balances, and altered the law so that the minimum currency reserve that has to be held in sterling was reduced. The Indian Finance Minister, Mr T. T. Krischnamachari, has meanwhile made it known that he is ready to use the whole of his sterling holding in London, if need be, to meet the bills for essential imports of goods required for the second Five Year Plan.

The Indian case is especially interesting because it has shattered a large number of illusions, formerly cherished in London, about the ability of the central banker of the sterling area to restrain its clients. It was commonly alleged, for example, that to take the total of £3,500m of London balances held by overseas countries as the real measure of Britain's liability was a gross exaggeration, since a large part of the money was held in the form of national currency reserves by sterling area members. The actual amount that could be spent was, it was said, much less. So that even though the total debt to the sterling area was four times as large as the gold and dollar reserve, it did not seem to matter all that much. But the Indian example suggests that this particular impediment is fairly easily removed. It is an example which other members of the sterling area in Asia and Africa are likely to follow in case of need; and the need will come as soon as they carry out their promise to accelerate sharply the pace of their economic development.

The Indian case also demonstrates that the British arrangements for the export of fresh capital into the sterling area do not in fact protect us from a sudden run-down of the existing sterling balances. We may have to take the strain of both a big outflow of British investment funds and a run on the bank at the same time. The reason why we have to reckon with this possibility lies partly in the way that the ownership of the sterling balances is distributed. The big holders of sterling assets are not necessarily the same countries as those which receive large amounts of British investment funds. Thus the movement of British capital into the new Australian motor industry, for example, or into Rhodesian copper does not help West Africa or Malaya or India in any way to conserve their sterling balances. The total amount of sterling held in London by these last three territories came to well over £1,000m in 1957, even after the big bout of Indian spending during the first year of the new Five Year Plan.

Indeed, there is something slightly disingenuous about the claim which is sometimes put forward for the sterling area – that it does at any rate provide for a ready flow of capital to the underdeveloped countries of the Commonwealth. The central principle of the sterling system, as we saw earlier, is the complete freedom of the British investor to transfer his money to any part of the area. This, together with the exclusive right of sterling area governments, denied to any government outside, to raise money by new issues on the London Stock Exchange, is supposed to look after the main part of their capital needs. But what happens, in practice, is that the greater part of British capital attracted into sterling area investment flows to the countries where it finds conditions for private enterprise most congenial. These are first of all the white dominions, and secondly the colonial territories where direct British rule still operates. The following estimates by Mr A. R. Conan of the amount of British capital, government as well as private, which went into the main territories of the sterling area between 1946 and 1955 show the pattern clearly[1].

CAPITAL FROM ABROAD

	From U.K.	*Total*
South Africa	£500m	£700m
Colonies	£450m	£500m
Australia	£350m	£600m
Rhodesia	£250m	£300m
India	£100m	£250m

India's relative position has deteriorated still further in recent years. What with the credit squeeze and the competing claims of British industrial companies in the London capital market, the right to make new issues on the Stock Exchange has been of little value. The same considerations apply to Ghana and to the other sterling countries now moving from colonial to dominion status. As soon as they come out from under the wing of the Colonial Office, these countries not only lose their share of British Government funds devoted to development and welfare in the colonies, but generally find their attractions to British private capital markedly reduced.

The conclusion is that whatever other purpose sterling area investment, as it works at present, may serve, it cannot be fairly regarded as an effective instrument for furthering the progress of the under-developed countries. If the colonies are treated as a separate problem – as they should be, since what matters here mainly is the Government's effort using British taxpayers' money, rather than the export of venture capital into the sterling area – then the system begins to look remarkably like an organization for the promotion of British investment in Australia and South Africa, with Rhodesia thrown in. That does not seem quite so important in ethical or political terms as the people who constantly stress the vital need for more investment in the sterling Commonwealth generally make out.

The main point, however, is that all the countries of the sterling Commonwealth – whether they are lucky enough to be able to attract British investment funds or have to rely on drawing on their own sterling balances – tend to run their balance of payments with a deficit on current account; and usually there is one of them at least, at any one time, which is running a very big deficit. The model which has impressed itself increasingly on the policies of these members of the Commonwealth is Canada, the country which has managed in recent years to maintain consistently one of the highest levels of investment in the world on the basis of the biggest of all deficits in its current balance of payments. In 1956 Canadian earnings of foreign exchange fell short of Canadian expenditure by some £500m. That is substantially more than the worst deficit incurred by Britain in any year since the war. Indeed, if Britain had even approached that figure in the past two or three years, the pound would have been devalued. The Canadians got away with it, of course, because of the vast inflow of American capital seeking employment in their country. When other members of the Commonwealth, like Australia, complain of the inadequacy of the British contribution in capital towards the development of their resources, it is this picture that they have in mind. Now, Canada's receipts of foreign capital are three times as large as the total British investment in all the sterling area countries put together. The truth is that if Britain were really in a position to match up to the investment demands of the rest of the sterling area, if it had a surplus which could sustain a run-down of the sterling balances on the recent Indian scale and also a flow of private capital large enough to satisfy the white dominions, then it would not be merely a matter of looking the dollar in the face; the pound sterling would be in a position to spit in its eye. Since Britain is itself another of the sterling area countries which stands desperately in need of more investment capital to expand its industries, there is no prospect of this exercise for many years to come. The pound is weak, because the sterling area is by its present nature a group of countries in deficit. No legerdemain by the Bank of England can cover up this fact. What can be done is to impose on Britain a régime of self-denial and penury, a continuing process of starving its industries of capital, which will allow the sterling area for a time, at any rate, to keep up appearances.

One thing is certain – that it is no use trying to slide out of the investment commitment to the sterling area and still hope to keep it together under British leadership. One of the conditions for British leadership is that Britain shall continue to supply the bulk of the foreign capital required by these countries. It is estimated that Britain's contribution to the capital invested in the sterling Commonwealth during the postwar decade, 1946–55, came to no less than 70 per cent of the total obtained from abroad, against 15 per cent from the U.S., 10 per cent from the World Bank, and 5 per cent from other sources.[2] It is becoming increasingly evident that the only way in which Britain could repeat this performance, or anything like it, in the second postwar decade would be by a process of self-mutilation.

THE DOLLAR GAP

The claim that is most commonly made about the advantage that Britain derives from the leadership of the sterling area is that it provides the means of meeting a dollar deficit in our trade, which would otherwise defeat us. Whatever burdens may be placed on the British balance of payments by the sterling area's investment needs are more than recompensed, it is argued, by the special facilities which the system gives to Britain for obtaining dollars earned by the other members. The point is that although Britain has an overall surplus on its current balance of payments in all currencies taken together, while the rest of the sterling Commonwealth often has a deficit, when it comes to the one narrow but crucial sector of the balance of payments with the dollar area, the relationship between Britain and the rest is reversed. Britain spends more dollars than it earns, while they, taken together, earn more than they spend. On this view, British capital exports are a kind of bribe to induce the other sterling countries to continue turning over their dollars to us.

Now this is a highly distorted picture, which reflects the situation as it was several years ago, in the period immediately following the war. There have been big changes since then. Today Britain is neither so dependent on extraneous sources of finance to bridge the dollar gap nor do the countries in the overseas sterling area make so large a contribution in dollars as seems to be generally believed. It is true that the members of the sterling area do deposit their dollar earnings with Britain as their banker and take sterling in exchange. The exception is South Africa, which looks after its own dollar bills and sells enough gold to the U.S. to pay for them. The South Africans only contribute to the sterling area dollar pool to the extent that they owe money to Britain, either as a direct result of goods and services supplied by this country or because Britain has settled some debt to another country on behalf of South Africa. In fact, Britain looks after all South Africa's payments to Western European countries which are channelled through the European Payments Union, and is reimbursed afterwards in South African gold. Thus South Africa's relationship is on a rather different footing from that of the other members of the sterling area. It is not really a full member of the sterling system, since it holds its own separate and substantial gold reserve, and has accepted absolutely no commitment to turn over any of its surplus dollar earnings to the sterling area pool in London.

South Africa is nevertheless, as we shall see later, the most important single outside prop – that is, outside the United Kingdom – of the sterling area's dollar balance of payments. But it does not accept the rule, which is the distinguishing feature of the sterling system, that London manages the dollar account, taking in the dollar earnings and paying out the money required to meet the dollar bills. Since the sterling area produces a number of important commodities which are sold in considerable amounts to the United States, such as jute, wool, rubber, cocoa, and various metals, it might seem to be a major concession on the part of the other members of the sterling area to leave the management of the big dollar funds to Britain. But once the matter is analysed into the particular contributions of individual countries, it takes on a rather different face. Indeed, it is highly misleading to talk about the sterling area as if it were one simple and coherent body with a single set of rules obeyed equally by all comers. A considerable effort has been made since the war to preserve the myth of its strictly non-political character, but in practice the realities of political and economic power are closely reflected in the behaviour of the system and its members. South Africa's special position is only an extreme example, which happens to be formally recognized. There are other oddities, which are not supposed to find a place in the pure doctrine of the sterling system, like the propensity of some of the dominions to build up their own separate gold and dollar reserves when the occasion offers. There is also the striking fact that the whole of the sterling area's dollar surplus – leaving aside South Africa's gold – is derived from the colonies, whereas the dominions are normally in deficit. This cannot be dismissed as a fortuitous circumstance, caused entirely by the fact that the Malayans happen to have rubber and tin and the West Africans cocoa. There are other equally important dollar-earning commodities produced on a large scale in the territories of the independent members of the sterling area, e.g. Australian wool and Indian jute. The decisive fact is the political one – that under the closer guidance of Whitehall, the colonies have been persuaded to be much more economical in the dollars that they *spend* on goods imported from the U.S.

Recently exports from the colonies have produced about £160m worth of dollars a year, against some £300m of dollar exports coming from the independent members of the sterling area, other than U.K. Both figures are of ordinary merchandise shipments only, and leave out of account all sales of gold. On the other side of the account, total dollar imports bought by the colonies have amounted to about £90m, and those of the independent sterling area to about £430m. Thus on merchandise trade the colonies' surplus of £70m covers a little over half of the deficit of the dominions and other independent sterling area countries, amounting to £130m. These proportions have varied from year to year, but the broad picture during most of the 1950s has been the same: the colonies' exports of commodities covering a greater or smaller part of the dollar deficit incurred by the rest of the overseas sterling area. This aid from the colonies has depended on the fact that while they export only a little over half as much as the independent sterling countries to the dollar area, they import about a fifth as much.

The question now is whether, with the achievement of political independence by two of the main dollar-earners in the colonial group, Malaya and Ghana, and the early prospect of their being joined by the third big dollar-earner, Nigeria, the arrangement which has provided such a steady support for the sterling area balance of payments since the war will remain unimpaired. The standard answer in Whitehall is that since all three countries have in effect been free for some time past to manage their own commercial affairs as they have seen fit, there is no reason to expect any drastic change in import policy as a result of the formal transfer of political sovereignty. The truth is, however, that although the responsibility for commercial matters was handed over to local politicians before the grant of independence, the influence of British officials and advisers in this field continued to be extremely strong. After all, it takes a little time before the new men in the colonies feel that they have acquired sufficient expertise in the mysteries of foreign commerce to challenge the judgements of their more experienced counsellors, and to impose their own wishes. But it does eventually happen. And among the new wishes that are likely to be asserted – especially by politicians intent on a big development programme requiring heavy imports of capital goods – is a desire for more supplies of American machinery, transport equipment, and so on.

Certainly in the West African territories the proportion of imports from the United States, compared with those bought from other sources, seems unusually low. Nigeria and Ghana buy from Britain more than twelve times the amount that they buy from the United States. It may be that British exporters will manage by an extraordinary sales effort to keep their overwhelming position in these markets intact. But experience of what has happened elsewhere makes it seem rather doubtful. Even in Malaya the share of U.S. dollar imports is already up to one quarter of the imports of British goods. In India and Pakistan it is about one half. On the other hand, the share of U.S. goods in the Ceylon market is still only one-eighth of the British.

The main practical conclusion, so far as the management of the sterling area is concerned, is that the arrangement whereby the dollar earnings of the colonies have been used to cover a large part of the dollar deficit of the dominions is in the long run highly uncertain. So far it has depended on the exercise of unusual restraint in importing dollar goods by countries which could afford to buy them. Since all the older dominions, with the exception of South Africa, have normally been in dollar deficit during the years since the war, they have had an excellent motive for pooling their dollar earnings in London. They have drawn out more than they have put in. South Africa, on the other hand, decided that it had no use for the pool – for obvious reasons. These were chiefly that the country could obtain greater freedom in the conduct of its dollar trade by staying out. It seems unlikely that the new dominions in Malaya and West Africa will in the long run remain indifferent to the same line of reasoning. They, too, will demand privileges commensurate with their dollar-earning prowess.

What this means for Britain is that the second prop of the sterling area, which I mentioned earlier, namely the right of members of the system to convert their sterling into dollars to cover any reasonable needs – the right of limited convertibility – will become more difficult for Britain to sustain. The significant fact is that the margin of dollar surplus provided by the colonial empire, as it was constituted up till the end of 1956, is rather slim. If, for example, the pattern of trade in these territories, which is at present so favourable to Britain, were to shift towards dollar suppliers to the same extent as in some of the Asian dominions, the dollar surplus would be completely extinguished. This is not going to happen overnight. But the British authorities, in considering the future cost of the rule of limited convertibility within the sterling area, ought at least to bear in mind the likelihood that there will be a gradual trend in this direction over the next few years. It would be extremely hazardous to assume that the colonial dollar surplus, which has been such a help to the sterling area during the 1950s, will continue to be the same solid asset in the 1960s.

It is perhaps worth emphasizing that none of the foregoing

argument provides any support for the familiar allegation that Britain has somehow been exploiting the colonies ever since the war, in order to maintain its own standard of living, through the medium of their sterling balances. The point that has been seized upon is that the sterling assets of the colonies held in London have risen by several hundred million of pounds over a period of years. This must mean that as a group they have been receiving considerably more income from abroad than they have spent. To that extent it is true that the burden on Britain has been less than it would otherwise have been, for this part of the sterling area has had a surplus on its balance of payments, which has helped to offset the deficit of the other part. But some people have gone so far as to suggest that the poor colonial citizen has in some way been the means of sustaining the spendthrift activities of the British welfare state. In view of the fact that Britain regularly puts into the colonies considerably more goods and services than it takes out of them, and so has a consistent balance-of-payments surplus with the group as a whole, this line of talk seems to be carrying the luxury of national self-mortification to unreasonable lengths. On the ordinary commercial account, Britain has an almost embarrassingly large current surplus with all the colonies taken together; in 1956, when Ghana and Malaya were still included among the colonies, this amounted to £180m. But the actual cash surplus was cut down to a much smaller figure by various forms of British Government expenditure. There was first of all, British military spending of rather more than £100m in the colonies, including the cost of direct contributions to the upkeep of local forces, and secondly, the direct grants of money by Britain, about £30m, to help various colonial governments balance their budgets. If these special payments by Britain were removed, the balance of payments of the colonies would look extremely unhealthy; and their main creditor would be this country.

As it is, the current account surplus earned by Britain on its transactions with the colonies, after deducting these special expenditures, has only been sufficient to buy from them a part of the dollars which the colonies earn. This part is usually more than enough to meet Britain's own dollar needs, after allowing for receipts of gold from South Africa and other earnings of hard currency by this country. The other part is a contribution to the rest of the sterling area. In return for it the colonies have received from Britain in recent years not goods or services, but money – pounds sterling, which they have set aside as a reserve for use later on. That is the source of their sterling balances. Countries like Ghana and Malaya have good reason today to be glad that the money was set aside in this way. They now need it. The truth is that if the colonies have by their efforts over recent years and their restraint in spending financed anyone's welfare, it is that of the dominions. While the colonies have been earning dollars and feeding them into the sterling area pool at one end, the dominions, who spend more dollars than they earn, have been drawing them out at the other. Britain's role in the business has been to underpin the exchange by providing the colonies with an acceptable currency in return for their dollars – acceptable in the sense that it can be transformed into the goods and services that the colonies ultimately want to buy. This is simply a deferred claim on British resources. In following through the detailed interrelationships within the sterling area, it is too easy to lose sight of the fact that it is Britain that provides the essential cement which holds the system together.

There has in any case been a tendency in recent years to exaggerate the role of the colonies in the solution of the sterling area's dollar problem. An even bigger contribution than that made by all the colonies put together to the sterling area's dollar income comes from South Africa. It looks slightly paradoxical at first sight that the chief support of the system is a country which only half belongs to it, a country which refuses to pool its dollar earnings. The truth is that the flow of gold and dollars from South Africa does not depend on a relationship with the sterling area as such, but on a purely bilateral arrangement with the United Kingdom. Britain *buys* the South African gold and diamonds, which help to sustain the dollar balance of payments. First of all, South Africa has a large trade deficit with Britain; in addition Britain looks after any trade debts incurred by South Africa with non-dollar countries. This is all paid for by shipping to Britain the necessary quantities of newly-mined gold. The South Africans do not do this as a favour; they would have to pay for the goods and services that they receive anyhow, and gold happens to be their staple product. The difference between them and the other members of the sterling area is that when Britain does not offer goods and services in exchange for the commodities that they have to offer, they are not prepared to take sterling instead and put it into reserve. They refuse to hold more than a fraction of their reserves in sterling. This means that any contribution that South Africa makes to the sterling area dollar pool in London is bought by Britain with cash on the nail.

TRADE WITH U.S. AND CANADA

So far we have been looking at Britain's indirect contribution towards the dollar balance of payments – the earning of dollars, at one remove, from countries which export to the United States and other markets in the dollar area, or which simply have a commodity like gold which can be turned into dollars at will. The sterling area certainly provides a useful piece of machinery for conducting these exchanges, as a result of which Britain receives a certain amount of dollar currency. But there is nothing unique about this arrangement. Many other countries outside the sterling area have been able to earn dollars at second hand in a similar fashion. For example, the European Payments Union, which covers all the main trading nations of Europe, has a standing arrangement whereby the creditor nations, those which achieve a surplus on their trade and payments with all the other members combined, receive the equivalent of 75 per cent of this surplus in gold or dollars at a general settlement which takes place each month. As to the remaining 25 per cent, the creditor is supposed to lend that to the less fortunate members of the Union for a time – but not for long. In the end these debts are repaid in dollar currency too. If the large surplus which Britain at present earns in its trade with the rest of the sterling area were earned with Western Europe instead, this country would receive at least as many dollars in its own right as now accrue to the sterling area dollar pool in London.

But it is not as if Britain were so enormously short of dollars anyhow. Circumstances have changed a lot since Sir Stafford Cripps launched the dollar export drive in the late 1940s – partly as a result of the drive itself. Somehow or other the old picture of a dollar-starved Britain, only prevented from falling flat on its face by the loyal support of the other members of the sterling area, has stuck. Meanwhile, Britain's own dollar earnings have been increasing steadily until they have now reached the point when they are greater than the dollar earnings of the whole of the rest of the sterling area combined. In 1956 Britain earned some $2,470m, against $2,180m earned by all the other sterling area countries together.[3] British exports of ordinary merchandise have increased most; such exports to dollar destinations were one-third larger in 1956 than those of the rest of the sterling area. But the sterling area produced a considerable addition to this dollar revenue, indirectly, by selling over $600m worth of gold to Britain (mainly derived from South Africa). Britain, for its part, produced some $800m by the sale of services to the U.S. and other dollar countries, including earnings from shipping, from American tourists, and, not least, from the American troops stationed in Britain.

On the other hand, Britain spends substantially more dollars than the rest of the sterling area combined. Moreover, imports of dollar goods have been rising sharply in recent years: they went up by 50 per cent between 1953 and 1956. This is one of the fruits of the policy of gradual liberalization of dollar trade, which has been pursued ever since the Conservatives came to power at the end of 1951. The Americans make a lot of things more cheaply or more attractively than anyone else, and when the restrictions are removed, U.S. exporters naturally find a large number of ready customers abroad, in Britain as in other places. All the same, in spite of the recent rush of North American imports as a result of these special influences, the rise in British exports has more than kept pace with the movement.

This is the picture shown by the 1956 figures: Britain's dollar income from exports and other commercial transactions amounted to £883m ($2,473m) and the dollar outgoings to £932m ($2,610m). The deficit was thus only £49m. And half of this was covered directly by American defence aid.

The trend of the dollar deficit in recent years, taking into account commercial earnings and expenditure only, and excluding British receipts of American aid, has been as follows:

1953	1954	1955	1956
£106m	£122m	£252m	£49m

The unusually low figure for 1956 is partly due to the fact that the U.S. and Canadian Governments waived the annual interest payments on the debt owing to them, which normally falls due at the end of the year; they agreed to do this in an attempt to bring some relief to sterling during the period of intense strain in the winter of 1956–7 after the Suez conflict. That saved about £40m, and it has been repeated in 1957. The dollar deficit in 1956 would, if circumstances had been normal, have been around £90m – that is slightly below, but in line with the order of magnitude of the deficit in the years 1953 and 1954. If these three years can be taken as at all typical, it looks as though Britain's dollar deficit nowadays is about the order of £100m – a wholly manageable figure. I exclude 1955 as an indicator of the size of the dollar problem, because it was a year of crisis in which the whole of the British balance of payments got temporarily out of gear; the rise in the dollar deficit in that year was part of the general problem caused by a burst of over-spending which was fairly quickly remedied. I do not mean to say that a situation like 1955 is never likely to occur again; it almost certainly will, when the momentum of some future boom turns out for a short period to be somewhat greater than was anticipated. It is, as was pointed out earlier, precisely in order to meet such contingencies that one bothers to keep a reserve of gold and foreign exchange. It is essentially a mechanism for allowing a nation to take risks.

In estimating the kind of dollar deficit that Britain must expect to meet in years of reasonable prosperity, it is fair to exclude the odd year in which the calculation of the balance of supply and demand at home goes plainly wrong. Such indications as are available of the further trend in 1957 continue to suggest that the figure is being kept within the compass of £100m or so. Now, this is an amount of hard currency that Britain should be able to earn without difficulty from a variety of non-dollar countries which depend on British supplies. South Africa is one such source: the gold earned by British exporters in the South African market in the normal course of trade would be sufficient by itself to meet a large part of the bill. £100m represents $2\frac{1}{2}$ per cent of Britain's total foreign exchange earnings outside the dollar area. It is not unreasonable to expect that, so long as some countries with which Britain trades are earning a surplus of dollars, it will be possible to pick up this marginal amount of dollar currency from them. After all, a sizeable part of Britain's dollar deficit is not incurred in buying things for British consumption, but in operations like the production of oil in Venezuela, which is then sold to other countries for sterling. If Britain did not spend dollars in producing sterling oil in Venezuela some countries, which at present pay sterling for fuel, would be forced to turn to a dollar source of supply.

The conclusion is that Britain does not need the sterling area in order to pay its way in hard currencies. That could be done by means of other arrangements. There are, of course, certain elements of instability in the present level of Britain's dollar earnings. Some of these earnings might fall and the dollar gap widen again. The most obvious uncertainty in the long run is about the future of American military policy abroad. At the moment the bases which the Americans occupy in Britain bring in over $200m a year. This is the value of the supplies bought by the American forces stationed here. Then there are the so-called 'off-shore sales' of British military supplies, which bring in another $100m. These are exports of arms and equipment to certain allied governments, which are ordered and paid for by the United States. The earnings from this particular source will almost certainly diminish in the next few years. But there is nothing to suggest so far that the aggregate amount of U.S. military expenditure in Britain is likely to be significantly reduced in the near future. It could of course drop sharply. But then so could the ordinary British commercial exports to the United States.

This is perhaps the more serious aspect of the matter, at any rate from a short term point of view. The American market is on the whole considerably more volatile than the American Government is when it comes to deal with long-term military policy. Many of the things which we sell to the United States are on the margin of consumer choice; they might suffer disproportionately with a drop in consumer incomes during a recession. However, this hazard is not peculiar to the American market. There is no reason to expect that the resultant fluctuations in sales will be any more violent than those which British exporters have experienced in Australia, for instance, in recent years. And meanwhile the secular trend of exports of British manufactured goods to the United States is rising strongly, whereas to Australia it is not.

However, that still does not dispose of the dangers of a recurrence of the world-wide dollar problem. Might it not catch us unawares again, as it did in the period immediately following the war? And in that case would it not be wise to cling to the dollar-earning capacity of the sterling area? In a recent study of the question[4] Sir Donald MacDougall has argued cogently that the dollar problem will sooner or later make a sharp comeback, and that it will remain with us for many years more. He bases his argument on a projection into the 1970s of postwar trends in world demand for American manufactured goods, and then shows that the probable earnings by the non-dollar countries together will not be nearly enough to meet the cost of these imports from the U.S. One of the chief reasons for this is that the U.S. is likely to satisfy the bulk of its increasing demand for raw materials from supplies provided by other countries inside the dollar area, like Canada and Venezuela.

But the nub of MacDougall's thesis on the inevitability of the dollar gap is the contention that the United States, as the most advanced industrial country in the world, will continue to provide the rest of the world with at least the present proportion of 5–6 per cent of its total consumption of manufactured goods. If consumption of manufactures in the world at large continues to grow at its recent pace, i.e. if the standard of living goes on rising, this will mean several billion dollars of extra imports from the U.S. in a few years' time. It is to be observed, however, that these imports of American manufactures are likely to be heavily concentrated in the less developed areas, and not in Britain or among the other industrial countries of Western Europe. Here the proportion of manufactured goods provided by the United States has always been, and will probably remain, much smaller.

In other words, if MacDougall is right, any benefit that Britain might derive from the rest of the sterling area during the years ahead in coping with a dollar shortage would rapidly diminish. Indeed, the less developed countries of the sterling area look like being among the chief sufferers. It is an industrial country like Britain standing on its own which is best placed to weather the storm. This is because the new dollar problem ahead will, if it materializes, be primarily caused by America's great commercial advantage as a supplier of advanced industrial goods, and not by its sales of certain scarce materials and foods, which made the decisive difference in the dollar crisis immediately after the war.

It is worth noticing, moreover, that the hard core of Britain's dollar problem is the unbalanced trade and payments with Canada, rather than with the U.S. This should help to make the local issue here more malleable, if there were a renewal of the dollar crisis on a world-wide scale. Indeed, such a crisis would probably galvanize the Canadians into a more active policy of diverting their trade into channels which would produce a better balance with the non-dollar world. If they did not do this, the new dollar shortage would mean the loss of even more of their traditional customers outside the dollar area, thus making them still more dependent on the U.S. market. The growth of this dependence over the postwar years is already regarded by many Canadians as both irksome and dangerous. The trade proposals made by Mr Diefenbaker, the Conservative Prime Minister, after he came to power in 1957, reflect this mood of anxiety. His idea, he explained, was that the British and Canadian Governments together should make a special effort to shift a substantial block of Canada's import trade from the U.S. to British suppliers. The equivalent of 15 per cent of U.S. exports to Canada was mentioned as the share of the Canadian market which Britain could reasonably aim to capture. That would represent about double the present value of British exports there.

The British response to the proposal, given when Mr Thorneycroft, as Chancellor of the Exchequer, went to Canada in September 1957, was equally interesting as an indication of one possible future line of approach to the long-term dollar problem. Mr Thorneycroft proposed a radical scheme for the removal of all trade barriers between Canada and Britain through the establishment, over a period of years, of a free trade area covering the two countries. Some people were inclined to dismiss the whole thing as merely fashionable talk. The new rule for British politicians when faced with an aggravating problem, it has been suggested, is to count ten and think of a free trade area. Besides, there was no doubt the purely tactical temptation to demonstrate to some of the old-fashioned commercial imperialists in Britain that the Conservatives were in fact ready to establish the same close trading arrangements with the Commonwealth as were being proposed to Western Europe, but that the hesitations came from the other side.

However, it is too much to believe that the whole idea was put forward by the British Government, without some thought, either as a frivolous diversion or a purely tactical manoeuvre. The underlying issue is too serious for that; and it is recognized as such. The British proposal is to be interpreted as an offer to the Canadians to lift from their trade alone all the discriminatory restrictions which are imposed on dollar imports into the United Kingdom, in return for a Canadian effort to buy a lot more goods than at present from Britain. Now, in practice the only way in which Britain could make sure that the projected freedom for Canadian imports did not interfere with the maintenance of the special trade restrictions on all other dollar goods entering this country would be by insisting on a far stricter control over the flow of goods from the rest of the dollar area into Canada. Otherwise U.S. exporters would get round the British dollar restrictions by sending their goods here via Canada. Indeed, unless the Canadians cooperated wholeheartedly with Britain, Canada would almost inevitably become a busy entrepot centre for U.S. exporters aiming at the British market; and Britain would find in the end that its whole policy of segregating dollar transactions and subjecting them to special regulations designed to economize dollar currency had been undermined. The basis for the present foreign exchange policy would have disappeared, because the pound would have been made convertible into dollars through the back door.

The truth is that the only way in which an Anglo-Canadian free trade area could be made compatible with Britain's existing currency policies would be by putting up a great new barrier on transactions between Canada and the rest of the dollar area. That would be the condition for keeping the pound sterling in its present inconvertible state. I do not suggest that the British Government seriously contemplates such an agreement at this stage, but that is the long-term practical significance of what it proposes. Translating the matter further into practical terms, what this would mean is that Britain would offer Canada a lot more trade, in return for an arrangement that would eventually detach it from the dollar area. This is the ultimate significance of the idea behind the free trade area scheme, whether it is explicitly realized or not. Canada would have to put up a line of exchange controls to conform with the sterling area's needs; otherwise there could be no real freedom of movement for goods, services, and money between Britain and Canada. The proposal would hardly stand a chance with the Canadians, unless some crisis occurred which threatened to destroy the present basis of their economy. A long-term dollar shortage, such as Sir Donald MacDougall foresees, with the prospect of a further loss of Canadian markets in Western Europe and elsewhere, would be just such a crisis. If that occurred, Britain might be able to establish some bilateral arrangement of this kind, which would deal with its own rather special Canadian dollar problem.

In the meanwhile, short of such a crisis and a radical reorientation of Canadian policy, there is still scope for a number of small measures which would help to reduce the present imbalance in Anglo-Canadian trade. Strong and sustained pressure by governments in a given direction does have an effect on businessmen – as the success of the dollar export drive initiated in the late 1940s has shown. Exhortation, especially of the vigorous kind which makes people feel morally uncomfortable, is not to be underrated either. Businessmen have patriotic feelings like anyone else, and like to feel that they are doing things which help the nation. The Diefenbaker initiative could provide the immediate means of still further narrowing Britain's dollar gap. This would be a useful insurance against the recurrence of a world-wide shortage of dollars in an acute form.

THE VULNERABLE POUND

But in the meanwhile, it is the sterling area, rather than the dollar problem, which imposes the heavy load on the British balance of payments. If this load is accepted, the reasons for the decision should be clearly stated, so that people inside Britain know the nature of the choice that has been made on their behalf. The nations that really need the sterling area, or some substitute for it, are the independent members of the Commonwealth, particularly the new dominions. They would suffer if they lost the convenience of an efficient multilateral trading system and the backing for their currencies of a common gold reserve, much larger than anything they could individually afford. But at present the accepted roles of the two parties to the arrangement are absurdly reversed. Britain staggers along holding a heavy umbrella over someone else's head; the rain drips and splashes off the edge of the umbrella onto the umbrella-holder's face; and the chap underneath keeps pointing out how nice it is to be holding an umbrella.

The odd thing is how easily the umbrella-holder has been convinced. The sterling area has been for years the focal point of British financial policy. We have already seen how British industry has been starved of investment, in order to keep the flow of capital going out into the sterling area through the ever-open door. We have also seen how this money is directed towards the rich countries of the sterling Commonwealth, rather than the poor; the effort cannot in fact be plausibly explained on purely philanthropic grounds. Then there is the obsession with the status of sterling as an international currency. It is hard to be sure whether the concern about British leadership of the sterling area led to the obsession, or whether pride in the international role of the pound sterling, as Britain's currency, came first. Anyway there is no doubt about the intensity of the national emotion surrounding the whole subject today. Perhaps the American commentator who referred to the sterling area as 'the third British Empire' –

the others being George III's, and its successor which survived until the Second World War – was not far off the truth. Certainly the pound sterling has come to be treated as a kind of flag. It is revered at home and brandished abroad. When the pound is strong the nation's spirits are supposed to be uplifted, and when it is weak it is assumed that they will be downcast. The Chancellor of the Exchequer's activities when he goes abroad are patriotically followed in the press as if he were striding forth in the guise of some new Saint George to smite the monster who is speculating with sterling in some vault in a bank in Zürich.

Indeed, the whole tone of the press on the subject of speculation against sterling has become faintly absurd. The picture that is presented is of a band of ruthless and cunning men, foreigners of course, whose sole business in life is to speculate against the pound. Every now and then these people are caught out by a shrewd counter-move on the part of the Bank of England; but whenever they get a chance, it is believed, they join together to hound sterling like a pack of dogs after a runnable stag. The truth is that with a currency that is so widely used in international trade as the pound, there does not have to be any active speculation one way or another to affect its fortunes in the foreign exchange markets. All that happens, when confidence in the pound is lowered for one reason or another and people begin to fear that it may be devalued, is that ordinary traders who use sterling try to look after their own interests. When a British exporter, for example, ships some goods abroad, there is normally a time lag before the foreign exchange paid for them is actually brought back to this country. The importer abroad usually obtains a short-term credit in sterling from a British bank to help him finance the operation. And if he wants to extend his credit, and hold off paying his own currency for a while longer, he has in the past usually been able to do so with ease, so long as he could offer reasonable security. That is exactly what he is inclined to do when the pound is weak. His calculation is that if sterling is about to be devalued, he will get more pounds in exchange for his own currency by waiting a bit longer, and so in the end he will get his British goods cheaper.

For exactly the same reasons, a foreign exporter selling goods to Britain has a strong urge in these circumstances to make sure that he gets paid as soon as possible – in advance if he can – and then changes the sterling at top speed into his own currency. He will get less money, if the pound is devalued. It is these two movements, the combination of paying out sterling faster and bringing back foreign exchange more slowly – known as 'the leads and the lags' – which are responsible for the bulk of the speculation that has caused so much trouble in recent years. When it is considered that the value of British trade alone which is financed in sterling – the imports, the exports, and the other overseas commercial transactions of this country added together – amounts to close on £10,000m a year, it is evident that the scope for leads and lags is extensive. Add to this the quantity of sterling used in transactions by the rest of the world and the amount outstanding at any one time on transactions awaiting settlement is probably of the order of several thousand million pounds. Even a comparatively small increase in the leads and lags may easily mean that in a matter of weeks, because the normal inflow of foreign exchange dries up and the outflow accelerates, the sterling area's reserves lose £100m or so. And that is an amount which makes a big hole in a reserve that varies between £600m and £1,000m.

The more extensively sterling is used in international trade and payments, the more Britain is exposed to speculative flurries of this kind. Each time they are countered by crisis measures of restriction, bearing inevitably on the investment programme as the biggest and easiest target immediately in sight, and the result is that British industrial development is held up again for another couple of years or so. In retrospect, the enormous effort made by the British authorities since the war to encourage the ever wider use of sterling in international trade payments appears an extraordinarily hazardous venture. Were the risks ever seriously measured? There is no sign that the policy was even mildly questioned by the leaders of either party during their tenure of office. Once again there is this characteristic mood of insouciance, the view that somehow or other a way will be found, that it is all a matter of morale, and that it is only necessary for Britain to assert its determination to return to the old position of world leadership. As a piece of sober commercial calculation, the policy of deliberately adding to the commitments of a currency, supported by a slender reserve, which was not even growing fast enough to keep pace with the natural expansion of international trade in the 1950s, hardly bears thinking about. The argument actually used to justify the policy is familiar enough. It is based on the kind of banker's reasoning that has guided so much of British financial policy since the war. If more foreigners use your currency, it is argued, then they will need to keep larger working balances of it; in order to buy the extra sterling to go into these balances, a lot of additional foreign exchange will have to be handed over to Britain, and this will give further support to the balance of payments and increase the currency reserve.

That is what did happen in 1953 and 1954, when there was widespread expectation abroad that the pound would be made freely convertible into dollars. The temporary success obscured the fact that this policy meant adding further to the already overwhelming burden of capital commitments for the future, while the foreign exchange that came into the reserve was treated as a windfall and not distinguished from other current income. A good deal of the subsequent speculative pressure on the pound in 1956 and 1957 was the result of the decision by many foreign users of sterling to reduce their working balances to a bare minimum. With no prospect of convertibility and the risk that Britain might be forced to devalue the pound, the currency became much less popular. Somehow or other the traders abroad managed to make do with smaller working balances of sterling, and they showed no signs of being unduly inconvenienced in the process. Month after month officials in the Treasury and the Bank of England were hinting confidently that it would not be very long now: that foreign banks and traders would soon be compelled to replenish their working balances of sterling. But it seems that a little sterling will, in case of need nowadays, go a long way further than the financial experts in London were inclined to suppose.

It is indeed the very efficiency of the international banking and credit facilities available in London which makes matters worse for sterling in these periodic crises of confidence. It makes it so easy for the foreign trader to speculate against sterling in the sense outlined above. No doubt, if sterling did not do the job of providing a smooth and readily accessible medium of international exchange, something else would be needed to put in its place. It might not be found readily, and if found, it might not be as good. But it is wrong to believe that foreign opinion is uniformly impressed by Britain's feat in running the whole business on a shoe-string. I recall the comment of an American businessman whom I had informed weightily that half of all international trade was still financed by sterling. 'Gee,' he said, 'I didn't know things were as bad as that.'

THE CITY OF LONDON

'It brings to us a great deal in the way of wealth, strength, and prestige.' This is Mr Thorneycroft, as Chancellor of the Exchequer, speaking of the sterling area in the Parliamentary debate on the financial crisis in the autumn of 1957. Analysis of the facts suggests that prestige is overwhelmingly the most important of the three considerations which he mentioned. It can be argued that Britain does derive a certain amount of additional strength because the gold reserve, which it commands on behalf of the sterling area, is larger than a purely British reserve would be. But against this must be set the fact that British obligations to the rest of the sterling area impose, as we have seen, a considerable strain on our balance of payments, and hold back the rise in the British standard of living. The suggestion that the strain is worth bearing, because the sterling system somehow brings us 'a great deal in the way of wealth' is the standard traditional view. It is only very recently that people have even questioned it. The great international financial centre in the City of London, the banks, the merchants, and the commodity markets, must surely, it is assumed, bring in a vast amount of foreign exchange; and all this money would be lost, if the City were not supported by a great international currency.

Part of the difficulty in moving towards a more rational economic policy for Britain is that there are no reliable figures at all on the contribution made to the balance of payments by the City of London. ('The City' is not to be taken literally, as the square mile in the centre of London; I use the term as a convenient short-hand to describe the various financial and merchanting services which earn foreign exchange for Britain). There is no doubt that in the past contribution of the City was large. That was partly due to the fact that at a time when the world trading system was still fairly primitive, when communications were difficult and methods of payment uncertain, the services of an efficient and trustworthy broker were much in demand. He would find a buyer for your goods, arrange for them to be shipped, and also make certain that you were paid – and paid quickly – without your having to chivvy your customers.

The declining importance of such brokers' services is clearly reflected in the statistics of British entrepot trade – that is the re-export of imported goods handled by merchants in this country. Such re-exports accounted for over 20 per cent of the total value of goods shipped out of Britain in the period 1880–84.[5] By 1913 the proportion had already declined to 14 per cent; by 1938 to 10 per cent; and by the middle of the 1950s it was down to 4–5 per cent. Some of Britain's share of this entrepot business, which had been such a speciality of London and Liverpool in the second half of the nineteenth century, was captured by rival traders, not-ably the Dutch. But the main cause of the decline in its relative importance in British trade was the reduced demand for the ser-vices of the middleman. Producers of commodities like wool and tea began to trade directly with their markets in continental Europe and North America, instead of passing everything through British ports and warehouses. Once they had set up their own marketing organizations, they discovered that they could make considerable economies on the cost of freight and trans-shipment in British ports by sending their goods, without intermediaries, to their ultimate destination. They might conceivably get a better price by putting their products through one of the highly organ-ized markets in Britain; but to many commodity producers this evidently did not offer sufficient compensation for the extra cost of freight and handling.

In the early days before the modern network of world trade was fully established, the middleman's profit may also have been rather larger than it later became. British traders at this time had a world monopoly of much of this business, and could charge monopoly prices for efficient and honest services, not available elsewhere. But by now the earnings of foreign exchange on this kind of transaction are fairly small. Brokerage commissions on most of the standard commodities come to only 1–2 per cent. Warehousing in Britain may add another 2 per cent, and other costs of handling, together with the profit, will bring the total to be added to the original price of the imported article to about 5 per cent. That is the Board of Trade's estimate of the average earnings on British re-export trade: each £100 of imported merchandise is sold abroad at £105.[6] Total re-exports amounted to £146m in 1956, so that the foreign exchange earned came to around £7m. In the previous two years the figure was rather lower.

But that is of course not by any means the whole story. There is a great deal of British merchanting activity, involving goods which never even touch these shores. The latest official estimate of this trade, for 1950, is in the Census of Wholesale Distribution of that year. The figure then was a little over £600m. A more recent unofficial estimate puts the total at £800m.[7] But no one has any accurate idea at all about the earnings of British merchants on this large turnover. The merchants are evidently pretty good at covering their tracks. The Board of Trade hazarded a guess at one stage that the average middleman's margin on this business might be about 4 per cent[6]; but this is an extremely uncertain figure. On the great bulk of transactions going through the international commodity markets in London, the merchant's margin is under 2 per cent. However, the 4 per cent figure appears to conform with the only official estimate so far made of British merchanting earnings – a 'broad estimate only', the Economic Secretary of the Treasury told Parliament.[8] He gave the total as £30m.

To this should be added the profits on the overseas operations of British banks. Once again there are no reliable figures. The official 'broad estimate' is £25m. This figure is intended to cover 'pure' banking income only, excluding any interest paid on money lent to foreigners by these British banks. Such loans are properly a part of overseas investment, the income from which was analysed separately in the last chapter. It is not possible in practice to draw a sharp line between what a bank charges for services rendered and what it receives in interest payments. Bankers live mainly on the difference between the interest that they pay to their depositors and the interest which they charge to borrowers. When the depositors are Englishmen and the money is lent overseas in overdrafts to foreigners, the banker may be regarded simply as an agent who helps to obtain part of Britain's investment income from abroad. But the business operations of British banks in foreign countries, turning over local deposits for lending on the spot, are a commercial enterprise of a different kind. It is the profit from such operations and from other local services supplied through these banks, which constitutes the genuine export earnings of British banking.

In addition, there are the banking services which foreigners buy in London – for example, the business in 'acceptance credits' of the merchant bankers in the City of London. This business is essentially one of guaranteeing to provide money in case of need, rather than actually lending it. The British accepting-house is simply a guarantor: it underwrites a promise to pay on behalf of a client, and charges a fee for its signature. This is of course an extremely useful service for anyone who has to obtain supplies on credit, and who needs the backing of an institution which is internationally known and trusted to support his own promise to pay. What the accepting-houses really do is to hire out their reputation for probity. When this facility is used by foreign traders in order to obtain credit from one another, Britain receives a certain amount of foreign exchange, without putting up any hard cash. The amount of acceptances outstanding on foreign accounts at any one time is estimated to be around £200m. The commitment usually runs for three months at a time – £200m therefore covers an annual flow of some £800m of transactions, which roughly corresponds to the estimated value of the international trade between foreign countries, handled by British merchants. The rates charged for acceptances change with circumstances and vary between different banks; at the end of 1957 the current range of charges was from 1 to 2 per cent. The foreign exchange income from the average £200m outstanding over the year would be about £3m.

Thus the total of the City's merchanting and banking earnings, on the official 'broad estimates', comes to £55m. It will be observed that two important activities associated with the City (in the literal geographical sense of the term) are left out of the calculation – overseas insurance business and the chartering of ships through the Baltic Exchange. The first of these is extremely lucrative: it produces about £40m a year. The brokerage fees obtained from foreigners who use the Baltic Exchange to charter ships add up to a smaller sum. One unofficial estimate puts it at £20m.[7] This seems to conform with the Government's figure for all brokerage services (other than merchanting) of £30m, in which the Baltic is known to be the larger part.

But it would be wrong to imagine that this useful business is really based on the glories of sterling as an international currency. The reason why people use the Baltic is firstly that it is an institution which has been established for a very long time. It is convenient to have *one* place where all the people who want ships and those who have ships to hire can meet and come to terms. It would need quite a lot of effort to get a rival institution going. Secondly, the Baltic offers a quick, honest, and efficient market service. Thirdly, it does so partly because the country in which it is located has a larger active merchant fleet than any other in the world. Britain still owns one fifth of the total tonnage operating on the seas. At the same time British importers and exporters provide a good deal of the business of carrying goods from place to place, and are especially important in the hire of ships for the carriage of bulk foods, like grain and meat. It is indeed only natural that Britain, which is both a massive importer of commodities in bulk and the world's biggest operator of liner services, should provide the location for the international shipping market.

Again, in the foreign insurance business it is the established position, the reputation for trustworthiness, and the sheer expertise in providing a reliable service, which count. Everything really depends on the goodwill that attaches to a few well-known British insurance companies. It is certainly true that they would never have been able to establish their position, if London had not at one stage become the world's commercial and financial centre.

But by now it would be extremely difficult for new competitors to come into the field and sweep them out. No doubt, the Americans or the Germans might make some inroads into their business in time, if either of these countries developed a network of international connexions and selling agencies such as the British insurance firms now command. It is also true that some of the insurance business comes to the British firms more easily, because they are conveniently placed in relation to other international commercial services provided by the City. But it is surely not to be supposed that an institution like Lloyd's Underwriters, providing a unique service, much of it on the basis of personal trust and goodwill, which has taken long years to establish, would close down all of a sudden, because Britain decided to go out of the international lending business and to treat the pound sterling as a domestic currency, like any other.

What would inevitably suffer is the City's banking and acceptance business. The combined foreign exchange income derived from these activities, it was suggested earlier, is of the order of £25m. In addition, the policy of pulling sterling back from its present too exposed position would mean closing down some of the commodity markets. At the moment there are dollar commodities, e.g. certain metals, which Britain offers to sell to the whole world for sterling in London. This is another way in which the pound is made effectively convertible into dollars, and therefore represents a potential source of strain on the reserves. Other merchanting activities outside the commodity markets would probably also suffer some restriction. But there is no reason to suppose that all the business would go, as soon as currency and credit arrangements in London were modified. Merchanting activity often depends on personal goodwill more than on any other factor. The re-export trade, which as we saw earlier produces some £7m, should not be significantly affected at all.

Perhaps, then, as much as £10m to £15m of the income from British merchanting might disappear under the impact of a new order in the City of London. Add to this the prospective loss of international banking business, £25m. There is also some foreign brokerage business in the London Stock Exchange which would go, if sterling ceased to offer the same amenities for international speculation. All told, the loss might, therefore, be of the order of £40m. But that would still leave over two-thirds of the total estimated £125m[8] of foreign exchange earnings of the City of London intact. The amount lost in the course of putting some armour on the pound sterling and withdrawing the country from a number of activities, which render its economic life intolerably exposed to international pressures, is about 1 per cent of Britain's annual income from the export of goods and services. To put the matter into an appropriate political perspective, this is the sort of loss of trade that the British Government accepts without further ado, when it decides to have a fight with Egypt over Suez, or, to take an earlier instance, to quarrel with Persia over oil.

NOTES

1. Mr A. R. Conan, *The Changing Pattern of International Investment in Selected Sterling Countries*, Princeton University, 1956.
2. White Paper, *The U.K.'s Role in Commonwealth Development*, 1957.
3. The two figures of dollar earnings are not complete, because some of the items in the invisible account, notably the earnings on oil investments overseas, are only calculated in the official statistics after the deduction of expenditure incurred. In other words, the totals given in the text understate the amount of *gross* earnings, since some included in the total are *net* earnings. They are, however, a fairly small element in the whole, and the aggregates probably reflect pretty well the comparative orders of magnitude of the dollar earnings of Britain and of the rest of the sterling area.
4. Sir Donald MacDougall, *The World Dollar Problem*, Macmillan, 1957.
5. Sir John Clapham, *An Economic History of Modern Britain*, Vol. II. Cambridge, 1952.
6. *Board of Trade Journal*, April 1954.
7. Mr John Wood, *The Listener*, 28 November 1957.
8. *Hansard*, 19 December 1957.

CHAPTER SEVEN

SOCIALIST AND CONSERVATIVE ECONOMICS

THE Labour Party's creative period in office was over by 1948. By then the major acts of nationalization had taken place, the state had acquired a commanding position in a crucial sector of industry, and the postwar advance in social welfare had reached its climax with the inauguration of the National Health Service. The following three years in which Labour held office, 1949–51, were in marked contrast to the earlier period of effective social revolution and spiritual certainty. They were occupied by an increasingly desperate attempt to discover some principle of planned economic progress at home, in the face of violent pressures from abroad. In the end, after two major crises in the course of these three years – the devaluation of the pound in 1949, Korea and rearmament in 1951 – the Labour leaders gave the impression of men who were intellectually exhausted, whose only ideas were about how to sit tight and ride out the storm. There was no evidence of conviction, other than the personal one that they were better than the people on the other side. When it came to the point, it required a jostle rather than a heave to displace them from office.

The Conservatives took over at the end of 1951, at an ideally favourable moment for their brand of creative experiment. This consisted in bringing the forces of the market-place to bear on an economy which had grown rigid in several of its parts, as a result of a long period of direction from above, guided solely by the principles of administrative expediency. For the truth was that Labour had no positive policy whatever for private enterprise, which was still responsible for 80 per cent of the output of the country. The original Labour programme said: nationalize the lot. However, few, if any, of the leaders really wanted to do that. And the more convinced they became that they would have to find some *modus vivendi* with the non-socialized four-fifths of the economy, the more they became separated from their most mili-

tant and vocal supporters; and therefore the less inclined they
became to propose openly any scheme that might have as a by-
product the outrageous possibility of more profit-making by
the private entrepreneur. There was thus a certain amount of productive potential ready to be released by the Conservatives in the
private sector of the economy, and some public waste caused by
the previous efforts to suppress it. The new Government set about
the task of getting rid of state controls over production and
distribution with great energy. It was cautious, though determined in its approach, and it handled the timing and the administrative arrangements covering the transition from controls to
freedom in one case after another with considerable skill. By the
middle of 1954 this job was more or less done. This was the date
of the final abolition of food rationing. It was the high point of
the Conservatives' popular endeavour. There is little doubt that
many people who had been sceptical beforehand, were by then at
least half convinced that, as the contemporary slogan put it,
'Conservative freedom works' – and more than half convinced
that some of the hardships of Labour rule had not been really
necessary.

The Tory Government was helped not only by a popular mood
which broadly favoured the objective of more consumer choice,
even at the expense of a little social injustice. More important
than this were the economic forces operating through the world
at the time when the Conservatives came to power. The fever of
the Korean war boom had begun to subside; it was followed by
the collapse of prices in world commodity markets. Britain as a
large importer of food and raw materials benefited at once. For
the first time since the war, after many years in which the cost of
things that were imported had been rising steadily much faster
than the prices of British exports, world prices started to move
sharply in Britain's favour. And they went on moving that way
for two and a half years. Thus throughout the creative first phase
of Tory Government, the period which lasts until about mid-1954,
the new policies of ease and expansion operated on a great
cushion of additional foreign exchange income, because of the fact
that most of the goods which the country had to buy abroad kept
on getting cheaper. This meant that we could afford to import

more, and so there were more supplies available to ease the transition from rationing to free markets. It also meant that when subsidies were removed, retail prices did not go up nearly as much as people had feared, for the prices of imported raw materials and food were coming down at the same time.

This piece of Tory good luck, which did so much during the years 1952–4 to make a success of the ideology of a return to the market-place, is analogous in some ways to Labour's luck in coming into office in 1945, with all the controls that it needed existing ready-made. If these controls had not been there to hand, as a result of the war, Labour's first three years of office would have been largely occupied in painfully forging the instruments that it needed to control economic activity, and its permanent legislative achievement would almost certainly have been less than that of 1945–8. Both parties in fact started off in office with the climate and the background that they needed in order to make their own characteristic contributions.

One consequence of this has been that both parties have subsequently been inclined to see their policies in the early successful years of their respective periods of office on a scale rather larger than life-size. They keep looking back to these years with a kind of nostalgia for a lost age of purity and simplicity. The aims then were so clearcut and the means adopted to achieve them were straightforward and readily comprehensible. It would have required an act of heroic self-criticism on the part of the politicians to admit that in both cases they were enormously assisted by luck. However, if the Conservatives had managed to make the necessary spiritual effort at the time and seen that the success of the disinflationary policy initiated in 1952 was due to the movement of world markets and prices, rather than to the concurrent raising of the bank rate at home, it would have helped to save them a lot of trouble later on, particularly in 1955, when the same domestic policy was confidently used again in much less promising circumstances. When the old successful formula failed to work, the leaders were temporarily at a loss. By then the formula had achieved a certain ideological sanctity. It required a spiritual upheaval before it could be admitted that Conservative freedom (old style) did not always work – and that it had to be abetted, quite generously on occasion, by direct government intervention.

Similarly the Socialists, after the astonishing economic recovery achieved by 1948 and the orderly redeployment of industry from a war to a peacetime footing, which went forward while the great transfers of industrial assets from private to public ownership took place, were inclined to give the credit to their own techniques of 'planning'. They came therefore to rely excessively on their powers as planners in approaching the second and more testing phase of Labour rule, 1949–51. It was more testing for two reasons: not only were there the external economic crises of 1949 and 1951, but also the immense recovery of production in the world at large raised the problem of consumer choice, and raised it in an increasingly acute form. It had been easy enough to cope with the consumer on a planned welfare basis, when there had not been enough to go round. The whole emphasis was then on the maintenance of minimum standards of health and comfort; and the rationing system which was designed to ensure this had a large measure of popular support. Britain was so plainly superior to any other nation in securing these ends that there was even a certain national pride about *our* rationing system and *our* price controls.

The Labour Party naturally took the full ideological credit for these achievements. Some of the credit fairly belonged to it: its leaders were providing strong government and were maintaining control over what was in effect a war economy with civilian purposes, at a time when everything else in Western Europe was slipping. But this was the combined achievement of able men ruling the country with clear objectives and of a people inured to wartime conditions, and had nothing to do with any discovery of a new technique of ruling. At the one end the consumer accepted the decision of the Government about how goods were to be distributed, because things were short. At the other end, the manufacturer was saved from a wild scramble for scarce supplies of raw materials by the Government's allocation schemes. These gave each manufacturer and trader an established position in a kind of industrial hierarchy: he was assured of a proportionate share of rationed supplies broadly corresponding to the position that he had occupied in the trade before the war. Some provision was made for new entrants into industries where supplies were rationed; but these postwar interlopers were not allowed to shake the privileges of the older inhabitants. Since the Government had control over the destination of so much of the country's resources, it was able to exercise an effective influence on the decisions of manufacturers, even in the fields where it was not armed with legal powers. The general feeling among businessmen was that even if they were not dependent on the good graces of an official controller at the moment, it always paid to keep in with the Government. You never knew what might not be rationed next. The probability was that at some stage you would come up against an official allocation scheme or a building control or some Government decision affecting your plant and equipment. The businessmen no doubt overestimated the extent to which the decisions of one official might be affected by the experiences of another. Some of the more naive seem to have believed in a kind of underground network by means of which an adverse impulse received at one point in the civil service in, say, Manchester or Birmingham was at once transmitted to an office in London – or wherever the relevant point for the next official request might happen to be. But even the more sophisticated spirits were often worried. You could never be sure when you might need an official's help. At any rate it did not pay, so it was felt, to be too difficult.

The Government thus had enormous powers of persuasion in its hands. In general the consumer was on its side, so long as things were genuinely scarce. Finally, it had a fairly straightforward order of priorities for production and distribution to guide its decisions. The early phase of reconstruction of a war-damaged economy does not present any really difficult problems of choice. The planner is not generally trying to project demand into some uncertain future ten years ahead – the kind of task that has to be faced nowadays in large-scale industry, like electric power or oil or steel – but to get to some point with which he is already familiar from past experience. In the first heroic age of

Labour planning immediately after the war, the Government did aim ultimately to lay down something like a Five Year Plan, which was to provide a detailed blueprint for the whole range of the country's productive activity over a considerable period ahead.[1] But it was soon discovered – at any rate by the people actually on the job – that one-year planning was quite hazardous enough.

The changing attitude towards the whole subject of planning emerges pretty clearly from the gradual alteration in the tone of the series of annual Economic Surveys, issued by the Government in the spring of each year, just before Budget time, from 1947 onwards. The 1947 Survey still strikes the authentic clarion note. Thus for example it asserts confidently that 'certain peacetime problems, such as control of balance of payments, can be handled by much the same techniques as were used for allocating our resources of manpower, materials, and shipping during the war'. It talks of an overall 'economic budget', by means of which the detailed objectives of a wide variety of industries and trades are matched with the resources available, and then scaled up or down by the planners. Even then, however, it was recognized, at any rate by some of the civil servants writing the Government's Survey, that there were limits to what the Government could do and their views do infiltrate into the document at one point. 'The apparatus of Government controls,' they say, 'is used to guide the economy in the direction which is indicated by the plan . . . But the controls cannot by themselves bring about very rapid changes or make very fine adjustments in the economic structure . . . Indeed, the task of directing by democratic methods an economic system as large and complex as ours is far beyond the power of any governmental machine working by itself, no matter how efficient it may be.'

But this brief burst of civil service caution is quickly overcome in the very next sentence of the Economic Survey. The clarion is brought on again to produce the necessary reconciliation between the aims of a far from omnipotent Government on the one side, and on the other, the impossible multiplicity of economic actions performed by millions of people, all pushing in different and unpredicable directions. 'Events,' says the Survey, 'can be directed in the way that is desired in the national interest only if the Government, both sides of industry, and the people accept the objectives and then work together to achieve the ends.' In other words, where controls do not work, unanimity of view about the correct course of action to be taken will operate instead. But this is not really tackling the essential problem at all. The idea only begins to make sense on the unspoken assumption that people's ordinary actions are constantly being considered by them in the light of some clearly understood notion of the collective good. And behind this there is the further delusion that economic actions are in some sense special and recognizable ones – different in kind from ordinary decisions like whether one will have a kipper for breakfast or whether one will walk, rather than take a bus to work. They very often are not.

The whole thesis is unmistakably stamped with the austere and devoted spirit of Sir Stafford Cripps, who was at that time rapidly moving up into the commanding position which he later came to occupy in the conduct of economic affairs. There is no doubt that by fostering these illusions about economic behaviour, by his ability to bring patriotic emotions into play in the economic field, he and the officials whom he inspired did succeed in making businessmen do things which they would not otherwise have considered. On the labour side, he managed to persuade the trade unions to accept a wage freeze in 1948, which although not complete, was a potent influence in keeping down the level of wages in this country for nearly two years. But the subsequent disillusion, which followed the demonstration that the Crippsian doctrines about economic affairs as a branch of patriotic activity did not really meet the bill, produced a strong reaction. Sir Stafford made his exit in 1950 at the right moment for his economic reputation. There is no doubt about his boldness. He was willing to accept the logic of his policies, even if this meant offending some cherished sentiment of the rank and file of his own party. There is the extraordinary statement in the Economic Survey of 1948 of his objective to increase the number of unemployed by 50 per cent in the course of the year, and to do so by deliberately putting a damper on the building industry. Unemployment was 300,000 at the end of 1947, and Cripps said that in order to achieve more mobility of labour it would have to go up to 450,000 by the end of 1948. No Cabinet minister, Labour or Conservative, since that time has been prepared to take his courage in both hands in any comparable way.

THE PROBLEM OF CONTROLS

The contradictions at the heart of Labour's economic policy became clearly visible in the uncertain attitude towards the whole issue of controls during the second phase, 1949–51. On the one hand, these controls were recognized as the dire accompaniments of scarcity. No decent liberal-minded person on the Left of British politics would want to go on interfering with people's right to consume what they wanted a moment longer than necessary. Once a reasonably equitable redistribution of spending power had been achieved through the taxation system and the social services combined, the function of the state, outside the industries which it owned and managed itself, was simply to give the producers the opportunity and the encouragement to satisfy consumer desires. Hence the fanfare emitted by the Labour Government when Mr Harold Wilson, who was President of the Board of Trade at the time, announced his 'bonfire of controls' in March 1949. The controls that he abolished on this occasion were mainly over the distribution of a variety of goods and materials used by industry. At the end of the previous year, 1948, he had got rid of a large number of direct government controls over the manufacture of certain goods. Indeed, the Labour leaders took considerable pride in the fact that they were giving back to manufacturers the freedom to produce what they liked and to use as much material as they wanted in the process.

On the other hand, these controls were the very stuff of economic planning. Somehow the Labour leaders managed to pretend to themselves that they could go on with their planning activities pretty much as before, and at the same time give everyone more and more freedom to produce, consume, and be merry. There were occasional doubts. There were some Labour politicians, notably Mr Aneurin Bevan, who believed at the time that the ideal remained the detailed control by government fiat over the whole range of goods produced by industry. There were others who argued that the rationing scheme, the utility scheme, and other wartime expedients were still essential instruments for the redistribution of the resources of society in favour of the poorer classes. Since the schemes were supported by state subsidies, which had precisely this social objective, it was hard to argue against this view. Abolition of rationing seemed to imply abolition of subsidies, and therefore a deliberate reversal of the policies of social welfare.

The Labour Party's effectiveness, especially towards the very end of its period in office, was stultified by such doctrinal confusion at the centre of its thinking. It represented a genuine advance that some of the relevant conflicting ideas became flesh, in the persons of Mr Gaitskell and Mr Bevan, during the struggle for the succession to the leadership of the party from 1951 onwards. That at least provided an opportunity for greater clarity. It was at this stage that the intellectual defects of Mr Attlee as leader, indeed his almost complete lack of interest in ideas, were revealed as a serious weakness of the party. The party was faced with the task of thinking out its philosophy afresh – no less – and to do so as an aid to good and effective government. Between the departure of Sir Stafford Cripps and Mr Ernest Bevin and the advent of Mr Gaitskell and Mr Aneurin Bevan to the leadership there was a spiritual interregnum. This intellectual failure was responsible for the inability of the Labour Government to develop any coherent policy on the great popular issue of food rationing. What did Labour propose to do when the shortages were over? Or did it pretend that they never would be, because some people would continue to be a great deal worse fed than others? Since no answers were thought out, there was a tacit agreement to leave things as they were and not stir up trouble. The result was that when the British balance of payments achieved its extraordinary surplus in 1950 – the biggest of any postwar year – no one even thought of using it as the opportunity for beginning a serious attack on the food rationing system. De-rationing was going forward in many other countries less well placed. World supplies of certain basic foods, for example eggs, had become noticeably easier, and an energetic British attempt to obtain more of these things abroad would almost certainly have met with some success. Instead, Britain's surplus of foreign exchange earnings was dissipated in a great buying spree of all sorts of marginal and expensive foods on the continent of Europe. Enough canned ham was stocked up by British importers then to last for several years. In the end the policy made the least possible contribution to social welfare at the greatest possible expense. The Labour leaders had convinced themselves that the abolition of food rationing presented such an impossibly difficult problem that they sincerely disbelieved in the ability of the Conservatives to keep their promise to get rid of it.

Because of this the Conservative Government was able to achieve a considerable popular victory by its success in removing the intervention of the state between the consumer and his purchases during the years 1953–4. The same doctrinal malady affected the Labour Party's efforts to deal with privately owned manufacturing industry, once the shortages of materials were relieved and the most urgent postwar needs of the community for basic essential goods had been met. The Labour Party planners wanted to keep some control over the activities of industry, whether by means of allocation schemes for raw materials, by building controls, or by some sort of supervision of standards through the utility scheme. But the planners realized as clearly as anyone else that through the system of fixing quotas of materials for individual manufacturers by reference to some pre-war situation, the economic system was in danger of being divided up into a chequer board of citadels of privilege. There was a new economic feudalism in the making. But what other simple and manageable criterion could an official adopt in distributing supplies among industrialists? The only real alternative was to let them compete for the market, and then give the prize to the most successful, which would very likely also be the richest, firm. That of course would not do at all. The socialist state could hardly abet the process of bankrupting the smaller and weaker firm through the pressure of the big and successful.

Increasingly, during the late forties and early fifties, the Socialists were faced with the need to make a clearcut decision about the future role of private enterprise in the economy. But so long as the party ideology continued in its pristine view that capitalists were functionless and evil, fit only for ultimate destruction, it was impossible to adopt any policy of active collaboration with them. Indeed, it was not until the decisions of the Labour Party conference of 1957 that it became officially permissible to sup with this devil – and even then only after careful washing of hands and other rituals. But at least the 1957 programme has got rid of the bogy of total nationalization, and so opens the way to a more rational policy of cooperation between private industry and some future Labour Government in the achievement of certain planned economic ends.

In fact, the Labour Government was at its most successful during the difficult years, 1949–51, when it was dealing directly with a typical modern industry dominated by a few large firms. It managed to induce the steel industry to invest heavily and expand its productive capacity at a time that many of the steelmasters regarded as unpropitious, and it persuaded the motor industry to continue year after year to send the great bulk of its output abroad, in the face of an insatiable demand in the home market. These successes should be compared with the total failure of Sir Stafford Cripps's attempt over several years to get the Lancashire cotton industry to modernize its equipment. A Labour Government with a psychological lever as its instrument, working by direct contact with a few powerful industrialists, was able to achieve more than an elaborate structure of planning machinery working full time. The lever for the motor industry was the Government's ultimate power to apportion the limited supplies of sheet steel in accordance with the effort being made by each firm to sell its cars abroad. In the steel industry it was the simple threat of nationalization. The big steel companies were determined that the Government should not be in a position to point to any failure of the industry to expand its output or capacity as justification for a decision to transfer them to public ownership. Indeed, the threat of nationalization appears to have been a more effective stimulus than nationalization itself. There is something in the quip that the only sure way of allowing a big and exposed industry to escape from the pressure of public opinion is to transfer it to public ownership.

It should be recognized that these successes of the Labour Government in pushing particular sectors of private industry in a given direction cannot be construed as a victory for socialist techniques. A very similar victory was won by President Truman in the early 1950s when, by a mixture of threats and cajoleries, he induced the American steel industry to undertake a vast scheme of expansion, and overrode the doubts of several of the industrialists concerned about either the wisdom or the ultimate profitability of the undertaking. There are several other instances of direct action by the U.S. Administration, under the Democrats, to make an industry obey its wishes. The great lever which the Democratic Administration possessed – and which incidentally President Eisenhower has not had at his disposal – was the generally understood fact that Democratic leaders like Mr Truman had no inhibitions about bullying, browbeating, and generally making life unpleasant for particular bits of private enterprise, if they felt that this would serve the public interest. The same kind of advantage was used by Dr Erhard, the German Minister of Economic Affairs, in the course of various disagreements with powerful German industrial interests about the prices to be charged for their goods. He had no qualms about bringing the strongest moral and political pressure that he could muster to bear on the coal-owners, for instance, in an effort to make them keep their prices down – or at any rate to moderate the price increase that they were planning to introduce. And he did not hesitate, either, to mobilize public opinion as an ally in his struggle, buying advertising space in the daily press and using it to put over his case in the most popular and partisan form.

Compare these rumbustious quarrels of the German arch-exponent of private enterprise, his unashamed attempts to twist the price mechanism to his own ends, with the timid and inhibited attitude of British Tory politicians in their dealings with businessmen in this country. They were so afraid of appearing to act as Labour had done that they failed to exert the influence of the state in the conduct of private economic affairs in the way that capitalist governments in Germany and the U.S. were doing as a matter of course. One glaring example will suffice to make the point – the failure of the British motor industry in the crisis of 1955 to make an adequate contribution to the balance of payments. While the expensive imports of sheet steel required to sustain the rising level of motor production added a serious load to the country's import bill, mainly payable in dollars, several of the firms in the motor industry were deliberately cultivating the home market at the expense of their export earnings. At this stage there was a strong case for calling in the people concerned and exhorting them, in the manner of Cripps, or bullying them, in the manner of Truman or Erhard, to mend their ways.

It is evident that direct intervention by the state in the business affairs of the private sector of the economy is not a special proclivity of socialist governments in the modern world. The Labour Government in Britain practised it more extensively than others; but on the other hand, it was less inclined than the non-socialist governments abroad to follow up the pressure on private enterprise by blandishments. It was inhibited by its anti-capitalist sentiments from offering British businessmen carrots as well as sticks. That in the end made its total influence on the private sector of the economy less than it otherwise would have been. For example, Labour failed to stimulate a general expansion of investment where it was badly needed – in ordinary manufacturing industry. The other general point that emerges from Labour's experience in trying to manage the economy during its last years, when shortages were being progressively relieved and the powers of direction inherited from the war constantly attenuated, is that the most effective method, at least in some cases, is to supervise or influence economic activity from the outside, rather than to control it directly or even, in the last resort, to own it. It is by no means clear, for example, that Socialist ministers were able to make their will more effective in the conduct of the affairs of the nationalized Bank of England than through the directives which they sent out to the private joint stock banks. The crude fact is that the banks felt that they had a strong motive for good and obedient behaviour. The Bank of England for its part, with its Governor, its staff, and its ideas intact, continued in large measure to act in the conviction that it had an independent role to play, regardless of the changing wishes of the Government of the day. It is arguable that un-nationalized, the Bank would have been a more obedient and pliable body than nationalized and holding the view that as the guardian of the nation's currency, it has a totally different relationship with the ministers of the day from any other Government department. The remarkable thing is, as one Bank of England official once said to me, how little difference nationalization has made to anything important that the Bank does.

Once again, the new programme of the Labour Party adopted in 1957, with its emphasis on the supervisory role of the state in private industry, rather than on direct control or public ownership, seems to be an advance towards more realistic thinking on this whole subject. Whether the type of supervision proposed, by way of a shareholder state putting in some of its nominees as directors of companies, will work out as the Labour theorists intend will depend, among other things, on the type of man chosen to do the job. For example, arranging for a number of retired trade union leaders to spend the evening of their days in the boardrooms of some rich and successful concerns will probably not make much difference to the way in which British industry is run. But the point of principle behind the new Labour approach, that as much may be done by exercising pressure as by giving orders, and that one of the ways of reinforcing this pressure is by greater public accountability of companies, is an important departure. It might mark the beginnings of a new attitude on the part of the Socialists to the whole problem of planning. Press and popular comment has been concerned chiefly with the question of how much public ownership Labour aims to achieve under the 1957 policy. But the important practical issue is how much influence it might allow the state to exert on the industrial policies of private enterprise, without involving it in the chore of detailed control, which it is not particularly well equipped to perform.

LABOUR'S COMPLACENCY ABOUT INVESTMENT

Looking back over the period of Labour rule from 1945–51, one cannot fail to be struck by a certain facile self-satisfaction constantly expressed by the party leaders about the results of their economic policies. They tended to understate the level of economic achievement reached before the war; and partly because of this, they grossly overstated the extent of the economic advance under their own leadership. This failing was particularly marked in Labour's approach to the problem of industrial investment. It is the central thesis of this book that the expansion of investment is the most pressing economic problem which Britain has to face today. The task is not just a matter of making good the ravages of a war, but of repairing many years of peacetime neglect during this century. It is to the credit of Mr R. A. Butler, when he was Chancellor of the Exchequer from 1951 to 1955, that he did show awareness of the urgency of this problem, and introduced the special 'investment allowance' to business – a kind of tax gift from the Government of 10 per cent of the value of any new capital equipment installed – in an attempt to deal with it.

The Labour Party leaders, especially Sir Stafford Cripps, were peculiarly complacent over this whole issue. Partly it was because they got the relevant figures consistently wrong, in a sense which allowed them to over-estimate their own achievement. In September 1949, at the time of the devaluation of sterling, Cripps was boasting in a speech in Washington that the British capital investment programme was absorbing 'more than one-fifth of the whole national output', and that this was a record performance in British history. He then came home and cut the programme back savagely. The figures presented in his last Economic Survey, on which Cripps was no doubt basing his statement, showed the following picture of investment at home as a proportion of the national product before and after the war:

1938	1947	1948
14%	21%	22%

Now, all these figures have been sharply reduced in later official calculations, partly as a result of a change in the definition of the terms. A note at the end of this chapter goes into some of the difficulties of making exact comparisons.[2] But the important practical issue is that there is no conceivable set of definitions which could, on the basis of the more exact statistical data available now, make the postwar performance look 50 per cent better than the prewar. This is a point at which statistics impinge directly on political decisions. If the Labour leaders had not believed that they were doing so enormously better than the Tory exponents of industrial stagnation before the war, they might not have been quite so ready to cut back British investment as the first move in the recurrent balance-of-payments crises – in 1947, 1949, and again in 1951. At any rate, it is reasonable to give them the benefit of the doubt. They believed themselves to be cutting down from an extremely high level.

It is true that they kept on repeating in public how important industrial investment was, vigorously disclaiming, whenever a new cut had to be made, any feeling of complacency on the subject. But the fact remains that they had got the order of magnitude of Britain's investment effort after the war profoundly wrong. One feels this at once in the kind of comparisons that the Labour Government made with the performance of other countries. Thus in 1948 it was comparing Britain's investment ratio of 'about 20 per cent' with what was going on in Russia, 'over 20 per cent' – and implying that it was a pity the Russians were getting slightly ahead in this way.[3] What we know now about the scale of Russia's effort at the time and about the failure of Britain to add to its stock of capital assets even to the extent that it had been doing before the war gives this kind of statement an air of wilful fantasy.

It is this question of how much is being added to the stock of assets from which the wealth of the country is ultimately derived that is crucial. It is the measure of economic growth. We saw in Chapter Two that Britain's growth had been disappointingly slow – slower than that of most other countries in Western Europe – during the 1950s. It was certainly no faster in the period of Labour rule during the late 1940s. The recent official estimates of net capital investment – that is, of the addition to the country's stock of capital, after deducting that part of investment which went to the replacement of worn out assets – show that we did not get back to the prewar rate of growth until 1953.[4] In that year, Britain's capital assets at home increased by the same amount as in 1938. But meanwhile the national income had increased substantially above the prewar level. Looking now at the proportion

175

of net investment to the total income available, this only gets back to the prewar ratio, and then moves a little beyond it, in the Tory investment boom of 1954–5.

Yet the figures used by the Labour Government at the time suggested that already by 1947 net investment in the British economy as a proportion of the national income was twice as large as before the war![5] The figures, when they were issued in contemporary official documents, were qualified by a careful warning from the statisticians, who were in any case working on very limited data, that the prewar estimates were probably an understatement, because of a difference in the method of calculating them. But this kind of thing made no impact on the politicians. They were satisfied on the main point – that they were doing extraordinarily well by any prewar standards. Their real success consisted in one thing only, in pushing a much larger proportion of a smaller total of investment into industrial plant and machinery. The volume of this kind of investment was well above prewar. The achievement lay essentially in holding back house building.

Sir Stafford Cripps, as Chancellor of the Exchequer, was still sufficiently interested in the problem of industrial re-equipment to present industry with the important concession of the 40 per cent 'initial allowance' on new plant and machinery, in his Budget of 1949. This in effect gave businesses a complete tax remission on 40 per cent of any profits ploughed back into new plant. The importance of this as a device for giving a tax bonus to firms which were expanding their productive equipment can be seen most clearly from what happened after 1951, when the concession was withdrawn by Mr Gaitskell in the emergency following the outbreak of the Korean war. In 1950 and 1951 the initial allowances granted by the tax authorities to British companies averaged £230m a year. Since at this time an average of about two-fifths of all company earnings went on tax, a tax-free segment of income of this size was well worth having. But in 1952 the value of the initial allowances granted to companies for new installations was reduced to £111m, and in 1953 to £104m, i.e., the tax relief granted to firms investing in new plant was cut by more than half.

It is no wonder that investment in British manufacturing industry was held back for several years, and did not recover to a respectable level until the boom of 1955. What is more puzzling at first sight is the comparatively small effect on industrial investment of the Cripps tax concession between 1949 and 1951. The explanation almost certainly lies in the unstable climate for business investment created by other aspects of Government policy at that time. The Chancellor might look as if he was trying to stimulate expansion all round, when he presented his Budget to Parliament at the beginning of April 1949, with the 40 per cent initial allowance. But there he was a few days later sternly ordering the Capital Issues Committee to restrain any exuberant demand for funds for investment, and to refuse permission to any capital development which could not be shown to be of an essential character. Thus a general curb was being applied to industrial investment at the same time as the general stimulus to invest. It is to be observed that the Government's definition of what was 'essential investment' at this time was extremely narrow, and left no room for a number of things which would have proved most useful in later years. But by the autumn of the same year, after the devaluation of the pound, Sir Stafford Cripps was cutting back sharply even on the narrow sector of essential investment. One of his main targets was manufacturing industry. The experts estimated at the time that the curb imposed on manufacturers' investment plans would take several months to become fully effective, but would make itself fully felt in the second half of 1950. No doubt it did. With the building controls and the other instruments at its disposal, it is hardly surprising that the Labour Government was more effective, in the climate of the 1940s and early 1950s, when it set itself the task of curbing the expansion of industrial capacity than when it was trying to stimulate business to invest.

CONSERVATIVE FREEDOM WORKS: 1952-4

'If only we could recapture the spirit of 1953 and '54!', says the younger Tory politician today. The nostalgia is wholly understandable. A party has rarely had the experience of being able to translate its declared policies so rapidly into action with such consistent and, even more important, such obvious success. Nobody could argue about the facts. By 1954 there was red meat in ample supply, many more houses were being built, the food queues had disappeared – indeed, most of the promises which had been jeered at by the Opposition had been overfulfilled. There was argument about exactly how this had been done – whether Tory policy had made a decisive and brilliant contribution or whether it had simply taken full advantage of a uniquely favourable set of circumstances – and this unsettled dispute did have an important influence, as we shall see, on the subsequent failures of the Conservative Government. But at the time, the Labour spokesmen who kept pointing to the large element of luck in the Tory successes appeared to an increasing number of people as somewhat pathetic figures, trying to keep their wilting ends up by constant carping. As one of the Conservative ministers pointed out gaily, the Labour Opposition would have to be careful about the political boomerang that it might be preparing for itself with this kind of propaganda: voters would be attracted to the Tories if they became too well known as 'the lucky government'.

There is no doubt that the members of the Conservative Government themselves underestimated the contribution of favourable chance in their impressive performance during these early years. Given half an opportunity, politicians, bankers, and the whole breed of men who earn their living by their judgement, will move rapidly towards the belief that they have some intuitive power, which allows them to ignore the views of people who simply think about problems in a more or less plodding systematic fashion. The bankers in fact came to exercise an unusual influence on the decisions of the policy-makers in the Treasury as time went on. And the unhappy conjunction of successful politicians' overconfidence and the intuitive certainties of influential people in the Bank of England played a large part in the debacle of the pound sterling from the middle of 1955 onwards.

But that belongs to a later chapter. It is easy to forget how splendid the bright years of 1953 and 1954 appeared, after the gloom that had preceded them. The starting point for the first experiment in postwar Conservative rule at the end of 1951 was an economic atmosphere of distress and anxiety such as had hardly been experienced at any time in the preceding six years of

Labour Government. In the previous nine months everything seemed to have gone wrong. The controls which Labour had been slowly and cautiously loosening were suddenly and drastically tightened up. The taxes which had been brought down from their early postwar heights were pushed up again. In the April Budget 6d had been added to the income tax, bringing the standard rate to 9s 6d in the £. And almost equally depressing from a popular point of view, the purchase tax on cars, radios, and a whole range of consumer durable goods, which the public was now getting ready to buy on a large scale, was doubled. Then in August the butter ration was cut to 3 ounces, and the cheese ration was reduced to only 1½ ounces – its lowest level since 1949. In September the exiguous bacon ration of 4 ounces was brought down to 3. In industry further restrictions had been imposed on the use of copper, zinc, and other metals. The steel rationing scheme had been extended to include certain items previously free. And business had been pummelled by a series of measures, starting with the abolition of the initial allowance for investment, the doubling of profits tax, and going on to the freeze on all company dividends imposed in mid-summer. Meanwhile prices were rising fast, in spite of food subsidies and controls, because the great hurricane of the Korean war boom in the world outside was carrying everything before it. It is scarcely any wonder that the feeling of many people when they went to the polls in November 1951 was : 'This is where we came in'.

But what the Conservatives actually did when they took over from Labour at the end of 1951 was to clamp down the controls still tighter. Imports were cut and slashed, and then cut again – three times all told – in the succeeding months. The tourist allowance for travel abroad was halved straightway to £50, and then later reduced to £25. New restrictions were imposed on hire purchase sales. And following up the body blow already given to investment by the Socialists in their last year in office, the Conservatives proceeded to block licences for new building still further, to order the banks to restrict credit, and to use the power of the Capital Issues Committee to deny finance for any industrial expansion not deemed to be absolutely essential. Finally, the Government intervened with fresh controls in the labour market.

There was to be no nonsense here about the free play of competitive forces; by means of the 'notification of vacancies order', it became illegal for employers to use any private initiative in obtaining the labour that they needed. All vacancies had to be reported to the Labour Exchange, and it was only through the Labour Exchange that the employers were supposed to engage workers.

Yet none of this seemed to count against the Tories. Indeed, it positively added to their record of virtue, once the turn came and the tight mesh of controls in which the economy was fixed began to be unravelled. The whole incident is rather like the Jewish story about a poor man who had the numerous family of a widowed sister take up their quarters in addition to his own large brood, in his two-roomed hovel. He went to the rabbi, told him that his life had now become quite intolerable, and asked for advice. 'You must empty that front room at once' he was told, 'and have all your sister's children – did you say there were seven of them? – to sleep with your family at the back.' The next day, still complaining, he was ordered by the rabbi to move all the furniture into the back room too. Then he was told to invite the considerable family of his brother to stay, and finally to bring in the goat from the yard. All were to live in the back room. After a fortnight of this life, the rabbi sent him a message – 'Take the goat out of the house'. The poor man ran shouting to his benefactor: 'I am free! The air is so sweet now that the goat is out! Rabbi, you are a sage as well as merciful.'

The Conservative leaders took their time about introducing the first measures of relief. The goat was kept in the parlour for quite a while. It took over a year before they began their serious attack on the controls inherited from the Labour Government. One has to recall the state of mind of the Conservative leaders in 1951, when they took office for the first time after the war and immediately faced a financial crisis, which put the pound sterling in serious danger. In economic affairs they were nervous and untried men. The commanding figures in the Cabinet, Sir Winston Churchill and Sir Anthony Eden, were either uninterested or uncomprehending on the subject. It was left to the Chancellor of the Exchequer, Mr R. A. Butler, a new reformist Conservative, and a far from popular figure with the traditionalists of the party, to do any creative thinking on an up-to-date Tory economic policy, adapted to the conditions of the middle of the twentieth century. No one else had any positive ideas. In the first phase, the Cabinet as a whole seems to have felt that the main necessity was to demonstrate as vigorously as possible that the Conservatives were not the class ogre of the 1930s, that they could get on with the trade unions as well as anyone else, and that they were not the friends of big business. It is doubtful whether the Excess Profits Levy, introduced in the first Conservative Budget in 1952, had any other purpose than that. The truth is that the Conservative leadership had not yet completely overcome the feeling of uncertainty that had depressed it during the late 1940s – a feeling which had been so strong then that it led at one stage to a proposal, which was seriously discussed within the party, to change its name, in order to get rid of the class stigma that went with the word 'Tory' or 'Conservative'.

In 1951–2 they were very much aware of moving into unknown territory. They were immensely concerned, for example, with the problem of keeping the trade unions sweet. It was only later, when they had proved to themselves that they could govern with remarkably little social tension, in happy relations with the Trades Union Congress, and after Mr Butler at the Treasury had successfully weathered his first economic crisis in 1952, coming through on the other side with a strengthened pound sterling, that the liberal counter-revolution began to gather momentum. For this new Conservative economic policy was wholly liberal in inspiration. It is hard to say exactly how this vicarious triumph of economic liberalism came about. The pursuit of *laissez-faire* principles became the conscious purpose of Tory economic policy only gradually. There have always been two distinct strands of thought on this subject within the Conservative Party: at different times the emphasis has been on the role of the paternal state, providing citizens with some measure of protection against the jungle of economic life, or on the dominant role of the market-place – the irresistible forces of world commerce swirling with particular ferocity around this island, because Britain is their natural storm centre. But perhaps the liberal ideology of the market-place never established quite so firm a grip on any Tory administration before that of 1951–5.

The reason may be simply that starting with the important political assertion that the welfare of all members of society could be secured with far less state interference than the Socialists believed necessary, the Tories were led on, by their very success in getting rid of so many controls painlessly, to elevate 'economic freedom' into an end in itself. Certainly it became increasingly common form in Government circles, as the task of economic emancipation proceeded from 1952 right through 1954, to indulge in confident doctrinaire talk about the beneficial powers of the market, as the means of coping with almost any situation. (I mean by 'doctrinaire' a tendency to base argument on *a priori* principles and to concentrate on the ingenious interpretation and use of such principles, rather than on the discovery of empirical matters of fact.) This kind of thinking readily takes hold of the civil service. In contradiction to the traditional view of the British civil servants as a body of men hopelessly devoted to empiricism in their work, eschewing any kind of general principles, the truth is that this body has a natural propensity, at any rate nowadays, to approach its problems in an ideological spirit. This became most evident when the change from a Labour to a Conservative Government took place at the end of 1951. Perhaps it had to be. In the economic field, at least, much of the direction from the Labour ministers had necessarily been in the form of broad lines of doctrine. When the Conservatives took over, the same civil servants looked for, and sometimes even invented, clearcut doctrines of another kind. One had the impression on occasion that the pure doctrinal essence of certain acts of policy was not absolutely apparent to the minister who was supposed to be responsible for them, until one of his more intellectual top civil servants had applied himself to the task of explaining it. This tendency was nowhere more in evidence than in the Treasury; and the influence of the highly intelligent, doctrine-conscious officials of the Treasury spread outwards into ancillary and subordinate Government departments during the period 1952–4.

The propensity of senior officials to supply doctrinal justifications and extensions to the thoughts of their masters played an

especially important part in the international financial policy of
the Conservative Government, which will be discussed separately
later. With the advantage of hindsight, it is perhaps all too easy to
smile at the tendency of politicians and officials during the early
years of postwar Conservative rule to exaggerate the virtues of
economic liberalism. At the time, those responsible for the conduct of affairs were chiefly aware of the fact that whereas the
majority of the people who purported to know had predicted one
failure after another, as each control was removed, the actual
results emerged as a series of brilliant successes. Moreover, the
removal of controls and the restoration of economic liberty
turned out to be so extraordinarily easy – when beforehand so
many of the pundits had been warning them that it would be
tremendously hard. It is perhaps not surprising that the experience of the rapid and painless abolition of all forms of food controls, starting with the egg ration in the spring of 1953 and
ending with the freeing of meat in the middle of 1954, tended to
go to the heads of the people concerned. The splendid fury of
decontrol continued apace during 1954: the international commodity markets were reopened one after another, building
licences were abolished towards the end of the year, and there
was the promise that the pound sterling would be finally freed
from exchange control sometime on the morrow. The mood of
the time was most enjoyable, while it lasted. It is, after all, much
more pleasant to believe that things will function smoothly,
without a lot of clever people interfering with many of the
ordinary activities of life. The cult of *anti-planning*, with certain
undertones of hostility towards the intellectual as such – a not
unfamiliar note in popular conservatism of the traditional kind
– developed strongly. The view was increasingly put about that
the whole economic paraphernalia of the Labour Government,
during the difficult period immediately following the war, had
been a kind of wilful imposition on the British people by politicians who were personal devotees of misery. The evidence for
this view seemed to be strengthened by the fact that whenever
the Conservatives got rid of an irksome control or turned their
backs on a piece of doubtful planning, the reaction of the
Labour Opposition was one of barely disguised satisfaction at

the catastrophe which it anticipated would follow, and which never materialized.

WORLD PRICES AND BRITISH PRICES

How was it, in fact, that Conservative freedom worked quite so brilliantly during this period? The answer is plain, and was propounded frequently by some of the wiser of the soured politicians on the Left at the time. The Conservatives benefited from a quite extraordinary windfall in British foreign trade, starting at the beginning of 1952 and continuing through until the middle of 1954. What happened was that the prices of the basic materials which the country buys abroad – costing some £1,500m in all in 1951–fell by no less than one-quarter over the period. That alone produced nearly £400m of extra purchasing power a year, without anyone lifting a finger. At the same time the prices that our exports fetched in overseas markets were edging steadily upwards. By 1954 the combined effect of the favourable bargain, which allowed us to sell our manufactured goods more dearly while buying our imports more cheaply, was to increase the foreign exchange earnings of Britain from the same amount of work done and the same amount of goods sold abroad by some 12 per cent. This meant that the country had at its disposal an additional £400m–£500m, which could be spent on importing more food and other commodities, as controls on consumption, manufacture, and trade were removed. But that was not all. During most of this period Britain was in fact exporting fewer goods than in the crisis year of 1951. Production meanwhile was rising; and the whole of the additional output was absorbed by the home market. Finally, investment remained low during most of this time. The re-equipment of industry made small demands on this additional output. So it is really no wonder that the British consumer, who was left almost in sole possession of the field, was able to go on a tremendous buying spree for a couple of years.

There were political windfalls too. Because world prices of the commodities that Britain has to buy abroad were falling, the Conservative Government was able to remove the great structure of consumer subsidies built up by Labour, without causing any serious distress to the ordinary housewife. Prices certainly went up during this period, but by a moderate amount. The cost of living index, which had jumped 10 per cent in 1951, the last year of Labour rule, continued to rise during the first six months of the Tory Government, until the middle of 1952. Thereafter it stabilized dramatically: over the next eighteen months, that is until the end of 1953, the total increase was only $1\frac{1}{2}$ per cent. And in the following year, which saw the final abolition of rationing and the development of the boom in cars and household goods, the increase was still confined to $3\frac{1}{2}$ per cent. This comparatively restrained movement – very restrained by comparison with what happened in the two succeeding years 1955 and 1956, when there were no special factors like the ending of food subsidies to give an artificial fillip to the process – was the outcome of two distinct forces, pushing individual prices in opposite directions. While the retail prices of foods and of most services went up, the prices of many manufactured goods came down.

The latter movement was to some extent a reflection of declining raw material prices. But it was powerfully assisted by the increase in productivity in British manufacturing industry during 1953 and 1954. After the decline in output during the recession of 1952, the hourly production of the average factory employee is estimated to have increased by 5 per cent in 1953 and 4 per cent in 1954.[6] The comparable figures for Germany during the same period were 6 per cent and 5 per cent. It was only in later years that the discrepancy between British and German productivity in manufacturing industry widened sharply. In 1955, the German increase at 6 per cent was twice as much as the British; and in 1956, when Germany's rate of increase did at last slow down, British productivity in manufacturing industry did not rise at all. It was also most unfortunate that just as the rise in productivity began to taper off, wages began to race ahead. Here was the exact recipe for a severe bout of inflation. But the point to observe is that the sudden change of fortune in 1955 did not happen quite fortuitously. It might indeed be argued that from 1952 to 1954 Britain had been benefiting from an exceptional run of luck, which had already gone on far longer than might reasonably have been expected.

There was nothing mysterious about the fact that after several years of low investment, productivity was rising too slowly in manufacturing industry. There was nothing surprising about the general rush to invest in 1954–5, once business had come to accept the probability of continued growth. Then all the bottle-necks littered right through the economy became painfully apparent. The introduction of the 'investment allowance' in Mr Butler's Budget of 1954 administered the final shove into the new boom. This important innovation gave to business for the first time an effective tax subsidy for any new piece of plant or equipment installed. Ten per cent of the value of the new asset was automatically taken off the tax assessment for that year. This was in addition to the normal depreciation allowances deducted from tax in each year of the life of the equipment. If, for instance, the estimated working life of a piece of machinery costing £1,000 were ten years, a firm installing it would get the normal tax relief for depreciation on this sum over a ten-year period (i.e. £100 a year) plus £100 of investment allowance in the first year – that is a total tax relief on £1,100. This was £100 more than the expenditure actually incurred – a tax bonus for expansion. It somehow clinched the issue. What with the talk of doubling the standard of living in twenty-five years, which was current at the time, and the open-handed way in which companies were distributing their considerably increased profits, after years of parsimony, a large number of people decided to follow the Chancellor of the Exchequer's advice, and 'invest in success'. As was pointed out in an earlier chapter,* this was a long overdue investment boom. Partly because it was overdue, businessmen discovered, once they got moving, that there was a vast amount to be done; and they were all suddenly in a tremendous hurry to do it. The result was that the order books of the machinery-makers, of the builders, and of the engineering industries generally became overloaded. The latter were already heavily engaged in trying to meet the new burst of consumer demand for motor cars and household goods which had been generated by the atmosphere of prosperity.

It was at about this time, in early 1955, that the movement of

* See Chapter 2.

world prices, so kind to Britain for so long, turned the other way. The average cost of our imports began to rise – not by much, but enough to add to the strain. In other industrial countries, this moderate increase in the cost of certain imports, mainly materials, was kept fairly well under control. The important difference was that the people of these countries had during the previous two years actually had the experience of stable or declining cost of living. They had discovered that prices could go down instead of up, even in the postwar world – not just odd prices, but the bulk of those encountered in an ordinary week's shopping, and above all the price of food. They were thus better prepared psychologically than people in Britain to take the comparatively small jump in import prices in 1955, following a period of decline, with reasonable calm.

In Britain it was treated as a kind of last straw. With high profits and companies hurrying to make up to the shareholders the ground lost during the years of voluntary or enforced dividend limitation, with the demand for labour unusually strong even for postwar Britain, it is not really surprising that the further rise in prices provided the occasion for bigger wage demands in 1955. Wage rates had risen by an annual amount of 4–5 per cent in the previous two years. This was not far out of line with the rise in productivity in manufacturing industry, though in industry as a whole, and particularly in the service industries like transport, productivity rose less. But the total inflationary effect was moderate; and in the event it was counteracted by the fall in import prices. In 1955 and 1956, however, the rise in wage rates accelerated to 7 per cent a year; and there was very little or no extra productivity this time, and no bargain prices for imports to offset the strain.

The great inflationary crisis, which came to occupy the centre of the political stage in 1957, is thus of fairly recent origin, and there is no mystery about its proximate causes. It is wrong to treat this particular phenomenon as if it was only a further extension of a familiar postwar inflationary movement – an annual rise of an average 4–5 per cent in retail prices. It is clear that what happened to prices in the first postwar decade was chiefly determined by the rise in the cost of food.[7] There were shortages, and there was a great upheaval in the world pattern of supply and demand. It now looks as if the decade of world food crisis may have come to an end. More worrying is the evidence that although the normal rise in productivity in manufacturing may be sufficient to offset a moderate annual increase in wages, there is no comparable offset in the important group of service industries, like transport and distribution. Any technological advance which succeeded in reducing costs in these fields would probably make the biggest contribution of all to an attack on the long-term problem of inflation.

THE WORSHIP OF THE MARKET

What seems so strange in retrospect is the heroic indifference of the Conservative leadership in the early years of its period in office to the psychological effects of rising prices. Indeed, they seemed positively to welcome higher prices because of their 'disinflationary effect'. This doctrine of disinflation through inflation of prices has played an important part in British postwar economic history, and it is worth exploring more closely. It is difficult to say who invented it. Certainly it was an economist; but he might equally well have been a left-wing as a right-wing economist. The view received open official recognition in the last Economic Survey issued by the Labour Government in April 1951. There it was argued (perfectly logically) that the Government would obtain some relief from the strain which would be caused by the prospective rise of spending power of £600m, unaccompanied by any increase in the output of consumer goods, because the rise in the prices of imports would mop up this amount of cash. The point of the argument was, however, quite specific. It concerned the balance of payments. If prices at home did not rise, then the additional purchasing power would have to be matched by extra goods obtained from somewhere: either there would be more imports or goods would have to be diverted from the export trade to the domestic market. In either event the balance of trade would suffer, and the country would have less foreign exchange at its disposal. Thus a rise in domestic prices in this context could be presented as a means of protecting the gold reserve.

Of course, it would be no use, if the higher prices charged to customers just went to British salesmen or manufacturers, who then spent their winnings in the home market. In 1951 the extra money paid by the British public was, on the argument of the Economic Survey, going to be sent right out of the country into the pockets of the overseas producers of raw materials and other commodities. But there is another and more general thesis, which at one time had a certain vogue, that rising prices are automatically disinflationary, because they increase profits at the expense of individual consumer incomes; and that means that more money will be saved. This is of course another version of the traditional argument for taking money away from the poor and giving it to the rich. The only difference is that in the past it had stronger and more explicit moral overtones. There is something in the argument – as an economic, not a moral proposition: one rich man does usually save more than a lot of poor men sharing the same amount of income. But in a democratic society the transfer of income by means of rising prices depends on the poor agreeing to the redistribution – or on their inability to obtain redress against it. The essential point is that the use of this particular disinflationary technique is a political act. The Conservatives refused to recognize this for a long time; the whole issue was treated as a piece of simple and inescapable economics. But it is no use expecting to convince people by talk about the impersonal forces of the market, when it is a well-advertised fact that the Government has deliberately let these forces loose.

There are only two ways in which it is possible to put through a redistribution of income resulting in a relative deterioration of the position of the wage-earner in a democratic society, where there is no large annual increment of wealth to be shared out. One is to obtain the assent of organized labour to the process, as a means of achieving some agreed national purpose. The other is by sufficiently weakening the bargaining power of organized labour. Mr Gaitskell was still trying the first course in 1951. He made it clear that he was not determined on his rise in prices: he was even prepared to bargain on an increase in the consumer subsidies, if the trade unions would do their part and moderate their demands for *real* wages. But it seems to have taken until 1957 for the

Conservative leadership to recognize that in rejecting the Cripps-Gaitskell alternative, they were in logic bound to turn to the second course, if they were after a significant redistribution of wealth between the middle and working classes. The issue had no doubt been obscured by the hope that a rapid expansion of production would provide an increase in wealth large enough to allow the redistribution of relative shares to proceed painlessly. Such an expansion did, in fact, cover the first phase of the Conservative redistribution in 1953 and 1954, when food subsidies were being abolished, profits were rising, and the ordinary shareholders of companies began to receive the benefit of higher dividends. But in 1955 the tempo of expansion slowed down, in 1956 it ground to a halt; and in 1957 the sputtering and uncertain attempts to stage a recovery encountered the sudden violence of 7 per cent bank rate in the autumn. Redistribution could no longer be carried through without friction. It required heroic measures.

In the years up to 1957, Conservative supporters had received middle-class tax reliefs from their Government, but the intended redistribution of wealth appeared to them to have been frustrated by inflation. Now the party platform became converted to the view that stable prices were the first objective of any economic policy, that no sacrifice of production or welfare was too great to secure it. Indeed, the new political propaganda rather suggested – in the face of much contrary evidence – that price stability had been the primary objective of the party all along, but that its efforts had been steadily frustrated by the greed of the trade unions. It became the established view that irresponsibility on the part of organized labour was the sole cause of the rise in British prices. What was left out by the Conservative propagandists was the part played by Government policy in the crucial price movements of 1952–4, when the rest of the world had the beneficial experience of the first postwar decline in the cost of living. That is not to argue that the decision of the Conservative Government to remove the consumer subsidies, which caused the price rise, was wrong. But the long-term psychological effect of what it did then should not be overlooked either. Organized labour in Britain today is not more irresponsible by nature than in other countries; it has just had a different set of economic experiences. Several

years of constantly rising food prices – continuing incidentally
into 1955, as a result of a number of special factors operating
after the subsidies had come off – create in the end a powerful
engine for the generation of massive wage claims.

What also tends to be forgotten nowadays is the positive zest
of the Conservative leaders in the earlier phase for policies which
raised prices, in order, as they said, to make people pay the 'true
economic cost' of the articles which they consumed. Again this
was in line with the post-1951 Tory economic philosophy: the
rehabilitation of the forces of the market-place, which had been
distorted by seven years of war, followed by six years of Labour
rule. But the search for hidden subsidies in unexpected places got
a little out of hand; it developed some of the characteristics of an
economic witch hunt. The market had to be king at all costs. And
behind this energetic pursuit of the free market ideal was the political belief that the people who had benefited most from the
whole paraphernalia of subsidies and price controls, which allowed the consumer to pay less than the 'true economic cost',
were the working classes. The middle class meanwhile had been
made to pay the taxes to support the system. Thus making the
market work was, apart from its economic merits, seen as a
powerful instrument for the Conservative policy of redistribution.

It is easy to understand, given the circumstances of the time,
how the Conservatives were caught up in the illusions of the
market – as the Socialists had earlier become involved in the illusions of 'planning'. Like the planners in their heyday from 1945
to 1948, the marketeers in 1952–4 managed to score some big
successes. As was pointed out earlier, both, being human, underestimated the contribution of fortuitous circumstance, and ele-
vated their respective doctrines into a kind of master key, which
would fit any door in the economy. The Conservatives during
their initial period in office did indeed manage to open several
doors which many people had believed to be firmly locked, and
probably boarded up as well. It is perhaps no wonder that the
Tory reaction against Labour planning, against subsidies and
directed consumption of all kinds, should have led some of the
leaders into a passionate and doctrinaire devotion to the price
mechanism as an end in itself. But putting the price mechanism

to work did almost invariably mean, at the start, raising prices.

The philosophy behind the new approach from 1952 onwards necessarily involved a more permissive attitude towards higher prices than there had been under Labour. After all, it was the Conservative view that price control – which meant the artificial compression of profit margins to something less than the market would bear – was bad not only for the individual firm concerned, but for the economy as a whole. It was this kind of molly-coddling of the consumer which distorted natural economic forces, and so held back the expansion of production and supplies at the points where they were most needed. When something was in short supply, the right answer, it was said, was to let the profit on producing it rise, as a result of higher prices, to the point where a lot of new people were attracted to come in and produce more. Their competition would soon force prices down again. Moreover, the result of price controls, which enabled consumers to obtain some essential item at an artificially low cost, was that they had more left over to spend on luxuries and inessentials. Since the prices of these goods were generally not controlled, there was in any case an incentive for businessmen in search of wider profit margins to go in and produce them. The end result of this process, it was argued, would be to concentrate more and more economic resources on the production of an ever larger volume of inessentials, while the necessities were starved. Then of course the state would have the perfect excuse to intervene with direct controls, in order to push resources into channels which served society better. There was plainly a good deal in this contention of the Conservatives in 1952. The Labour Government had tended to ignore the secondary effects of state controls on the business decisions being made in the large and growing area of the economy which had been freed from control. There were some serious distortions.

But in the process of getting rid of these distortions, the Conservatives carried the doctrine of non-intervention in the market to extreme lengths. In this they were markedly different from the champions of private enterprise and capitalism abroad, notably from Dr Adenauer's Government in Germany. The Conservatives in Britain also developed an extraordinary shyness about any form of state encouragement of specific kinds of productive activity, which might be thought to be in the nation's economic interest to foster. That would have meant bringing the judgement of the 'gentleman in Whitehall' into the picture; and it was notorious that he knew nothing at all about the rough and tumble of commerce. All this kind of thinking was backed up by the economic argument that price controls and artificial stimuli to certain kinds of production do not work in the end, anyhow. Unless the state takes over completely, private enterprise is bound to operate in such a way as to maximize its profits. If the price is not right, production of the article in question will diminish; and artificially stimulated industries will not grow, unless there is a demand to match the additional output at a profitable price. However, the practical qualification that has to be made to all these arguments showing the pointlessness of interfering with prices is that what is true in the long run is not necessarily true in the short. Businessmen are in general extremely eager to raise the prices of their products, whenever they see half an opportunity. It is after all their function to get the highest possible return for themselves or their shareholders. On the other hand, they are immensely reluctant to lower a price in response to pressure from the market. The common feeling, at any rate in British industry, is that it is better to drop production when demand goes slack, and wait hopefully for a revival, rather than drop prices. When so many prices are fixed by collective agreement, as they are in Britain, this means that prices tend to be mobile in an upward direction and sticky downwards. Again, this only applies to the short run; but price movements in the short run may determine the psychological atmosphere which eventually sets the pace of an inflationary boom.

This fact was ultimately accepted by the Conservative Government in 1956, when Mr Macmillan, as Chancellor of the Exchequer, instituted his 'price plateau'. But it took until then to become established. For a long time the ruling doctrine had been that the function of government was solely to hold the ring while the wisdom of the market wrestled to assert itself. This doctrine was first seriously questioned in the crisis of mid-1955. By the end of that year the Conservative leadership had already moved to the conclusion that economic wisdom might be sought by other means.

But by that time much of the psychological damage had already been done. There is no doubt that what the Conservatives called 'the discipline of the market' and what Labour calls 'the free for all' did go with a new and more permissive attitude towards wage claims. This is another aspect of Tory economic policy in the period immediately following the party's advent to power which is sometimes forgotten nowadays. It was implicit in much of what the Conservatives said and did that wages, too, would have more freedom to move up in the new era when the price mechanism was allowed to operate through the economy. It was just as wrong-headed, it was suggested, to try and moderate the rise in wages by agreements with the trade unions – as Cripps had done – as to try and counter the natural pressure of economic forces in the markets by means of price control. The freeze was over. Long live the thaw!

NOTES

1. *Economic Survey, 1947.*
2. *The Difficulty of Measuring Investment.* In the early postwar years the figure for British investment used in Government calculations included the cost of repairs and maintenance to building and works. This is one reason why the estimate of investment expenditure at the time was about one-third larger than subsequent official calculations shown in the Blue Books on national income. Since 1952 repairs and maintenance have been excluded from investment, and treated as an item of current cost. It would be wrong to be dogmatic and say that the earlier practice was incorrect. After all, it is not easy to distinguish clearly as a matter of principle between the activity of replacing a whole roof of tiles, because they have fallen in, and building a new house, because it has fallen down. The former is just repair, and the latter is a piece of fixed investment on currently accepted definitions.

The important point is that these definitions are now accepted by a considerable number of countries, and therefore provide a basis for some kind of international comparison. Immediately after the war no such agreement had yet been established, and it was much more difficult to see exactly who was doing what. But it was, as one can see clearly now, wrong to compare Britain's inflated figure of 20 per cent of the gross national product devoted to investment – inflated by the inclusion of expenditure on repairs and maintenance – with the Russian figure of their 'new investment' or even with U.S. estimates of American *gross* investment. This made the British figure look far too favourable. There are other factors, like the inclusion of capital investment on behalf of the armed forces in the British figures and their exclusion from the statistics of investment in other countries, which tend to distort the picture in the same way.

The calculations of *net* investment used in the early postwar years also produced a bias in a similar direction. In this case, the question of repairs did not enter into the calculation: the cost of all depreciation was deducted in order to arrive at the net figure – the house built to replace the one that had fallen in, as well as the repairs to the roof. The Government economists responsible for these calculations in the 1940s certainly did not intend their figures of net investment, derived from the arbitrary depreciation allowances granted by the tax authorities on the basis of the historical cost of capital assets, to be taken as a true measure of the amount added to the stock of the country's capital wealth. Their method of calculation necessarily involved an understatement of the true cost of depreciation of existing assets and so led to an overstatement of the share of net investment in the sum total of gross capital formation. Unfortunately, the policy-makers appear to have been fascinated by the overstatement, and failed to notice the qualifications. It was only when more refined statistical data became available in the 1950s that it was realized just how low net investment in Britain had really been in the years immediately following the war.

3. *Economic Survey for 1948*, Chapter III.
4. *National Income and Expenditure, 1957, Blue Book*, table 45.
5. *Economic Survey for 1948*.
6. *Europe Today and in 1960*. O.E.E.C., 1957.
7. R. G. D. Allen: *On the Decline in the Value of Money*. Stamp Memorial Lecture, 1957.

CHAPTER EIGHT

THE CLIMACTERIC OF 1955

THE years 1955–6 were a spiritual climacteric for the Conservative Party. The process is more evident in 1956, when the débâcle of Suez suddenly and sharply brought into the light a whole collection of unquestioned assumptions about Britain's place in the world and the future of British foreign policy. But a similar, though much more confined and less publicized, crisis in the Tory leadership occurred in the field of domestic policy in 1955; and it has continued with varying degrees of agony ever since. Briefly, 1955 was the year in which it was discovered that Tory freedom does not always work. The question that follows is what to put in its place – how much state intervention and in what form? What system of priorities for economic policy should be established, since the forces of the market did not always produce the right choice? And finally what cherished objectives would have to be given up, in order to concentrate effectively on the narrower front? It is at this point that these two crises, in foreign policy and in economic policy, meet and intermingle. For, as the argument of earlier chapters has tried to show, the choice that has to be made in order to pursue a policy of concentration means giving up a number of traditional objectives of a political character, above all in the sphere of international affairs. Several of these objectives are plainly worth while; if Britain does not fulfil them, someone else will have to. That makes the process of surrender all the more painful.

That is not to say that the leading Tory politicians are all explicitly aware of the process. But they have, most of them, become increasingly concerned about the problem of choice. The way in which this has come about in the sphere of economic policy is the subject of this chapter. In order to explore the subject, it is necessary to look in greater detail at what happened in 1955, the year of the great economic disillusion. The essential nature of the choice, which emerged with increasing starkness as the year progressed, was between two major objectives that Mr

R. A. Butler, the Chancellor of the Exchequer of the day, had managed to pursue simultaneously from the end of 1951 to 1954. They were on the one hand, the objective of high investment and economic expansion at home, and on the other hand, a very strong and ultimately convertible pound sterling abroad. What the events of 1955 showed was that these twin objectives were beckoning Britain in opposite directions. The external policy had a simple and straightforward aim – to restore to sterling exactly the same role as it had played in international trade and finance before the war. Sterling was still the most widely used international medium of exchange after the war, but plainly it was no longer so attractive to foreigners, hobbled by a variety of regulations restricting its use in certain transactions. The bait that was now offered to the foreigner, who was to be induced to make still more extensive use of sterling in international trade and finance, was more freedom through the gradual relaxation of exchange controls. And the final freedom which he was to be offered was the restoration of the prewar arrangement for exchanging pounds sterling into any other currency, including dollars.

Once the pound sterling was made convertible, so the argument ran, it would become again the only effective international currency; and then all countries would find that they had to replenish their working balances of sterling, in order to have a sufficient supply of 'real cash' ready to hand. This they would have to buy from Britain, and in the course of the operation the British gold and foreign exchange reserve, which had been depleted by the war and its aftermath, would be built up again. But the price that would have to be paid for this benefit was the relinquishment of the various controls that had since the war been exercised by Britain over the flow of sterling currency around the world. There was, and still is, a very large amount of sterling owned by governments and institutions outside Britain. This money is mainly derived from British expenditure abroad during the war. When the Conservatives came to power at the end of 1951 a considerable portion of these sterling holdings was effectively frozen in blocked accounts at the Bank of England. They had been blocked by the Labour Government, which had tried, wherever possible, to reach an agreement with the owners on the amount of sterling that Britain was to release to them each year. But it was part of the policy of exchange freedom and the gradual approach to convertibility to liberate these assets, too. All this meant that Britain's liability to provide a lot of foreign exchange quickly was greatly increased. First of all, several hundred millions of pounds, previously frozen, were now liquid; and secondly, a large number of regulations governing the use of sterling abroad, which had been designed to limit Britain's liability to provide a lot of dollars at short notice to foreigners, were abolished.

Everything might still have been all right, if there had been an increase in Britain's reserves proportionate to the increased liabilities. But that was not part of the plan. The idea was that the lifting of the exchange controls would itself produce an inflow of gold and dollars into the reserves, not that we should wait for an increase in the reserves sufficient to eliminate any additional risks that would arise from the wider international use of sterling. It was, in other words, a huge gamble; and the odds were never explained to the British public. Moreover, there is no evidence that the Government itself had thought the matter out at all clearly. There was once again the characteristic mood of insouciance, the indifference to any rational calculation of probable loss or gain, given an objective of international prestige. But what had really been put at risk, once the gamble on external financial policy had been taken on without the cover of an adequate gold reserve, was the whole domestic policy of expansion. If things went wrong, and for one reason or another confidence in sterling weakened, the only way in which the greatly increased liability to foreigners could be met quickly would be by cutting back Britain's own domestic demand on the national resources. And it is the dismal moral of the whole of the postwar period that investment invariably presents itself as the easiest thing to cut in a hurry.

THE STERLING FIASCO

That is the sequence – beginning with an external crisis and proceeding to an assault on investment – which started in 1955; and the assault was pressed harder and harder during the following years in the face of remarkably determined drive for re-equipment by business. The policy of liberalizing Britain's external arrangements in finance pursued since 1952 – the lifting of many of the exchange controls, the greater freedom to transfer capital sums abroad, the deliberate reversal of the previous policy of supervising the use of sterling in transactions between foreign countries outside the sterling area – had made the pound much more sensitive to any adverse current of world opinion. It had of course been vulnerable to external pressure, even when the exchange controls were held very tight, as the devaluation in 1949 had shown. But on that occasion the pressure was at least partly derived from the hard commercial fact that the pound was overvalued, in terms of what you could buy for it, compared with the dollar. The over-valuation was certainly not anything like the difference between the old pre-1949 rate of $4 to the pound and the new rate of $2.80 to the pound. Sir Stafford Cripps, who was Chancellor of the Exchequer at the time, deliberately went further than was necessary, in order to give British exports to the dollar area an extra competitive margin. Most of the countries outside the dollar area devalued at the same time, following Britain either the whole or part of the way down. But in the crisis of 1955 there was no evidence that British or sterling area costs were excessive and needed to be reduced in order to sell more goods abroad. There were, it is true, certain temporary weaknesses in Britain's trading position at the time, caused largely by the rapid growth of imports, as the book at home gathered momentum. But the point to notice is that the pressure on sterling continued in 1956 and most of 1957, after the trading weaknesses had been completely removed. Similarly, the pressures began to be felt right at the start of 1955, before the trading deficit had appeared.

Of course it is the business of people who make their living out of dealing in currencies to sense which way the wind is blowing well in advance. By the end of 1954 it was already clear to anyone who cared to look that the British balance of payments was no longer as strong as it had been. But the change in the demand and supply of sterling resulting from this temporary commercial development was not sufficient, either then or later in the year, to account for the strain that was suddenly put on the reserves. It is hardly worth labouring the point that the trouble which hit sterling at the beginning of 1955, and caused the three-year crisis which followed, was primarily of a speculative, rather than a strictly commercial, character. And speculation against sterling had been made a great deal easier, as a result of the policy of loosening the exchange control. This had been consciously done by the Treasury and the Bank of England as a preparation for the advent of sterling convertibility. Each new control removed was hailed as one further step towards a convertible pound sterling. And the prospect of convertibility naturally attracted foreign holders of sterling. They bought more pounds, and the British reserves received a windfall of £200m–£300m worth of gold and dollars. 1953 to 1954 were years of mounting confidence in sterling – mounting in this quite specific sense: that more and more people believed that it would soon be possible to turn pounds freely into dollars.

Now, when the pressure started on the balance of payments in 1955, the British authorities at once found themselves in an awkward spot. The foreign holders of sterling, observing that the balance of payments was no longer as strong as it had been, would conclude that there was no prospect of early convertibility for sterling, and a lot of them might in their disappointment be tempted to sell their pounds. The inference that was drawn, especially by the people in the Bank of England responsible for the day-to-day management of the currency, was that it was necessary at all costs to demonstrate to the world that the momentum towards convertibility, the policy of breaking down exchange controls, continued in all its vigour.

The impression of many observers at this time, in the first half of 1955, was that the Bank had more or less taken over the direction of British policy, and that the Chancellor of the Exchequer was prepared to do whatever was necessary at home in order to sustain the appearance of a continued movement towards sterling convertibility abroad. In fact, there seems to have been inadequate liaison between the Bank and the Treasury at this period. That became very evident when the Chancellor of the Exchequer,

Mr Butler, went out of his way at the world assembly of bankers and finance ministers in Istanbul in September 1955, where the International Monetary Fund was holding its annual meeting, to make it clear that there was no imminent prospect of a convertible pound sterling. The Bank's line up to that point had been to insist on all possible occasions in the course of its extensive international contacts on the imminence of convertibility.

The effect of Mr Butler's announcement was, paradoxically, to check the wave of speculation against sterling, which had been gathering strength since the early summer. Now, the main reason for this speculation was the story, which had got around abroad, that when the pound was made convertible, it would be subject to a 'floating exchange rate'. Instead of there being an established parity of $2.80 to the pound, with a maximum movement permitted in the foreign exchange markets of no more than 1 per cent on either side (i.e. $2.78 to $2.82), the value of the pound would be allowed to move up and down freely over a much wider range in response to changes in supply and demand. The accepted guess at the time was that Britain was preparing to set a limit of a 5 per cent fluctuation either way. Now this meant only one thing in the conditions of sterling crisis which had developed by the middle of 1955 – that anyone dealing in currencies must expect the pound to lose 5 per cent of its value, and possibly more, in the exchange market in the near future. The purveyors of confidence in sterling had overplayed their hand. No one doubted at the time that if the pound were set free in the way suggested it would immediately bump all the way down to the lowest permitted level. There are not sufficient facts available to make it possible to pinpoint with certainty the people responsible for putting this disastrous story about. Mr Butler himself specifically denied having countenanced it in any way at the crucial meeting of the European finance ministers in Paris during the summer of 1955. On the other hand the system of floating rates was known to be a pet scheme of several powerful people inside the Treasury. The matter had been discussed by these officials, in a more or less hypothetical fashion, on a number of occasions both at home and abroad. One way or another, the impression had been formed on the continent of Europe that *if* the pound was made convertible, there was a high probability that the exchange rate would be set free to fluctuate much more widely than before.

The reason why many of the responsible people on the British side, including, it was believed, the Chancellor of the Exchequer himself, were attracted by the idea of floating exchange rates is not far to seek. The scheme seemed to offer a kind of built-in protection against a sudden wave of speculative pressure against the pound, after it had been made convertible into dollars. There was, and still is, a real problem here. At the first sign of weakness, some foreign holders of sterling, at least, might well think it wise to insure against the possibility of the suspension of convertibility. With the reserves supporting sterling so small, such a suspension might be forced upon Britain as a result of even quite a short run on the bank. People remember that this is precisely what happened when Mr Hugh Dalton, as Chancellor of the Exchequer, tried the experiment of convertibility back in 1947. The most convenient way for a foreigner to insure himself against this eventuality would be to convert into dollars any part of his sterling holding that he did not require for immediate business purposes, and then patiently wait. If nothing happened and the pound recovered its former strength, he could always buy his previous holding of sterling back later. So long as the exchange rate could not move more than a very small amount either up, when the pound was strong, or down, when it was weak, it would be extremely cheap to cover risks by going in and out of sterling in this way.

In other words, there would be every incentive for foreigners to cut down their normal working balances of sterling at the first breath of rumour; and that might itself cause the run on the bank, against which people were trying to insure. The virtue claimed for the floating exchange rate was, and still is – for the scheme is supported by many financial experts today – that it would exact a severe penalty from the people who were, wittingly or unwittingly, speculating against the pound. As the wave of speculative selling developed, the exchange rate would drop, in response to the state of supply and demand in the market. The operator contemplating the sale of his sterling holding would then be deterred by the thought that he was going to get poor value for his money; if the pound recovered later on, when the operator found that he needed sterling again in order to meet his commercial obligations, he would have to pay a lot more foreign exchange to acquire the same amount. In other words, by letting the rate run free you expose the speculators against the pound to the risk of bigger losses. This would not of course stop a serious run on the bank, based on the expectation that the currency was about to collapse. But it might stop the minor speculative movement from growing into a major crisis.

Objections have been urged on the other side against floating exchange rates – the chief perhaps being that if the value of the currency did fluctuate at all widely, the foreign governments and institutions, which at present hold sterling balances as a usable form of ready cash, would be put off. However, the inherent merits and demerits of the proposal were not the main issue in the context of the sterling crisis of 1955. It was sufficient that an impression had been built up that British official opinion, for reasons which it regarded as sufficiently compelling, was on the whole favourable to the idea of floating rates. This was the background to the wave of speculative pressure against the pound which developed in the summer of 1955. But it was only the background. By itself, it would not have been sufficient to generate and sustain the pressure. For it had been generally accepted until then that the British Government would not move into convertibility – whether with a fixed or a floating rate – unless it could do so from a position of strength. All the discussions about fluctuating exchange rates, as a useful adjunct to a convertible pound, had taken place on the supposition that, whatever might happen later, the first movement of the rate immediately following convertibility would be upwards. In other words, it was believed that the British authorities would time their announcement at a moment when the U.K. balance of payments was favourable, when international confidence in the pound sterling was firmly established and was tending to strengthen rather than weaken.

All that looks, on the face of it, like a thoroughly plausible supposition. But, as will appear in a moment, it was by no means unanimously accepted by the men who were actually playing the game of freeing the sterling exchanges on a knife-edge of hazards.

Their view was that having gone so far in freeing the pound from the encumbrances of exchange control and thus exposing it to additional risks, the only possible move to inspire further confidence in sterling was forward – into a still more exposed position. For them the growing weakness of sterling in the foreign exchange markets became the most compelling reason for making it convertible at once. Here in fact is the key to the exchange crisis of the summer of 1955. It was not the preference for fluctuating exchange rates, which had been known for some time, but the authoritative whispers, going the round of the bankers on the continent of Europe, that Britain was about to make the pound convertible, because of its weakness. If the whispers were to be believed, the only sensible thing for a foreigner to do was to get out of sterling – before it lost 5 per cent or more of its value on being set free.

THE BANK OF ENGLAND'S ROLE

There is little doubt where the whispers originated. They came from Basle, where there is a kind of club of central bankers meeting once a month in order to conduct the affairs of the Bank for International Settlements. This institution, which was set up in 1930, originally to deal with German reparations, owes a great deal to the initiative of Montagu Norman, the Governor of the Bank of England of the day. His aim from the beginning was to use the occasion of these meetings for a far larger purpose – to ensure that the central banks of Europe were thrust into close and informal contact with each other's ideas and problems. Norman himself was particularly successful at running this kind of international collaboration between central banks, by-passing and even on occasion overriding relations between mere governments. He managed to generate some of the atmosphere of a bankers' trade union.

There were, it is undeniable, considerable benefits as well as dangers in these close relations between the central bankers, which he did so much to foster. These men were at that time far more independent in their dealings with their respective governments than they are today. They had much power, without responsibility

to any electorate. They were able to do things, quickly and inform-
ally, which are often not done nearly as well through the formal
processes of international collaboration operating between governments nowadays. For example, they were able, when they
wished, to cope with any movements of speculative capital, which
threatened to disrupt the international exchanges, a great deal
more efficiently than the governments which have had to rely on
the ponderous techniques of open economic diplomacy since the
war. Perhaps the most striking demonstration recently of the
incapacity of postwar governments in the face of problems such
as these was provided by the total failure of their attempt to miti-
gate the disruption of the exchanges in the summer of 1957,
caused by the outburst of speculation in favour of the German
Mark. This was a crisis which could have been avoided, if there
had been effective cooperation in the day-to-day supervision of
the exchanges by the central bankers. In the event it put the trade
and finances of two-thirds of Western Europe under severe
strain, and its further effects were felt in the outer reaches of the
sterling area.

There was a strong tradition of British leadership at Basle before the war. This was no doubt helped by the excellent relations
between Montagu Norman and Dr Schacht, the President of the
Reichsbank. But the most important point was that Norman, who
as Governor of the Bank of England had some pretty big guns at
his disposal at that time, was determined to make the club of
central bankers an effective force in world affairs. In his approach
to the problem of imposing discipline upon some of the smaller
members, he would assume at times all the airs of a head prefect.
He was capable of calling the bank governor of a lesser country
to his hotel room, and giving him a dressing down for some piece
of policy of which he disapproved. He once told the Bulgarian
governor in this determined manner that his bank rate was too
high and that he would have to reduce it. It was important for
these financially weak countries to keep on the right side of the
irascible Governor of the Bank of England. It would have been
surprising if Norman's successors, living in reduced circumstances in the 1940s and early '50s, had not hankered after some of
the old glories of undisputed international leadership. They were,

it is true, still the guardians of the most widely used currency in international trade; but it was far from being the most sought after. Their comfort was that it would become so once again, as soon as the pound sterling was made freely convertible into dollars. It is important for a proper understanding of the situation to recognize that there was this large element of pure prestige in the pursuit of convertibility – and not only among the bankers, though they were the people most directly concerned – as well as the practical aim of bringing sterling into wider use, so as to attract foreign money to London.

Indeed it is no exaggeration to say that, from the Bank of England's point of view, convertibility was an end in itself. It was necessary in order to re-establish the international status of sterling, which it was, after all, the Bank's business to protect and enhance. In interpreting British financial policy abroad, no one ever doubted that the Bank of England desperately wanted to make the pound convertible – and the sooner the better. The only question was whether the British Government would give the Bank its head. And the significant fact about the speculative crisis which hit sterling in 1955 was the firm impression abroad that the British Government had. This was the conclusion arrived at by the other central bankers, who attended the meetings with their British colleagues in Basle.

There was indeed considerable evidence at the time that they were right. A number of signs pointed to the conclusion that the Bank had obtained the dominant voice in determining the direction of British economic policy. This may now seem to have been an absurd view – just the sort of thing that a foreign banker would think. But there were after all familiar precedents for it, notably in the 1920s, when the decision to return to the gold standard at the old prewar parity, largely for prestige reasons again, imposed a policy of deflation on British industry, and held back the country's economic growth at a time when other nations were expanding fast. Chancellors of the Exchequer, like Sir Winston Churchill, who held that office at the time, are sometimes prepared to abdicate control over a crucial segment of economic affairs to the requirements of the Bank of England, seeking to enhance the international status of the currency. Indeed, behind the foreign exchange policies pursued by the Bank in the 1950s, it was possible to discern the same larger objective as that which was ultimately attained by Montagu Norman in the 1920s. The advent of convertibility, like the restoration of the gold standard in its day, would prove to be a ruthless and effective disciplinarian of the home economy. Once sterling was exposed, without the shield of exchange control, to every slightest movement of confidence in the international market, the country would find that it could no longer afford many of the things which it had come to take for granted after the Second World War. There were, and still are, many business people – not all of them bankers – who hold this view.

The political context of early 1955, when it seemed that the Bank had been given its head and was going to make a dash for convertibility, was also of some importance. The leading figures in the Government at this time were all preoccupied by the problem of the imminent departure of the Prime Minister, Sir Winston Churchill – or rather with the problem of turning the endlessly imminent into the actual. Sir Winston was enormously reluctant to go. Ministerial decisions were hampered during this period leading up to the general election in May 1955. What with the slow-motion exit of Sir Winston Churchill and the preparations for the election, these months had some of the atmosphere of an interregnum. In the field of economic policy, the evidence of indecision came right at the beginning of the year. In January, after more than two years of bounding prosperity and optimism, the Government gave the first explicit warning that something was wrong by raising the bank rate. But the operation, as an instrument of warning, was muffed. The increase in the rate was confined to $\frac{1}{2}$ per cent – from 3 to $3\frac{1}{2}$ per cent – and the City of London took hardly any notice. The amount of the increase was too little, and the accompanying official publicity was not nearly forcible enough. In February the rate had to be raised again, this time by a full 1 per cent. The second attempt was more effective as a measure of publicity; the Stock Exchange, at any rate, was severely shaken. Even so, ministers were anxious above all, with a general election ahead of them, to assert vigorously that Conservative prosperity and freedom were still working fine.

Out of this atmosphere of ministerial confusion one thing emerged, which impressed itself on the mind of the foreign bankers. It was a new financial measure, introduced at the same time as the second increase in the bank rate in February 1955, and it considerably increased the Bank of England's powers. Since it was of a somewhat technical nature, it received little publicity and discussion inside Britain. The bare fact announced was that henceforth the Bank was to be allowed to use funds taken out of the gold reserve, in order to intervene in the unofficial markets abroad, where pounds were being exchanged for dollars on an extensive scale. The main centres for this business are New York and Zürich, and the point to notice is that it is strictly illegal for an Englishman to take any part in these transactions. From a British point of view these are black markets. They deal in a distinctive variety of pounds sterling, 'transferable sterling', which is the currency used to pay for goods or services supplied by countries *outside* the sterling area. This money can be used pretty freely in international trade. If Japan buys something from China or Russia ships some goods to Argentina, as likely as not the payment will be made in transferable pounds. But there is one important restriction imposed by the British exchange control regulations: this sterling is not supposed to be used in transactions with dollar countries. A foreigner can bring the pounds to London and exchange them legally through the foreign exchange market there into any currency, except dollars. The consequence is that the Russians, for example, are not able to pay in transferable sterling for the Canadian wheat which they have imported in recent years; the Canadians would not accept it, because they know that they would not be able to turn this money into London and get the dollars that they want in exchange for it.

This is, after all, only another way of saying that the pound is still not fully convertible. To put the matter more strictly, what inconvertibility means is that although some pounds can be converted into dollars at the official rate of exchange (for instance, pounds earned by Americans and Canadians by exports to Britain), the majority cannot. However, when the practical issue is examined still more closely, it is found that if someone is really anxious to do so, all pounds can be exchanged into dollars in some market somewhere at some rate of exchange. You get less for your pounds than the official price, but you do get dollars. Now, the most active unofficial markets for changing pounds into dollars at a discount are precisely these centres in New York and Zürich, where people deal in transferable sterling. Moreover, these centres are often watched by the foreign exchange dealers as a better indication of the state of commercial demand and supply for sterling than the official market in London. And when the gap between the official rate and the rate for this cheap sterling becomes at all wide, this can be a source of embarrassment to traders trying to sell sterling area commodities at the official rate of exchange. The outsider, buying his pounds on the cheap, is in a position to obtain the commodities more cheaply than the insider. For there is no legal way in which a merchant working in Britain or in any of the main sterling area countries can operate in the unofficial market for transferable sterling.

The new departure in February 1955, which brought the Bank of England into these markets as an active operator, had the declared aim of ensuring that the unofficial rate for transferable sterling would in future be kept up close to the official rate. When a lot of people in Zürich wanted to sell pounds, the agents of the Bank were to go in and 'support' the market. They would do this by handing out dollars, taken from the British reserve, in exchange for the pounds. It was regarded at the time by many people in Britain simply as a psychological move designed to give some extra protection against speculative strains on the pound, and no special significance was attached to it. But this is not how it was regarded by those actually responsible for the execution of the new policy in the Bank of England, or indeed by the bankers and businessmen directly affected by it in the world outside. By these it was seen clearly as the penultimate move before convertibility. The subsequent meetings of the bankers at Basle in 1955 can only have served to reinforce the conclusion and drive it home.

Indeed, the British bankers kept pointing out that the pound was already convertible in practice – only the British Government refused to take official cognizance of the fact. If the decision to support transferable sterling were examined closely, it would be apparent that what it meant was that the Bank of England had entered into an arrangement to supply dollars to any foreigner who had sterling to sell, and to do so at a very small discount on the official rate of exchange. Soon, it was generally believed, even this discount would disappear. There was no secret about the ambition of people in the Bank of England to push up the transferable rate for the pound in the New York and Zürich markets, until it was level with the official rate of exchange, and then by keeping the two rates together, get it finally recognized that the pound was officially, as well as unofficially, convertible. Everybody would be able to buy dollars with sterling at the same price. Some financial commentators were already speculating about the possibility of opening a market for transferable sterling and dollars in London, although the whole of this business was then, and still is, barred by legal penalties to Englishmen. The mood of the time was expressed for me in a startling fashion in a remark made in the spring of 1955 by a man holding a high and responsible office in this field. We were discussing the position of sterling in the foreign exchange market under the new arrangements, and there was one point at which I tried to raise an objection to a line of argument which he had developed. 'Surely,' I said, 'what you are suggesting would mean that someone would have to contravene the exchange control regulations?' I received a brief pitying look. 'Nobody but small fry,' he said, 'takes any notice of exchange controls now.'

The new permissive atmosphere about foreign exchange dealings which was established then has certainly been one of the factors making it more difficult to defend the pound sterling against speculation during the period of strain that followed in 1956 and 1957. First of all, foreign bankers and dealers were encouraged to think of transferable pounds – that is broadly any sterling that came into their hands in the course of an ordinary commercial transaction – as being convertible into dollars. Previously there had been strict rules imposed by the Bank of England, in order to prevent the sale of cheap sterling for dollars, and those countries which did not maintain an effective exchange control to this end were refused certain facilities by Britain. Secondly, there was a feeling engendered in Britain and in other parts of the sterling area that the currency regulations no longer mattered so much. It was always wrong to suppose that privileges could be given to foreign businessmen outside the sterling area, allowing them to use their pounds more freely, without people inside the sterling area demanding, and then taking, the same rights. The idea of 'convertibility for non-residents', which was the official objective during the early years of the Conservative Government, was psychologically obtuse. The notion that it would be possible to abolish all exchange regulations for the lucky people outside the sterling area, while maintaining the full rigour of the controls inside it, argued an extreme view of the docility of British and Commonwealth businessmen. They are not as desperately law-abiding as that.

THE BANK AND THE TREASURY

The situation in mid-1955, when the financial crisis broke with full violence on the calm and even complacent mood of the Conservative Government, was that a strong rumour was running round the world that sterling convertibility was imminent, combined with a drop in the value of the pound. British economic policy was in fact being tugged in two different directions. There was the Bank of England line, which demanded a bold stroke, a big risk, with the possibility of a glittering prize at the end of it. And on the other side a Treasury view had gradually crystallized, that the time had come to pull back and consolidate, and above all avoid adding to the already considerable risks that had been assumed. Relations between the Bank and Treasury were extremely bad. A certain undercurrent of rivalry and opposition is indeed normal between these two great institutions. Only occasionally does it erupt into open hostilities, such as occurred in the incident between Lord Cunliffe, the Bank Governor, and the Chancellor of the Exchequer, Mr Bonar Law, in 1917, when the Bank refused to supply the Treasury representative in Canada with the gold that he required in order to conduct certain operations on behalf of the British Government at a difficult stage in the First World War. On that occasion the Chancellor demanded the deposit of a signed letter of resignation from the Governor, as a surety for more cooperative conduct in the future. But generally the urge to competitive coexistence triumphs. Montagu Norman's approach to the relationship with the Treasury was rather milder than that of Lord Cunliffe – perhaps because he was so consistently successful in getting his way in Whitehall. He would describe the proper relationship in cricketing terms. 'It is like two elevens,' he said. 'So long as the best players on the Bank side – the opening batsmen, the wicket keeper, and one or two more – are better than the people in the Treasury team, everything will be all right. But if not . . .'

The effect of this rivalry between the Treasury and the Bank on British economic policy during the present century would make an interesting subject of study. Unfortunately too few facts are known about it. For civil servants and bankers, unlike generals, maintain the gentlemanly tradition of sealed lips even in retirement. The Bank's advantages in the unending cricket match with the Treasury, of Lord Norman's fancy, are very considerable. To begin with, there are none of the civil service limitations on the size of its staff or on the amounts that it pays them. No account is rendered to the public of the Bank's expenditure, since it all comes out of business earnings. One becomes aware of this atmosphere of freedom and ease as soon as one enters the Bank's premises. The contrast with the Treasury building in Great George Street, where people are still living very much in the Gladstonian tradition of saving candle ends – and, one sometimes suspects, working by candlelight in order to give themselves the opportunity for doing so – is overwhelming. As one enters the unnaturally tall door of the Bank, let into the fortress wall facing on to Threadneedle Street, and comes into the large vestibule, one is struck at once by the considerable crowd of pink-coated messengers in top hats standing about in attitudes of respectful waiting. These are mostly men of impressive size and personal appearance possessed of a notable aplomb, apparently derived from the genius of the place, and good firm manners, who lead the visitor to his appointed destination with sureness and dispatch. The Bank has more clerks at its disposal for the amount of work to be done and a more elaborate filing system than the Treasury; its offices are much better, and so are many of its other amenities. Its solitary apparent handicap is its inability to build up a staff of bright young men from the universities. But this is perhaps because it does not try very hard. The graduates whom it recruits do not seem to have much encouragement to stick. Many of them go. The Bank tends to acquire such trained intellectuals as it needs, and can tolerate, from other walks of life, where these men are already established. It does not reckon to build them up on the premises. The result is that the hard core of the executive hierarchy is still public school, rather than university.

They are in fact very different people from the prize-winning university graduates who are recruited into the Treasury. It is no wonder that each shows a certain jealousy about its domain. The Bank's official task is to look after the 'day-to-day' management of currency and credit, while the Treasury is supposed to concern itself with the broader aspect of financial policy. But who is to say what exactly constitutes a day-to-day issue? Many such issues merge imperceptibly into longer term questions of policy. A strong Governor, people in the Bank will say confidently, can always impose his own delimitation of the respective areas of authority on Whitehall; Montagu Norman certainly did; the only question about the present occupant, Mr Cobbold, is whether he is quite firm enough. The reality is thus a far cry from Sir Stafford Cripps's confident description of the relationship: 'The Bank is my creature.' More to the point is the remark made to me subsequently by a Conservative politician with more exact knowledge of the inner workings of the institution: 'Somebody may have to nationalize the Bank of England one of these days; the Socialists don't know how.'

All these sources of friction between the Bank and the Treasury were exacerbated in the strained conditions of mid-1955. They added to the appearance of indecision and confusion in British policy at a critical moment. But it is unfair to put the blame for this entirely on the initiative taken by some of the Bank's officials in the conduct of external financial policy. The whole mood of the Government at the time fitted in only too well with the Bank's conception of 'a dash for freedom'. Indeed, it was the Treasury itself which had developed to a high pitch of oversimplification the theory of the maximum exposure of the British economy to the forces of the market, both at home and abroad. The pure theory, which became increasingly fashionable as the Conservative experiment moved forward from success to success in 1952–4, was that the economy was to be governed ultimately by two levers only. These were the rate of interest and the variable rate of exchange. The first, by fixing the cost of money at home, would regulate the supply and the demand for it, and would therefore determine the level of economic activity, which would in turn exercise a decisive influence on wages, investment and consumption. But if any one of these did not respond fast enough or fully enough to the pressure of rising interest rates, the other automatic lever, the exchange rate, would start pressing down. If, for instance, British workers obtained an increase in wages in excess of the increase in their productivity, and the resulting inflationary purchasing power began to pull in more imported goods than the country could afford, there would never be any need to introduce import cuts. The drop in the exchange rate would do the trick. More pounds would flow into international currency markets as British imports rose; and as the supply increased without a corresponding growth of demand, the price would adjust itself. This would automatically reduce the volume of British imports by the necessary amount. With the fall in the exchange rate the pound would be worth less in terms of foreign currencies, and so the foreign goods would cost more. British consumers would thus be restrained by the rise in price level, just as the businessmen, when they were inclined to overspend, were to be kept in check by an increase in the cost of borrowed money at home. There was, the civil servants would point out proudly, no need for any kind of Government action, except to ensure that the market was allowed to determine the correct price of money at home and abroad.

There are numerous flaws in this baby model of an economy with two levers – which would become immediately apparent as soon as anyone tried to drive it in the real world of grown-ups. But the important fact in the historical context of Britain of the 1950s was not so much its mechanical imperfections, since no one was really going to try it out, but rather that this device represented the current ideal among top British officials of how the economy would work under the best of all possible governments in the best of all possible worlds. Rarely, at any rate in modern times, can the doctrine of *anti-planning* have been carried to this degree of excess. And the new philosophers, it is to be observed, were the same people who had carried out the Labour policies of state intervention during the period 1945–51. It represents a startling reaction to this experience on the part of the people who probably had as much direct day-to-day contact as anyone with the operation of Labour's experiments in planning. However, it would be wrong to suggest that these men were moved solely by spontaneous moral revulsion to the mistakes in the policies which had been pursued under the Labour Government. They were, as good civil servants ought to be, keenly aware of the advent of a new lot of masters, and they conscientiously set out to formulate a set of principles to conform with what they conceived to be the changed needs of the Government. It may be that the ideas and policies of the Conservative ministers were in any case more congenial to many of the senior civil servants. But the striking fact to an outside observer at this time, that is in the period 1952–4, was that they tended to be much more extreme in the doctrines which they propounded than their political masters. That is partly because they were deliberately looking for a doctrine, whereas their masters were not.

Perhaps the civil servants had no option, faced with the problem of putting the whole of their great machine into another gear and guiding it in a new direction, after six years of doctrinal instruction from the Labour Government. But they certainly fell on their new intellectual task with enthusiasm. To some extent they were, no doubt, whether consciously or unconsciously, anxious to demonstrate their loyalty to the new Government, after serving Labour's postwar social revolution. There is almost bound to be some anxiety, even under the British system, where civil servants have a secure guarantee of permanent employment, whenever there is a radical shift from one government to the next. After all, ministers being human look for willing and even enthusiastic collaborators in carrying through their policies. The result has been a tendency for civil servants to over-react to changing political needs in a way that a person with overt political loyalties would not. It is a noticeable fact that when President Eisenhower takes over from the Democrats in the United States in 1951 and brings in a new set of economic advisers on the Government payroll, who are frankly Republican in their personal politics, they do not feel the need to demonstrate constantly that the Government's Republicanism is reflected in every piece of economic advice given. It certainly seemed to me at the time that Dr Burns, the head of the U.S. President's Council of Economic Advisers appointed by Mr Eisenhower, was less concerned to prove that the policies he proposed were untainted by the views of the other side, than the permanent and unpolitical chiefs of the economic departments of the Government on this side.

The British practice has paradoxically served to aggravate the ideological approach to economic policy. Britain seems to have run more easily to extremism and doctrinaire decisions in this field than the allegedly anti-empirical nations, like the French or the Germans. There is a unified and consciously coherent view of policy cultivated in the civil service in this country, which is absent both in continental Western Europe and in the U.S. Gunnar Myrdal, the former head of the Economic Commission for Europe, who has had a great deal of experience in comparing the intellectual manners of the officials of different countries, once summed up the matter admirably. 'Your country,' he said, 'is the only totalitarian democracy in my experience. Whatever the occasion, it has never been known that a British official deviates from the party line.'

OPERATION ROBOT

Perhaps the most characteristic specimen of the ultra-liberalism which the civil servants tried to wish on to their Conservative masters was a scheme which went by the dramatic title of 'operation robot'. This was a code name, most secretly kept at the time. Even now, when it has become very ancient history in terms of practical policy, many of the details are still carefully concealed. But there is no doubt what 'operation robot' was intended to do. As its name suggests, the scheme was to bring suddenly into play as supreme controller one of those impersonal mechanisms, so much favoured at the time.[1] This was early on in 1952, just after the Conservatives had taken office and the pound sterling was still under strong speculative pressure, as a result of the aftermath of the Korean boom. The way of salvation that was proposed was essentially the doctrine of the two levers – only this time the economy was not to be given the benefit of any gradual extension of freedom, before it was subjected to the full force of the market mechanism at home and abroad. On the contrary, an essential feature of the scheme was that some controls were to be clamped down tighter still. Chief of these was the control on the sterling balances. All were to be blocked. But at the same time the pound sterling was to be made fully convertible (for 'non-residents' only, of course), the exchange rate was to be set free to fluctuate, and the Government was to raise the rate of interest to whatever height was necessary in order to hold the position at home.

The full story of how this scheme was scotched has never been told. The evidence is that there were some exciting moments in 1952, when it was touch and go for 'robot'. It is believed that Mr Butler, the Chancellor of the Exchequer, was in favour of the plan at the time when the pressure on the pound became acute, and he thought that this might be a way of stopping it. But in that case, the views of the other members of the Cabinet – particularly, it seems, that of Lord Cherwell, the scientist and friend of Sir Winston Churchill, who was Paymaster General at the time – evidently prevailed against him. Although the plan itself was shelved once the speculative pressure on sterling eased and the condition of the gold reserve began to improve in 1953, the mood that conceived it remained. And it was this mood which was chiefly responsible for the confusion in British policy when the next crisis came round in 1955.

In fairness it should be said that this robot scheme might well have worked and altered the whole course of British economic history. Once a large measure of convertibility for the pound sterling had been established, it would have been extremely difficult to go back. Indeed some officials, and even ministers, still look back with a hankering eye to the desperate days of 1952. There is something in the view that if the bold stroke had been taken then, with everything risked on a single throw, it would have imparted a sharp point and a coherence to Conservative policy, instead of the havering and flabbiness that came upon it in subsequent years. Given the fact of convertibility, there would have been no room for argument and hesitation on a number of vital issues of policy. The Government would have been compelled to act quickly and with the utmost vigour, in order to save the pound each time that it came under the slightest international pressure. We would not have had to wait until the autumn of 1957 for a bank rate of 7 per cent. With a slender gold reserve, and a pound sterling exposed in such a way that every breath of international rumour could be turned into a hurricane of speculation, there would have been only one course open to the defenders of the pound – to cut and cut expenditure at home, until we had built up a siege economy, which could withstand any violence that might come from abroad. This was of course not the explicit intention of the protagonists of this policy. But it was the inescapable logic of what they proposed: henceforth whatever the Government might wish to do at home would be *absolutely* limited and subjected to the views of foreigners holding convertible pounds sterling. The Government would find itself increasingly forced into demonstrative acts of deflation, designed to show that it was sufficiently hard-faced to inspire confidence among the bankers in Zürich and elsewhere.

It may be argued today that the British Government has manoeuvred itself into this position anyhow, and has done so without obtaining the benefits that would have flowed from full convertibility. The abolition of many of the exchange controls, the weakening of others, and the pursuit of a whole range of commercial objectives, which only made sense if accompanied by a currency that could be freely used by the foreigner, have brought on Britain the pains and anxieties of convertibility, without the prestige. There is no doubt that the Government has allowed its domestic policy since 1955 to be determined largely by the movement of international confidence in the pound sterling. It is the thesis of this book that such a situation is both tragic and absurd, and that a means of escape from it must be devised. The last minute refusal of the Conservative Government to embark upon the hazards of full convertibility in 1955 does now leave the way open for a rational policy of retreat from a too exposed position. If the exponents of the dash for freedom had had their way, there would now be no possibility of retreat without a cataclysm. The basic structure of the exchange controls is still in existence – we have fortunately not replaced it by a robot – and the system can now be strengthened to provide an increasing measure of protection for sterling against short-term speculative movements abroad.

The essential fallacy of the financial technicians who argue that since we already have informal convertibility of sterling for foreigners, as a result of the decisions of 1955, we might as well advance to formal recognition of the fact, is that they ignore the human realities of the situation. They do this partly because of an exaggerated belief in their own ability to translate these neat bankers' categories – finance being a field which readily sprouts metaphysics – into the disorderly world of business, where people shift money about, and neither know nor care how the banker has classified it. Thus for example the technician's rigid distinction between convertibility for non-resident sterling (that is pounds held by people outside the sterling area) and no convertibility for resident sterling (money held inside the sterling area) would rapidly become blurred, once people saw an advantage in blurring it. To take the very simplest case, there are many British companies which contain within themselves both 'resident' and 'non-resident' business organizations. It would be extremely difficult in real life to prevent the 'residents', if they were determined, from obtaining all the currency advantages given to 'non-residents'. As was pointed out earlier, it never was a very clever idea to have a scheme under which the British authorities deliberately handed out privileges to foreign holders of sterling, which were denied to Englishmen and other members of the sterling area. The only way to stop the 'residents' from obtaining parity with the foreigner in this matter would be by a vast reinforcement of the system of exchange controls within the sterling area. Relations between businessmen inside it and those outside it would have to be much more closely policed than before; and this would largely stultify the purpose of the whole exercise. The odds are that if the bankers had had their way in 1955, they would have gone to the Government, after a few months of 'non-resident' convertibility, and said: 'We really must be realistic about this thing. The truth is that the residents are managing to make their pounds convertible too, and there is no way of stopping them. So why not recognize the fact, and go on to full convertibility for everybody?'

There has indeed already been a dangerous movement in this direction, as a result of the successive relaxations in exchange control. A big market in what is called 'resident sterling' has grown up in New York, fed by illegal exports from Britain and other sterling area countries. Dealers on the spot claimed that by 1957 it had become the most important unofficial channel for the exchange of pounds into dollars. Now, 'resident sterling' is just another name for ordinary pounds, shillings, and pence owned by people holding bank accounts in Britain and elsewhere in the sterling area. There are various ways in which they can, under the present loose system of exchange controls, sell this money and obtain dollars for it at something less than the official rate of exchange. When the Americans subsequently use this sterling to pay for British goods and services, the current balance of payments receives no benefit whatever from such dollar exports. The people who will have benefited are those who managed to sell their 'resident sterling' in the first instance, got dollars for it, and presumably spent them. Our dollar exports in this case simply sustain a flight of capital. This could prove extremely troublesome in a political emergency, or even in a period of political uncertainty like a general election.

However, for the moment the movement of such capital funds is still being kept under some sort of supervision. With full convertibility for non-residents formally established, effective supervision over such transactions as these would become much more difficult. Here indeed is another one of the banker's sharp theoretical divisions, which become hopelessly blurred in practice – the distinction between money which is *capital* and money which is *current* commercial earnings. The technicians who prepared the currency plans for the Conservative Government proposed only that there should be convertibility *on current account*; and they let it be understood that when it came to the point, they would be able to identify with certainty the capital element in money transactions and deny it the privilege of convertibility into dollars. They can in practice do nothing of the sort. Indeed, the whole distinction between what is current income and what is capital presents considerable theoretical difficulties. The borderland between the two concepts is highly uncertain. After all, it is a familiar fact of experience in postwar Britain that the really big fortunes are built up by converting current earnings into capital, which is free of tax.

If the realities, rather than the metaphysics, of international finance had been properly explained to the politicians, it is at least doubtful whether they would have deliberately courted the risk of being asked to convert all the world's sterling holdings, including a lot held inside the sterling area, into dollars. There was certainly a feeling among some members of the Conservative Government in 1955 and afterwards that they had been insufficiently informed, if not positively misinformed, by their banking advisers. Part of the trouble lies in the fact that often the influential bankers are not the flexible and empirical spirits of the popular imagination, but rigid theorists, sometimes of a quasi-mystical character. Unfortunately the theories and the metaphysics have important practical consequences, which properly belong in the domain of political choice. Thus, for example, the series of technical decisions affecting the exchange controls from 1952 to 1955 would, if they had been carried much further, have exposed Britain without any defence to the full violence of a flight of capital out of sterling, both at home and abroad. The only way to prevent such a movement, once the controls are down, is by making Britain as attractive a place to the owners of capital as any possible alternative abroad. This at once sets pretty narrow limits to what the Government can do about taxation, about social expenditure, about nationalization, and a number of other major political issues. Here in fact is the vicarious reassertion of the political power of the owners of wealth – not businessmen or people active in any way, but just owners – which the postwar social revolution in Britain had set out to prevent. The Conservatives, when they came to power, gave no hint that it was part of their purpose to undo the *fait accompli*. It was certainly not the conscious purpose of the party leaders, either then or later.

The other answer to those who lament the missed opportunity

of 'operation robot' is that if they had had their way, the Conservatives would never have experienced their golden years of expansion 1953–5. No Chancellor of the Exchequer, knowing that he had a convertible pound to defend with a hopelessly inadequate gold reserve, would have dared to stimulate an industrial investment boom in the way that Mr Butler deliberately set out to do. His confidence in these years, it is fair to say, was partly due to the fact that he had not grasped the essential nature of the choice between expansion at home and the establishment of an absolutely safe, convertible pound abroad. He thought that he could easily have both, and he pursued both aims indiscriminately. But somehow his instinct, rather than his judgement, warned him just in time against jeopardizing the home programme, which was nearest to his heart, for the sake of the external prestige of the pound. In a sense the exponents of convertibility were more sophisticated. They saw clearly that there was a choice which would have to be made sooner or later. When the crisis came in 1955, they were prepared to carry the logic of governing the economy by means of the automatic market mechanism to the extremes of deflation. Mr Butler and the group of regenerate postwar Tories around him were not. Hence the confusion of British policy in that year, and to a lesser degree ever since. Extreme deflation was the logical answer to the problem of sterling, as it had been in the 1920s, but none of the succession of Tory Chancellors, neither Mr Butler nor Mr Macmillan nor even Mr Thorneycroft, was ready to embrace it with the enthusiasm and constancy necessary to carry such a policy through. This is the essential contrast between their record and that of the Tory Chancellors of the twenties, notably Sir Winston Churchill. They were not prepared to sacrifice the growth of the productive capacity of the country to the exigencies of its external financial relations.

This would have been more to the credit of the Conservative Chancellors in the difficult years from the middle 1950s onwards, if they had translated their unwillingness to make the sacrifice into something more tangible than personal emotion. During 1955–7, it is possible to point to one important practical effect of their views about the necessity of expansion – the refusal to commit the country to the ultimate step to convertibility. For the rest, in spite of the continuing and no doubt sincere public statements of these men that economic expansion must be resumed as quickly as possible, the measures which they actually took during this period were a succession of attacks on the forces making for growth in the economy. It now looks as if these forces have at last been broken – to the accompaniment of a mounting volume of exhortation from the members of the Conservative Cabinet about the urgent need to expand. The moral is that having the right sentiments is not enough. A choice has to be made between expansion at home and other desirable objectives; and it ought to be made before a government starts confidently embarking on all the desirable objectives in sight at once.

WHY CONSERVATIVE FREEDOM CEASED TO WORK

This was the essential tragedy of 1955, the year when Conservative freedom failed to work: no one had seriously contemplated making the choice between conflicting policies. It is therefore wrong to look for the real explanation of the record of failure in that year, as some Conservative commentators do, in the events of 1955 itself. It is true that there were a number of special misfortunes of a more or less fortuitous character for the Government in that year. Some of them – the confusion caused by the protracted departure of Sir Winston Churchill from the premiership and the general election which followed – have already been discussed. There was also the series of strikes, involving comparatively few men but a number of vital activities, starting in the late autumn of 1954 with a dispute in the docks, which paralysed foreign trade for a month, and continuing into the summer of 1955, when the train drivers struck and the railways were brought to a standstill. In between, there was a strike which stopped the production of newspapers at the time of the Budget in the spring, and thus effectually stilled the critical comment and discussion that would certainly have been evoked by the tax concessions and the lax economic policy of the Government at this time. It is perhaps not sufficiently realized how much cabinet ministers rely on the printed word in newspapers to turn their ideas over. Most of the time, they are so busy acting that they have no opportunity to think much beyond the next decision. Newspapers, and conversation with those who write them, often provide the stimulus for self-examination in the context of a somewhat longer perspective. I have come to the conclusion, as a result of my own experiences as a journalist, that the considerable risks which politicians take when they talk in their characteristically uninhibited fashion to newspapermen are not by any means always, or even mainly, motivated by the hope of favourable publicity. What they want above all is a mirror. Where else are they to find one?

Finally, there were the personal difficulties of the Chancellor of the Exchequer, Mr Butler, who had been the creative force behind the Party's new economic policy both before and after it came into office. There is no doubt that by the summer of that year, the Chancellor was an over-tired man. He was still able to produce, on occasion, flashes of the old brilliance – as for example at the meeting of the International Monetary Fund in Istanbul in September 1955, when he deliberately set out to check another violent wave of speculation which had started up against sterling, and succeeded in doing so. I witnessed this performance myself. After seeing Mr Butler arrive in Turkey, haggard and careworn off the aeroplane from England, I was astonished at the jauntiness with which he responded to an extremely difficult task of public relations forty-eight hours later. But it is doubtful whether even in more favourable circumstances, he would have been capable at this stage of carrying out the still more exacting intellectual task of going back to the essentials of Conservative policy, and thinking out the problem of choice afresh. He had developed over the previous years two separate lines of policy and treated them as if they were one – economic liberalism and industrial expansion. Then somehow the liberalism got on top. The process of reversing these priorities – or at any rate of curbing the primitive faith in the efficacy of market mechanisms free and unrestrained – which began in the latter half of 1955, was a hesitant and painful one.

There were at the time inhibitions of the most powerful kind against letting the Government lay its unhallowed hand on the sacred machinery of the market. The people who had been responsible for bringing the markets back into operation felt intensely about the subject. They were determined to defend the point of principle, which they believed they had gained. Their exaggerated concern for the punctilio of the market-place emerges clearly in the furious arguments about the use of hire purchase restrictions as the crisis developed during 1955. The first lot of h.p. regulations were issued in February of that year. The more extreme liberals, among whom the Economist newspaper was included, said that such restrictions were bad in themselves, because they interfered with the free functioning of the market. However, the followers of the true faith could at least console themselves that the Government had been careful not to introduce any serious discrimination between the various articles on which the restrictions had been imposed. The 15 per cent legal minimum deposit operated right across the board. Two things became clear almost as soon as the order was in force. First, it had no noticeable effect on the demand for cars, and very little effect on a number of electrical household goods, which were also big users of sheet steel. And it was the large import of sheet steel, required for the production of these goods destined for the home market, which was one of the causes of the crisis in the balance of payments. The second point was that furniture sales, which had already tapered off from the high point of their boom in 1954 even before the restrictions were imposed, were depressed still further by the h.p. regulations. Thus the net effect of the policy of non-discrimination was that an industry whose operations did not strain the balance of payments found itself in trouble, while other industries, which were adding to Britain's import bill and failing to contribute adequately to exports, got away scot-free. Yet it took until July before the Government could bring itself to discriminate against cars and electrical goods by putting up the minimum h.p. deposit on these to 33⅓ per cent, without giving the unfortunate furniture-makers the same treatment. The measure was preceded by furious argument, which went up to Cabinet level. Afterwards some of the officials concerned seemed to treat the decision that had been taken as a sin against the light.

It was in fact the breaking point of the policy of doctrinal economic liberalism. That was not immediately apparent at the time. Indeed, the doctrine celebrated one of its spectacular triumphs in that same month of July, with an increase in the price of coal by no less than 18 per cent, in response to the forces of supply and demand. There were of course cogent reasons for raising the price of coal in this country, the same reasons that have existed ever since the war, namely that it is hard to justify the sale of coal below world market prices to British consumers, who are particularly wasteful in their use of it. But coming in the middle of an inflationary crisis, at a time when the costs were rising and wage claims were growing dangerously, the deliberate and violent increase in the coal price in the summer of 1955 can only be regarded as an act of bravado. It was certainly treated as such by the people who fix prices and demand wages. For them this was a clear signal, which indicated the official climate on costs and prices. It was evidently a permissive climate. Anyone who had been hesitating about whether to raise his prices or not now had his mind made up for him; and if his customers grumbled, he could always say: 'Well, look what the Government is doing.'

On the labour side, matters were made worse by the enthusiastic argument used by economists of the liberal school, guided by official inspiration, that here was a striking example of courageous disinflationary action. It mopped up inflationary purchasing power. The extra money that people would be forced to spend on coal would, after all, have to be subtracted from other kinds of spending, which had no doubt been adding to the excessive pressure of consumer demand. Once again there was the characteristic propensity of these market economists to ignore the human and political realities of a situation. It should be noticed, however, that it is characteristic only in this country. In Germany and the United States the exponents of the virtues of the market have been chary about provoking a price rise out of devotion to an abstract principle. The inevitable political counter to this abstract principle was put by Mr Frank Cousins of the Transport and General Workers Union some time later. 'If there is to be a free for all,' he said, 'we are part of the all.'

It is a measure of the speed of the reversal in Tory economic policy that less than a year later, in the spring of 1956, Mr Macmillan, as Chancellor of the Exchequer, was appealing for a régime of administered prices, regardless of the market forces, as a means of creating a 'price plateau'. The Government itself was prepared by this time to make its own contribution to price stability by asking the nationalized industries to cut their rate of profit, rather than raise their prices to compensate for rising costs. In the particular case of the railways, it was decided that the increased losses would be met directly out of Government funds. It was no longer fashionable to recommend the splendid disinflationary device of raising the prices of essential goods and services.

NOTE

1. It was rumoured at the time that ROBOT was a cryptogram formed of the initial letters of the names of the three men concerned in the policy – Sir Leslie ROwan, Second Secretary at the Treasury, Sir George BOlton, director of the Bank of England, and Mr OTto Clarke, another senior official of the Treasury. The unity between Threadneedle Street and Great George Street appears, however, to have been temporary.

CHAPTER NINE

TORIES IN SEARCH OF A POLICY 1956–8

IT would be wrong to suggest that the policies of the years 1956 and 1957, when the Government was consciously moving back from the extremes of *laissez-faire* where it had landed itself in 1955, were all of a piece. The economic liberals continued to fight a powerful rearguard action. They found it more difficult to make headway with the new Chancellor of the Exchequer, Mr Harold Macmillan, who took over from Mr Butler at the end of 1955, for Mr Macmillan had never been personally sympathetic to their views. Another personal factor of some importance was the influence of the Economic Secretary of the Treasury, Sir Edward Boyle, who had been appointed to this office in the spring of 1955 and soon showed a decided temperamental opposition to the philosophy of *laissez-faire* extremism and the current obsession with markets, as the only means of guiding the economy. He was an effective administrator, and he was able to do something to resuscitate the influence of the Economic Section of the Treasury, which had been eclipsed during the earlier period of Conservative rule. The Economic Section was regarded by many as an alien imposition on the Treasury – it was a band of professional economists brought in during the war to assist the process of planning – and it had few defenders within the permanent civil service organization. Boyle made a point of bringing it into the centre of Government policy-making again, and of showing that he took its views seriously. Meanwhile it was characteristic that Mr Macmillan introduced an entirely new emphasis on the need to collect more and better statistics as an aid to Government action in the conduct of economic affairs. He made it clear that he had no faith in automatic market mechanisms as the sole regulator of economic progress.

This Macmillan-Boyle team at the Treasury was rather demonstrative about its lack of doctrinal inhibitions on matters like the reimposition of building licensing, which filled many of the party faithful with almost religious horror. They were even prepared, it seems, to defy the party's strong feelings on the subject of income tax. At any rate there is a good deal of reliable evidence that an increase of 6d in the standard rate of tax, bringing it back to 9s. in the £, was seriously considered in the spring of 1956, before the Budget, as a means of combating inflation. It was, apparently, turned down at the last moment. The reasoning behind this suggestion was almost pure Crippsian theory. It was a far cry from the type of argument which had accompanied the Budget of the year before, in April 1955, and had been used to justify the cut in income tax of 6d in the £ introduced then. At that time the Government felt able to contemplate such a tax concession in the midst of a difficult inflationary situation, when high spending at home had helped to tip the balance of payments the wrong way, because it relied confidently on the indirect pressures of monetary and credit policies, operating through the market, to put matters right.

The 1956 approach is also very different in spirit from the new financial policy, presented by Mr Peter Thorneycroft, the third Conservative Chancellor of the Exchequer, in September 1957, when he raised the bank rate to 7 per cent – the highest level for thirty-seven years. Mr Thorneycroft intimated that the Government had decided once again to rely on monetary measures to restrain the supply of credit, as the main instrument for guiding the economy in the right direction. In the financial press and the City of London, this was hailed – and in some cases lamented – as a return to the old orthodoxy. In fact, there was no such orthodox intention on the part of the Cabinet as a whole; there were profound divisions within the Government. But for the moment the reins had been handed to the Chancellor. The autumn of 1957 was a period of perilous crisis, when the pound sterling was subjected to one of the most severe bouts of speculative pressure that it has experienced at any time since the war, and no one was going to argue with the Chancellor about the kind of public relations activity that he thought appropriate for the defence of the currency. In fact, the various gestures and speeches made at the time did have the desired effect, and the speculative wave which had almost engulfed sterling retreated sufficiently to allow the underlying strength of the British balance of payments to come into view. The gold drain of the late summer and autumn of 1957, brought on partly by the devaluation of the French Franc and partly by a general expectation that the German Mark would be increased in value, was halted and then reversed.

However, the danger with talented practitioners of public relations is, it has been observed before, that they often display a special talent for convincing themselves. Characteristically, the Thorneycroft announcement that measures to stabilize the supply of credit to the market were now going to halt inflation once and for all was converted almost overnight into a fundamentalist dogma by Government officials and Conservative Party militants. The doctrinaire overtones in the discussion of this policy were particularly evident in the financial press. The Government as a whole was, however, chiefly concerned, in this new phase of the credit squeeze, with the practical issue of improving the bargaining position of the employers against excessive wage claims – excessive in the sense of being more than the prospective increase in productivity – in the period immediately ahead. Its direct means of influencing the situation were very limited – they existed chiefly in the negotiations on the railways, because there the employers happened to rely on a direct Government subsidy to pay their bills – so official spokesmen determined to do what they could by means of appropriately menacing noises and gestures. Meanwhile, the division of views within the Cabinet, the failure, for tactical reasons, to face the essential issues, were bound to produce more intellectual confusion, of the kind which had already reduced the effectiveness of the Conservative Government during its second postwar period of office.

What is more, the departure of both Mr Macmillan and Sir Edward Boyle from the Treasury – the former to become Prime Minister after the Suez crisis and the latter resigning office because of his disagreement with the Government during the crisis – meant a change in the directional thrust of official economic policy. One of the replacements, Mr Nigel Birch, the Economic Secretary of the Treasury appointed in early 1957, was by training and temperament a City man. The views which had flourished under the previous régime at the Treasury – that rates of interest were only of marginal importance in economic policy and that market forces, however well managed, ought ideally to be reinforced by direct Government controls, in order to make them work effectively – were not given quite the same ready acceptance by the new men who took over at the beginning of 1957. That was not evident at once. One of Mr Thorneycroft's first actions after he became Chancellor of the Exchequer was to reduce the bank rate, in February 1957, at a time when any orthodox hard money man would have warned him against it. He then proceeded to encourage the economic expansion, which got under way in the spring and summer of 1957, after two years of stagnation. The index of manufacturing production, which had remained static from the second half of 1955 onwards, in spite of the considerable growth in the country's industrial capacity, began to move upwards again – during the summer months it was 4 per cent above the level of the previous year – and the Government seemed to accept the view that the answer to inflation lay in increasing the volume of supplies to match a demand which could not in the end be controlled.

But in the autumn of 1957 all this changed. If one trusted solely to official statements, one received the impression that the Government had decided all at once that the only thing to do with demand was to sit on it. Since the demand which was thus to be suppressed was mainly in the form of additional wage claims from the trade unions, this was bound to be a hazardous operation. But there were other reasons for surprise at this apparent reversal of a policy which had achieved considerable success up till then. The current balance of payments had responded satisfactorily to the final dose of restrictions administered by Mr Butler during the second half of 1955, towards the end of his period of office at the Treasury. From the beginning of 1956 onwards there was a steady recovery. Imports were curbed and exports went ahead. The disturbance to the balance of payments in 1955, although it looked serious enough at the time, was not of a fundamental character. It is possible to sympathize with Mr Butler's frequent and slightly hurt insistence at the time that this was 'not a crisis'. He was right in the sense that there was no basic defect in the balance of payments, which could not be put right by comparatively minor measures of restraint. What had happened was that a great spending spree on consumer durable goods, coinciding with a delayed upsurge of industrial investment, had created a volume of demand temporarily beyond the capacity of the economy to fulfil; and the overspill had gone into the balance of payments. Once the curbs were imposed with sufficient firmness in the second half of 1955, discriminating sharply between those industries which needed to be squeezed and those which did not, the balance between imports and exports was fairly rapidly restored. The only trouble was that the speculative movement against sterling abroad, for which Mr Butler's earlier policy had provided so many additional facilities, continued to offset this improvement. The gold reserve remained precariously small; there was very little margin in hand with which to meet the violent crises of confidence when they came, first over Suez at the end of 1956, and then over the rumours of devaluation in September 1957.

But by the time that the second of these crises arrived, the internal situation in Britain had become pretty sound. The strain on sterling could by no stretch of imagination be attributed to an overloaded economy at home. It was impossible to point to any industrial development or set of consumer demands which were imposing a special burden on the balance of payments, as in 1955. The measures of restriction had done their work remarkably well on these identifiable soft spots. The outstanding softness had been in the motor industry. In 1955 it had weakened the balance of payments in two ways. On the one hand, the enormous growth of home demand for cars necessitated big imports of sheet steel, particularly from the U.S., and on the other hand the excessive concentration of British motor manufacturers on an easy home market noticeably diminished their competitive performance in export markets. The main pressures of the credit squeeze, the curbs on hire purchase and consumer credit of various kinds. were specifically, and rightly, directed against motor cars. They worked. The motor industry was forced to cut back its output, and to cut its inflated costs at the same time. Under the pressure of the domestic squeeze it was compelled to push outwards, into markets overseas. And it did so with spectacular success. The growth of British exports during 1957, particularly to the United States, the improvement in the models, in the sales service, and in the general

standard of attention to foreign customers have provided heartening evidence of the reserve of energy and initiative in British
industry which can evidently be mobilized in an emergency. By
the autumn of 1957, the strong revival of home demand coming on top of the exports had pushed motor output back to its
peak of two years before, but – and here is the significant point –
using 30,000 fewer workers. Productivity, aided by a lot of new
machinery installed during the years of heavy investment from
1954 onwards, had advanced sharply, and costs had been cut.

THE CREDIT SQUEEZE – THEORY AND PRACTICE

The moral for policy-makers, to be drawn from the experiences of
1956–7, was that the controls which are quick and effective are the
ones which are specific, aimed at some identifiable object in a
particular sector of the economy. The general squeeze on credit
operating through the money market and the banking system
worked uncertainly and slowly. The rise in interest rates, which
was treated as the primary instrument of the squeeze, when it
was inaugurated in early 1955, had no visible effect on investment.
Again, in so far as the control of credit worked, it did so as a result
of the direct order of the Government to the banks to cut down
the overdrafts granted to their customers by a stated amount. The
cuts fell most severely on personal overdrafts and on the finance
houses providing funds for hire purchase; so it was private spending that was chiefly affected. Now, this result was totally different
from that which had been anticipated when the credit squeeze was
originally set in motion in the heyday of economic liberalism
at the beginning of 1955. At that time any direct Government
intervention, ordering the banks to do some specific thing, which
they were not compelled to do by the pressures of the market
working through their profit and loss accounts, would have been
regarded as a flat contradiction of all the rules of the game. When
Mr Butler, after hesitating for six months while the position of
sterling got worse and the promised reduction in bank lending
failed to materialize, did eventually issue a directive to the banks
in the summer of 1955 about how much they were to lend in the
future, their response was one of profound shock. The subsequent

speeches of the bank chairmen to their shareholders made it clear that this was not the sort of behaviour that they had expected from a Tory Government and a gentleman. They had real grounds for their sense of grievance. The directive was part of the new interventionist economic policy – its other aspect was the imposition of stiffer hire purchase controls, discriminating openly against cars and metal goods – and the bankers had not been warned in advance that the orthodox liberal inhibitions of the earlier period could no longer be relied upon to palsy the Government's grip on the economy.

The truth is that the monetary policy of 1955–7, on which the Conservatives had pinned their hopes – primarily as an alternative to the policy of high taxation pursued by the Socialists – worked out in a totally different manner from that originally intended. It is extraordinary how confident the bankers and the officials were that they knew how the bank rate and the whole money machine really worked, when they started to apply the credit squeeze in early 1955. Two years later, the Government more or less admitted that it was now satisfied that it knew hardly anything about these matters, and decided to set up the Royal Commission under Lord Radcliffe to inquire from the ground up into the working of the banking and monetary system. As originally conceived, the theory of how to curb a boom by means of monetary policy worked as follows. First, a rise in the rate of interest would make businessmen more reluctant to borrow money to invest in stocks or fixed capital. Stocks were expected to be particularly sensitive to an increase in the cost of borrowed money, and some highly placed officials were predicting optimistically in the early months of 1955 that the increase in the British bank rate would bring about a fall in world commodity prices, because businessmen would try to save money by thinning out their stocks of materials. The reasoning was based on a totally false analogy with 1952. Then commodity prices were already falling rapidly after the collapse of the Korean boom, and the increase in British bank rate happened to coincide with this movement. Anyway, the second leg of the orthodox monetary theory was that higher interest rates would cause Britain to import less, and as demand fell off, foreigners would tend to charge less for the goods that they sell to this country. Thirdly, at a later stage, the pressure on domestic business in Britain would be passed on to the British consumer. In the first stage, he is not supposed to be affected at all, except if he happens to be buying a house and needs to borrow money for it. But gradually, as stocks of all kinds of goods are thinned out by businessmen anxious to save money, and the decline in fixed investment affects the engineering and building industries, the demand for labour slackens off. Some unemployment appears.

This process of lowering the economic temperature of the whole community by curbing the borrowing activities of businessmen is supposed to be assisted by action on the part of the central bank, aimed to make money scarce as well as dear. The commercial banks have to be kept short of cash. This can be done by a variety of techniques known as 'open market operations' – no doubt because they are generally conducted in a clandestine manner. The simplest case, which really is open to full view, is when the Government offers new securities at an attractive price to the public, so that investors take their money out of their bank accounts in order to subscribe to the issue. The banks now find they have less money at their disposal, and have to reduce their loans to customers. Thus even if the high rate of interest does not deter all the would-be borrowers from asking for loans, the banks' own shortage of funds is supposed to force them to cut down the overdrafts which they grant to businesses. There are several more or less sophisticated variations on this simplified version of orthodox monetary policy. But the causal sequence remains the same: the ultimate drop in consumer spending is to be brought about by attacking investment first. As a result of the cut in investment, the tempo of economic activity slows down; the incomes of consumers are affected through the fall in wage earnings and the growth of unemployment; and so finally, less is spent in the shops.

Now it is undeniable that this chain of events might well occur – in the long run. But in the particular run from 1955 to 1957, things turned out quite differently. The banks did go on lending, until they were forcibly stopped by Government decree. Businessmen showed no inclination to thin out their stocks or to reduce their investment in fixed plant, because it cost more to borrow money. On the contrary, they went on adding generously to their stocks of raw materials, steel, and finished goods right through 1955 and 1956. An investigation conducted in early 1956 by Mr H. F. Lydall among a large sample of businessmen showed that the rise in interest rates had had no effect on the investment decisions of the great bulk of manufacturing firms questioned.[1] It is evident that these people were playing for bigger stakes than could be affected by a 1 or 2 per cent rise in the cost of borrowed money. By the same token, at a time when prices of materials are expected to rise, businessmen will hold on to their stocks and even add to them, reckoning that the extra 1–2 per cent which they pay the bank will be more than compensated for by the extra profit they will ultimately earn on their cheap materials. This is where the climate of prices, which in modern conditions depends so much on the actions of government, is so important. If the British authorities had been in closer touch with commercial realities in 1955, they would hardly have indulged in the flamboyant gesture of an 18 per cent increase in the coal price in July at the very climax of the struggle against inflation. If they had not been mesmerized by the unreal sophistication of their favourite mechanical model of the economy, they would have realized what any simple man would have told them – that you can only make disinflation work, if you first create the *feeling* of price stability. The ineffectiveness of British policy at this stage was chiefly due to an intellectual failure. The people in power were not thinking straight. Anyone suggesting that the Government ought to intervene directly at this crucial stage in the psychological struggle, either by exhortation and moral pressure on particular groups of producers, or by subsidies, or by a limited measure of temporary price control over some critical items, would have been howled down as a traitor to Tory principles.

In truth, these particular Tory principles are of very recent invention; traditionally, the Tory Party is paternalist by instinct and upholds the positive role of the state as moderator of the economic system. In this instance, the Tory politicians and their supporters were caught up in the full violence of an emotional rebound from the long years of state intervention under Labour.

The emphasis was all on getting rid of 'suppressed inflation', of forcing the ordinary man to face up to the true cost of the things which he consumes, of making him feel the pinch immediately in his own pocket, when the country was in difficulties. Hence the sorry miscalculation in the emergency autumn Budget of October 1955, when the Chancellor, Mr Butler, clapped an extra purchase tax on pots and pans and other household utensils, and tried to present the measure as a poor man's contribution to the fight against inflation. Once again disinflation was being pursued by putting up prices. The measure in fact served no serious financial purpose; it was designed as a gesture. And as a gesture it was, predictably, a total flop. The poor are not likely to be impressed with the argument that by having the prices of essentials raised against them, they are making a splendid contribution towards lower prices for everybody.

It was not such measures of spiritual correction which brought the British economy back into balance in 1956 and 1957, producing again a healthy current surplus in the balance of payments; nor was it the squeeze on industrial investment postulated by the orthodox theory of the credit squeeze. The squeeze worked, instead, directly on the consumers – they spent less and saved more – and much the most important instrument of pressure proved to be the direct restrictions on hire purchase. It came therefore as something of a shock in the autumn of 1957 when the Chancellor of the Exchequer, Mr Thorneycroft, reverted to a statement of the orthodox theory of monetary policy in its purest and most intransigent form. The principle which he now enunciated as the supreme guide to future economic policy seemed, in the popular form in which he presented it, innocent and straightforward enough. Whatever anyone else might do, he said, henceforward the Government would not 'help to finance inflation'. What this meant in hard practical terms, as he later explained, was that the Government would bend all its efforts to ensure that the supply of money was held absolutely constant, so that any general rise in prices became impossible. If one imagines the supply of money as a tankful of water above a bath, and then thinks of the water being drawn off in spurts, sufficient to pay for the various goods bought by the community, then whatever happens to the prices of individual goods sold, the final level of the water in the bath, after the tank is emptied, will be the same. If the total volume of goods sold is constant, and the volume of money spent is constant, then any rise in the price of one product must be offset by a fall in the price of something else. The average level cannot be raised.

CONTROL OF WAGES

Similarly any rise in wage-earnings not covered by a corresponding increase in output will be made self-defeating on this theory. With a constant wages fund, somebody earning more in one place would automatically mean somebody else earning less in another. That is what the policy aims to secure. The mechanics of the process by which any general rise in wages is to be frustrated depend once again on the control of credit. If the theory of the 'bath of water' worked perfectly, then higher wages on the railways, without an increase in output there, would mean that the railways would have less to spend on the maintenance of the track, on new equipment and so on. The result would be less work for the people who supply the railways with such goods and services. If the suppliers concerned tried, nevertheless, to maintain the same volume of output and employment, they would have to obtain credit from somewhere; but there would be no money to be borrowed. In the end they would be forced to do one of two things: either cut down production and lay off workers or lower their prices, so that the railways would be able to buy the same amount with the reduced funds at their disposal. In order to cut its prices, a firm would either have to get its workers to accept lower wages, or succeed in raising output per man-hour, or sacrifice profits in order to keep output up. In other words, unless businessmen are prepared voluntarily to sacrifice part of their income and hand it over to the workers, a successful wage claim which is not covered by an equivalent increase in output per man, must – if the bath of water does its stuff – mean a drop in the general level of economic activity.

Now, the most important thing about this economic theory is its political implication – that it is up to organized labour to decide what level of economic activity the country is to have. The

Government, after all these postwar years of active interest in full employment and expansion, suddenly turns up in the guise of a neutral. It depends, it says, exclusively on the sense of responsibility of the trade unions in wage negotiations whether industry is to be busy or slack, whether Britain is to be prosperous or full of unemployed men and idle machines.

This monetary technique for establishing control over wages and prices is evidently something which can only be expected to work in the fairly long run. No doubt it is possible to conceive of a situation in which the demand for labour is so weakened, as a result of the deflation caused by the monetary authorities, that the trade unions are unable to obtain wage increases in excess of any increase in productivity. Indeed, there is no reason why they should in these circumstances be able to obtain any wage increases at all. In which case it would no longer be a question merely of price stability; we should enjoy the benefits of falling prices, as technology advanced and productivity increased, while wage rates remained unchanged. But before we rejoice at this glimpse of a golden age for consumers, we ought to consider carefully all the other things which are going to be lost in the process of weakening the demand for labour to this extent. The cost to society would be appalling. I am not now thinking of the spiritual damage which would be the inevitable consequence of a revival of class warfare on the scale required to push such a policy through over a number of years. An equally frightening prospect is the material, countable loss that would be incurred in making the demand for labour weak, and keeping it so. It would have to be kept weak, in order to prevent a revival of the bargaining strength of organized labour. The only formula for doing this in a free society is by forcing down the general level of demand, first of all by squeezing investment, and in the second stage, as the reduced economic activity affects people's incomes, through the consequent drop in consumer spending.

It is a dangerous fallacy to suggest, as some economists have done, that the whole issue is one of a marginal adjustment between the supply and demand for labour. That does not reflect the situation in the real world. The economist's model, which has been used to mislead the politicians, suggests that the market for labour is like any other market – a shortage of even 1 per cent may send prices sky-rocketing, while a surplus, however small, will tend to depress prices sharply. It must be evident to anyone not dazzled by the mechanical perfection of a toy model that the price of labour is not in fact determined in that way at all. The whole business of fixing its price is institutionalized; and the bargain ultimately struck between the various organizations concerned is influenced by a large number of factors which have no relevance to the imaginary sum that a marginal worker seeking employment could squeeze out of a businessman, who was just then tossing up whether it would pay him to incur the cost of taking on an extra man. These are the two fictitious characters whose encounter in the market-place is supposed to be watched by the millions of workers, standing ready to adjust their own prices to it.

The truth is of course that although there is a market for labour which influences wages, in the sense that employers are prepared to pay more or less in different circumstances of demand and supply, the market forces are crude and blunt and tend to operate in a violent manner. There is no possibility of a fine adjustment at the margin. In a boom when labour is short, employers use special inducements, such as the promise of a lot of overtime work or the offer of wage rates above the level negotiated by the trade unions, and at times when trade is bad and unemployment growing, the unions use their characteristic weapons – the strike, the picket, and the strong emotional appeal to workers' solidarity in the struggle with employers – to obtain the best bargain they can. The practical conclusion for British economic policy at the moment is that the ruthless use of monetary deflation as a means of weakening the demand for labour probably would, quite rapidly, stop the payment of any premium over union rates by employers, who have hitherto been using this as an inducement to their labour to stay put; but that it would take a long period of steady pressure, involving strikes and lock-outs, to compel workers to accept lower money wages as the production of goods and services declined, under the pressure of the tightening credit squeeze. On the assumptions made in the official monetary policy of the autumn of 1957, the only hope of avoiding the dismal cycle of tightening squeeze and diminishing industrial activity would be the acceptance by the trade unions of an immediate standstill on all wage claims, other than those that could be sustained by increased output per man. Cost-of-living claims would have to be excluded too.

All this would be a lot more disturbing, if there were not good reasons to suppose that the 'bath of water' theory of money only works in practice with a considerable amount of uncontrollable leakage. To take the simplest case: say all the workers making toys and other articles used as Christmas gifts receive a wage rise shortly before Christmas, and the employers decide to finance the extra cost by raising the prices of their goods. All that happens is that the workers with more money in their pockets pay more for the toys which they buy for Christmas. The employers never have to turn to a bank or any other lending institution to finance them, because the time taken over the production of the finished article and its sale is very short. The employer is able to reimburse himself pretty well at once for his extra wage costs. The point is that this kind of wage increase – and it applies in many consumer industries and trades – is self-sustaining. The monetary authorities have no means of intervening. Their only answer to this autonomous increase in money wages and prices is to be more savagely deflationary in those sectors of the economy which they do control, through the machinery of providing credit. Investment and growth are thus once again the victims.

WAGES AND PRICES

Is there then no way of achieving price stability without halting our economic growth? In practice, there does not seem to be much hope of keeping prices absolutely static in conditions of full employment. If it is the aim of economic policy to apply a sufficient stimulus to keep production constantly expanding, then there will be occasions when buoyant demand exceeds productive capacity; the overspill will be taken up in rising prices. But there is absolutely no reason why prices should increase on anything like the scale that we have witnessed in this country during the 1950s. It is wholly misguided to suggest that this high degree of discomfort and frustration is part of the necessary cost of maintaining full employment. But the way to a spirit of moderation, which will consciously relate wage increases to the prospective rise in real output *of the community as a whole*, is not going to be cleared by the violent exertions of hard money beating and flattening everything around it. That bulldozer is altogether too destructive. After all, it is a simple enough fact to understand that if wages and other incomes go up all round by 5 per cent, while the volume of output goes up by only 2½ per cent, then part of the additional wages will disappear in higher prices. The rise in real incomes is limited to 2½ per cent – whether money incomes go up by 5 or 10 or 20 per cent.

But even when this truth comes to be generally accepted, the problem of sharing the extra 2½ per cent of real output among the competing claimants will remain. The chief source of rising productivity has for some time past been in the manufacturing industries. It would obviously be foolish to expect the teaching profession, for instance, to show anything like the steady increase in output per man-hour that has been achieved in steel or in motor manufacture. So that if teaching as a profession is not to suffer, the workers and employers in the manufacturing industries must not try to absorb the whole benefit of their increased productivity in higher money incomes for themselves. There is room for only a certain number of workers in motor manufacturing, steel, and so on; and the rest of the community will not allow them to set up as a privileged minority – the only group whose living standards go up. If they want the things provided by other people, who are not in a position to make use of technology to raise their output – or at any rate, to the same extent – they must be prepared to offer them the same opportunities for improving their living standards. Otherwise they must face the fact that services like transport, retail distribution, medical attention, teaching, and so on, will no longer be provided in the same volume, while the standard of these services will decline as the abler people are attracted into other more remunerative forms of work. To some extent it is possible to replace services by manufactured goods, and thus transfer the benefits of rising productivity in the factory to the rest of the community. This has been one of the achievements of American civilization, which we are all now busy copying in Europe. Vacuum cleaners, washing machines, and electric polishers replace an army of domestic servants, the garbage grinder reduces the call on the dustman, and then the deep freeze with the opportunities which it offers for purchases of food in bulk cuts down retail services. It is some measure of the economy that can be achieved by bringing the machine into our daily lives, instead of relying on services provided by other people, that we naturally think in spendthrift terms of one such machine per household. If they were more expensive to buy, people would more readily consider the obvious ways of sharing their use among neighbours.

But in spite of these technical achievements in the kitchen and about the house, the demand for services of the kind which cannot easily be replaced by factory products continues to grow rapidly as civilization advances. This is nowadays particularly true in North America. A moment's reflection convinces one that this is the sort of development that must be expected when an industrial civilization gets its second wind. Once people have accumulated a lot of goods, they want more amenities, the pleasures of a cultivated and interesting life. They want to travel, they want their children – and sometimes themselves – to be better educated, they demand more medical attention. Unless the workers in manufacturing are prepared to adopt some kind of self-denying ordinance on wages, so that the benefit of their productivity can be shared out, they will find that the sharing out is done for them by a sharp increase in the prices charged by the people providing these services. But the problems involved in an approach to a more rational wages policy belong properly in the next chapter, in the discussion of a practical policy for economic expansion.

BREAKING THE WILL TO INVEST

Meanwhile, to complete this account of official economic policy up to the end of 1957, it is necessary to put on record the series of attacks on industrial investment delivered by the Government from 1955 onwards. The first blows aimed against it were largely frustrated, because they relied almost exclusively on the weapon of interest rates, which left the businessman, who was seriously bent on expanding his plant, unscathed. This whole incident prompted the reflection that investment is altogether too serious a matter to be left to bankers. But the next phase in the second half of 1955, when the Government intervened directly and ordered the banks to cut down their loans, was much tougher. All the same, the investment boom had by then acquired sufficient momentum to overcome the obstacles placed in its path. It was the ordinary private individual whose overdraft was chiefly affected by the banks' effort to reduce their loans. In consequence, spending by ordinary people, rather than investment by businessmen, felt the squeeze. Manufacturing industry went on increasing its outlays on new plant and equipment at an impressive rate during 1956. In February 1956 Mr Harold Macmillan, who had just taken over as Chancellor of the Exchequer, abolished the 'investment allowance' – the tax subsidy given to businessmen on the installation of new plant and equipment, which Mr Butler had introduced two years before.* This incident had the sad quality of *déjà vu*. It was altogether too much like the effort made by Sir Stafford Cripps to stimulate industrial re-equipment through his 40 per cent initial tax allowance on fixed capital investment in his Budget of 1949, which was followed after a fairly short interval by the abolition of all initial allowances for investment by Mr Gaitskell in 1951.

But still, by 1956 the expanding manufacturing businesses of Britain were in a much more robust mood than they had been five years before, and it was no longer so easy to smother their bright visions of the future with the Exchequer's wet blanket. Industrial investment went on rising right into 1957. And in his April Budget of that year Mr Thorneycroft, who had by then taken over as Chancellor, felt impelled to take another swing at it. This time the Capital Issues Committee of the Treasury was ordered to ensure that the banks cut back their provision of finance for industrial expansion. Evidently some of the banks had been flouting the British convention which confines their lending strictly to short-term activities. They had, it seems, begun to look with more favour on the practice, which is common in European banking, of

* See page 186.

lending money to industry to put into plant and equipment. Or perhaps they simply felt that they ought to try and help out the more pushing and vigorous of their clients during a period when their capital commitments were particularly heavy. A characteristic example of the kind of problem that was now occurring was provided by the great engineering firm of Vickers, with an ambitious programme for extending manufacturing capacity on its hands: in the course of twelve months, the company had managed to run through its cash balances, and needing more funds, had moved into bank overdraft to the tune of £8,700,000 by the middle of 1957. This was the sort of borrowing facility which Mr Thorneycroft set out to check. And there is little doubt that the check administered to some of the bolder companies, which in their determination to expand had allowed their finances to become extended and exposed, has been since then to make the typically cautious business, with a chronic tendency to underinvest, more timorous still.

The final blow against industrial investment in this recent series came in the autumn of 1957, when the Chancellor of the Exchequer followed up the introduction of 7 per cent bank rate with a number of cuts in the programmes of the nationalized undertakings. The form which this took was an order that aggregate state spending for investment purposes was to be stabilized at the 1957 level during 1958 and 1959. If prices went up, the physical volume of work to be done would be less than in 1957. This was in fact a further extension of the 'bath of water' principle of finance. One of the ways in which the Chancellor hoped to ensure a static money supply was by taking the figure for total state investment at some point in time – this came to £1,500m – and refusing to spend one penny more than that, whatever happened to prices.

In practice, this huge and variegated mass of investment will not be quite so easy to discipline, at any rate in the short run. It is not possible to curb something of the scale and complexity of the railway programme, for example, at the drop of a Chancellor's hat. It takes many months before a cut in the new orders placed by British Railways has any effect on what actually happens on the ground. There are so many things already in the pipeline, so many projects which can only be halted suddenly at the cost of great waste.

But the delayed action effect in the present case makes matters, if anything, rather worse. To see why this is so, it is necessary to look at the development of British industrial investment as a whole since the attempted squeeze on it was begun back in 1955. Although investment in private manufacturing industry went bounding ahead right through 1956, regardless of the impediments which the Government put in its way, the nationalized industries had no means of avoiding the tight rein applied to them by the Government itself. Once again it was the direct physical control, the order from above, which worked, while the great monetary squeeze on the private sector of industry failed to act. But of course a manufacturing investment boom of this kind does not remain impervious for ever to the steady pressure applied against it. In 1957, although the expenditure on factory plant and equipment was once again higher than in the year before, the drive gradually lost its momentum and by the end of the year it had petered out. All the signs were that investment by manufacturing industry would turn down in 1958.

However, during 1957 the long delayed programmes of the nationalized industries were at last beginning to come to fruition. The plans for the railways, for the roads and other forms of transport, for electricity and coal, which came out in early 1957, suggested a new surge of investment in the public sector, which would more than offset the decline in private manufacturing industry. Moreover, since this was to be a continuing programme of public investment, increasing from year to year, the likelihood was that it would in time apply just the stimulus required to stir private manufacturing industry to renewed effort. If orders for new equipment for the nationalized industries were going to grow steadily over a period of years, the chances were that private manufacturing industry would pretty soon feel the urge to expand its own productive capacity once more. The end of the first investment boom in 1957–8 would then turn out to be a pause before the second drive for British industrial re-equipment.

But all these hopes were destroyed in the sudden violence of the 7 per cent bank rate in the autumn of 1957. It was not only that the halt to the further plans of the nationalized industries made it certain that the growth of industrial investment, which had been proceeding steadily since 1953, would now be reversed. The Government this time succeeded in creating an atmosphere of industrial anxiety, and this went a long way to remove any lingering enthusiasm for expansion in private manufacturing industry. Everyone suddenly felt the wisdom of postponement. The impression at the time of writing, at the end of 1957, is that many of the firms which had plans to increase their productive capacity have now put them off. Others, who are involved in projects which cannot be stopped, without wasting the money already spent, are trying to trim them wherever possible.

The era of Conservative expansion, which was started by Mr R. A. Butler back in 1953, has now come to an end. Its final death blow was celebrated amidst a chorus of frenzied middle class voices shouting that no sacrifice of real wealth was too great so long as the price tags on goods in the shops could be kept the same. The Conservative Party, which had struggled successfully to adapt itself, after its electoral victory in 1951, to the conditions of the welfare state, had reverted (it is to be hoped, temporarily) to the worship of its primitive idols. For the new deflation was motivated neither by the needs of the balance of payments nor by the purpose of relieving a strain on the productive resources of the economy; in 1957 these resources were plainly under-employed. The objective this time was social rather than economic: stability was an end in itself, the condition for an orderly society with a hierarchy of relationships which were comfortable and fixed. If Conservative official statements on economic policy were to be taken at their face value, 1957 would stand out as the year of the delayed counter-revolution from the Right. Fortunately they need not be so taken; there is sufficient disagreement within the Conservative leadership to guard against excess. 1957 stands out only as a year of confusion.

THE CRISIS IN THE TREASURY – JANUARY 1958

The resignation of Mr Peter Thorneycroft, together with the other two Treasury ministers, Mr Nigel Birch and Mr Enoch Powell, in January 1958, brought some of the strains and differences within the Tory Party, which have been described in this chapter, more into the open. But true to the traditional Tory way – not entirely into the open. The parties to the dispute behaved altogether too well to one another at the time for an outsider to achieve complete clarity on what issues were really involved. Ostensibly, the difference within the Cabinet which led to the rupture was about the size of the Budget estimates proposed for the year 1958–9. Mr Thorneycroft insisted that total expenditure should not increase, even by the slightest amount, above the sum spent in the Budget year 1957–8. Since prices had risen in the interval, this would have meant various cuts in the *real* services provided by the state. Some of these cuts Mr Thorneycroft's Cabinet colleagues were not prepared to contemplate. They argued that certain economies, in the social services for example, would have a serious inflationary effect in the end, because they would make the wage claims put up by the trade unions larger and more intractable. Mr Thorneycroft, on the other hand, insisted on the principle of stabilizing the money value of Government expenditure at all costs.

But beyond this argument about the Budget estimates, which brought matters to a head, there was a feeling within the Government that Mr Thorneycroft was trying to use the special and ephemeral circumstances of the exchange crisis of autumn 1957 – an external crisis of confidence in the value of the pound – to foist a new internal policy on the Cabinet. The Thorneycroft measures, it was felt, had done a good job of public relations. The wave of speculation against sterling had ceased – though the cessation had not been solely due to the gesture of 7 per cent bank rate and the further deflationary actions at home. There were other factors in the situation, notably the growing conviction that the German Mark would after all not be up-valued, which halted and then reversed the earlier movement of speculative funds out of London into Germany. It seems that the view gained ground among a majority of the Cabinet that whereas Mr Thorneycroft's strict monetary policy – the 'bath of water' theory – was a useful tactical device for resisting and then moderating a number of dangerous wage claims immediately ahead, it would be disastrous if it was treated as a piece of grand strategy. They were not, and never had been, converted to the idea of holding the supply of money absolutely stable as the answer to all our inflationary ills. It was thought of, in so far as the monetary technique was seriously considered at all by the Conservative leaders, as a means of mitigating the trouble, not as a sovereign cure. Hence their air of pained surprise when Mr Thorneycroft insisted on resigning over a few million pounds, which was, as they pointed out, well within the normal margin of error in the process of Budget accounting.

The trouble was that Mr Thorneycroft, and his fellow-ministers in the Treasury, apparently believed that their theory had been accepted as official dogma. They took it for granted that there had been a genuine change from earlier Tory policies – of economic expansion, combined with social welfare and increasing scope for private business enterprise – to a party line which put price stability before everything else. But the Macmillan-Butler group, which had provided the creative energy for the earlier revolution in Tory thinking during the late 1940s, were not to be overcome as easily as that. Their difficulty, however, was that in the circumstances of early 1958 they had no clear-cut alternative to the Thorneycroft policy. All they could do was to express their determination not to permit this policy to be driven to extremes. The effect of the resignation and of the changes in the Treasury which followed was to establish a bias towards letting up on the measures of deflation early rather than late – as soon as the measures had done their main work of moderating the demand for higher wages. The chief purpose of the policy of the reinforced credit squeeze adopted in the autumn of 1957 was now regarded as being psychological. The Thorneycroft school, solidly backed, it would appear, by the upper ranks of the hierarchy of Treasury officials, had thought of it as an automatic and foolproof mechanism which would, if properly used, clear inflation out of the system.

But a determination on the part of a Government not to let a monetary theory be pushed to extremes of social discomfort, although commendable, does not by itself make a policy. The confusion in early 1958 has been deepened by the fact that while the Government continues to pursue deflation on the domestic front, it shows growing anxiety about the deflationary conse-quences, in the international field, of the business recession in America. It hardly seems the right answer to a spontaneous business recession in the U.S. to bring on an induced recession in Britain. Yet within the framework of currently accepted as-sumptions about British economic policy, there appears to be no alternative.

NOTE

1. *Oxford Bulletin of Statistics*, November, 1957.

CHAPTER TEN

A WAY FORWARD

THE central failure of postwar Britain is inadequate investment. So many of our difficulties flow from this. Because our wealth grows more slowly than the wealth of other countries, our prices rise faster; industrial relations have grown strained, and now many people have come to be positively afraid of full employment. The Government's policies both in home and external affairs are constantly constricted by penury; the balance of payments is like a raw and exposed nerve: with the first breath of adversity the economy is wracked and convulsed. It is bad for the spirit of any country to live with so little room for manoeuvre. There is a noticeable meanness of attitude in the official British approach to the arts, to public buildings, to almost any kind of cultural activity. The terror of making any kind of splash with public money eventually robs the community of major pleasures. It has been pointed out that whereas the Arts Council in this country spends altogether about £1m a year on the public patronage of drama, opera, ballet, music, and touring art exhibitions, the small German province of Hesse, with a population of 4 million and not exceptionally liberal-minded in its budgeting, spends £700,000 of public money on its theatres alone.[1] For West Germany as a whole, the expenditure of public money on the arts per head of the population works out at about nine times as much as the corresponding figure in this country.

It is the spiritual consequences of living in a country with a slow rate of growth, which are most worrying in the long run. It is a great depressive to live in a constant atmosphere of 'make do', to exist in a place where almost any effort to do anything or to go anywhere leads you pretty soon into a bottleneck of some kind. The way to escape from this situation is by a determined effort to get a lot richer, and to do it quickly. The first move must be to step up the rate of productive investment sharply, and then to use part of the additional wealth accruing in order to keep the volume of investment up to this higher level.

There have been two occasions since the war which might have served as an opportunity to do precisely this. The first was the American £1,000m loan in 1946 and the second was the Marshall Plan, under which Britain received a further large sum in dollars from 1948 to 1950. If all this money had been absorbed into investment and so transformed into an addition to the country's productive capacity, the British industrial dynamic might well have been on the scale of Germany in the 1950s. But in fact – and for quite respectable reasons – the money which the Americans provided was deliberately turned to serve other ends. Britain's international obligations, particularly in the sterling area, Britain's desire to free itself from dependence on any form of external aid at the earliest possible moment, regardless of the level of output and growth, Britain's military obligations and the need felt to fulfil them as an absolutely independent sovereign power – all contributed to the result.

The essential truth which has to be faced is that Britain's failure to grow at an adequate pace since the war flows largely from a series of *political* decisions. It is not that these political choices were necessarily wrong – though we did see earlier that on more than one occasion, reasons of state were extended to cover some pretty narrow nationalist motives – the real complaint is that nobody bothered to count the true economic cost of international commitments which carried a traditional stamp. There was no one to remind the Government that, for example, the maintenance of our extensive overseas garrisons meant that British exports had to be boosted, to meet the foreign exchange cost, by the sale of machinery and equipment abroad, which was badly needed at home – and to ask whether it was, after all, desirable to slow down our own rate of industrial growth in this way. Similarly, nobody stopped to inquire into the wisdom of the sterling area arrangement, and above all into the system of the open door for British capital going overseas, while it was being closely restricted at home. These, and many other things like them, were part of the accepted pattern of life; they were not, until recently, subjected to the test of rational query by people in the universities or by writers of books and learned articles – least of all by the politicians. Surprisingly, one is driven to the conclusion that the failure of British policy is, in large part, intellectual weakness – a failure of the spirit of inquiry.

It is heartening to be able to record the recent change in the spiritual climate, which has now brought many of these established ideas under sharp questioning. The mood seems to have altered most markedly after the Suez episode at the end of 1956. But there were signs of change before that. The long drawn out agony of sterling from mid-1955 onwards led to increasing doubts about the policy of currency convertibility and the whole ideology that had gone with it. There was a good deal of vestigial imperialism – of a civilized twentieth-century kind – in this ideology. Another sign of the new mood was the sudden radical twist given to the Government's European policy in 1956, when Britain became the main protagonist of the creation of a European Free Trade Area. That decision has already stimulated British industry into an unusual activity of critical self-examination. Whatever happens to the European free trade scheme itself in the end, the effect of simply proposing it will have been worth while. Somehow, the bare threat of competition from Europe has provoked more interest among industrialists than the whole long series of British studies of American productivity from 1948 onwards. Thinking about the possible strength of a Continental sales drive in the British market has brought home, as nothing else before had done, the fact that much of industry is now under-equipped for the struggle.

This healthy mood of anxiety is however by no means universal yet. There is an inclination in some quarters to argue that after the fine burst of investment activity of the Butler era and after, roughly from 1954 to 1957, we can pause and rest on our oars for a time. This was the argument used by Mr Thorneycroft, when, as Chancellor of the Exchequer, he made his last violent assault on industrial investment in the autumn of 1957. He was not, he averred, cutting anything; he was simply preventing British investment from going beyond the high level already reached. This is fallacious. By comparison with the standards steadily maintained over a period of years in other industrial countries, notably on the continent of Europe, the rate of growth of capital assets in this country, even right at the peak of the recent boom, was not high. Then there are the economists who argue that the kind of comparison between investment in different countries, which I have been using in this book, is so full of statistical uncertainties as to be quite untrustworthy.[2] Now, it may be that the British statisticians are more rigorous in excluding certain doubtful items from their calculations of investment expenditure, which other countries like to see included in theirs. This may mean that Britain may not be quite so low down in the 'investment league', as the tables in Chapter Two suggested. But it is surely implausible to suggest that so much evidence, coming in over a very long period indeed, should be consistently biased in one direction only – and that one unfavourable to Britain. For the really striking thing, once one begins to examine the historical evidence, is how far back the same signs of trouble appear. Britain's low industrial investment and comparative slowness in the development of modern techniques of production was widely remarked in the 1920s, and before that in Edwardian times. If it had not been for the industrial stimulus of a couple of major wars, particularly the second, and the depression of the 1930s, in which the other advanced industrial countries, notably the U.S. and Germany, suffered more damage than Britain, the situation would almost certainly be much worse today. It is interesting to recall the comment of the German businessman made before the First World War, which is quoted by Sir John Clapham in his 'Economic History of Modern Britain'; 'Give us a hundred years of peace, and we'll kill England stone dead.' ('Wenn wir noch hundert Jahre Frieden haben, werden wir England tot gemacht haben.')

THE GREAT SLOW-DOWN

There has been much discussion in recent years about the date when the decline in Britain's tempo of expansion set in. At one time it was fashionable to point to the First World War as the source of the trouble, and to look back to the year 1913 as the apex of a golden age. But closer analysis demonstrated that the 1900s were in fact a period in which Britain's industrial performance showed up particularly badly. Output per man was either static or declining. It was bounding ahead in other countries.

This led certain economic historians to propound the theory of the great slow-down of the 1890s, at the latter end of the Victorian age itself.[3] What had happened, it was argued, was that Britain had come to the close of a period of technical innovation during the nineteenth century, based on the inventions making use of steam and steel. The country had run through the benefits derived from the 'massive application' of the techniques of steel and steam – railways, turbines, industrial furnaces, etc. – and so for a while productivity stopped rising.

The very latest investigations, however, suggest that the original source of the trouble must be pushed back still further into the nineteenth century.[4] The implications for Britain's long term industrial growth are also rather more disquieting. It seems that after several decades of extremely rapid expansion of British output throughout the early and middle parts of the nineteenth century, something happened in the 1870s, and the whole process was slowed down sharply. We have never again captured this early *élan*. Others have. First the U.S. and Germany in the closing years of the nineteenth century and the early part of the twentieth, then Japan, then Russia, then Germany again after the Second World War, have managed to achieve the tempo sustained by British capitalism in its heyday, and frequently to better it. There is little real comfort to be found, either, in economic metaphors of an organic character, suggesting that societies, like living creatures, inevitably grow more slowly beyond a certain stage of maturity. There may conceivably be such a point of maturity, but it is quite clear that Britain has never got within sight of it. One should beware of people who compliment one about being mature; they often mean that one is merely decrepit. As Mr Coppock points out in his striking analysis of industrial trends in the late nineteenth century,[4] Britain, U.S., and Germany were in 1880 producing roughly the same amount of steel – about 1 million tons each; by 1913 the figures were: Britain 8 million tons, Germany 17 million tons, and U.S. 31 million tons.

The cause of the great slow-down in British industrial growth in the last quarter of the nineteenth century certainly does not lie in the limitation of the scope for the massive application of steel. On the contrary, the evidence suggests that at this stage

Britain was not exploiting the new technical possibilities opened up for the use of steel in industry to the same extent as other countries. The same sort of lag occurred in the development of the new techniques in chemicals and electrical engineering. It is interesting to observe that these three relatively neglected industries – steel, chemicals, and electrical engineering – played an outstanding role in the British industrial advance after the Second World War. In each case the expansion was achieved through a large and costly programme of investment, conducted by giant companies, which had evolved out of the mergers of earlier years and were now financially strong enough to carry the expense. Indeed, the size of some of these corporations, like Sir Alexander Fleck's Imperial Chemical Industries and Lord Chandos's Associated Electrical Industries, is now so great that they are constantly in danger of attracting the attention of the Monopolies Commission. There is no doubt that bigness is a great help to expansion.

Equally important is a specific incentive to invest. In electrical engineering, the incentive came from the vastly increased programme of electricity generation, started by Lord Citrine, when he became chairman of the nationalized Electricity Authority in 1948. Initially a lot of people in the electrical industry refused to take Citrine's ambitious programme seriously. But in fact by uniquely energetic management, combined with a rebellious attitude towards a succession of Government attempts to cut back his investment programme in the course of its economy drives, Citrine got rid of the plague of the postwar power cuts in a remarkably short space of time. The big makers of electrical equipment responded rapidly to this stimulus, as they did to the further stimulus provided by the atomic energy programme in the middle 1950s. These are extremely progressive firms with large, up-to-date ideas about the amount of money that has to be spent on investment and research. In the chemical industry, the incentive to invest and expand at an accelerated pace came through the removal of German competition during the war and for many years after it, combined with a world shortage of chemicals. The postwar years were also a period of rapid development of many new chemical products, in which the British industry used its considerable resources for research – much expanded during the war – to notable effect. The steel industry, facing similar conditions of shortage both at home and abroad, also had the threat of nationalization hanging over it. For half a dozen years after the war, the steelmasters were under close Government supervision. In recent years, however, there have been signs that some of the earlier momentum of the industry has been lost. In particular, it has failed to start work on the building of a fourth integrated steelworks of 1 million tons capacity, with a continuous strip mill, in spite of the fact that the Government-controlled Iron and Steel Board has made it clear that it regards this project as urgently necessary. Meanwhile the Germans, whose steel output had been steadily surpassed over a period of years after the war by the expanding British industry, have moved ahead again now, as a result of the vast investment programme undertaken by the Ruhr companies, benefiting from generous tax concessions, in the 1950s.

Turning back to the earlier period, the explanation of the drop in the tempo of British industrial expansion at the end of the nineteenth century offered by Professor W. A. Lewis is that it was the direct consequence of the slowing down in the growth of world trade, after the free trade movement of the 1850s and 1860s had spent itself. Britain stood completely exposed to the fluctuations of world trade – it deliberately bared its breast to these forces, as a matter of principle – whereas other countries proceeded with the expansion of certain crucial industries and with new technical developments, under the shelter of tariffs and other forms of protection.

There is a further factor which probably exercised an important influence on the technical development of British industry – the decline in the relative importance of Europe as an export market for its manufactured goods. During Britain's great industrial age, exporters turned naturally to Europe rather than to the Empire. It is only in the closing years of the nineteenth century, and then increasingly afterwards, that the main export drive comes to be directed towards the undeveloped countries in general, and the imperial possessions in particular. In the 1850s, '60s, and early '70s, it was the markets in the advanced countries of Western Europe which provided the springboard for Britain's industrial triumphs. Afterwards, as the more distant agrarian markets assumed a growing importance, with their simpler demands notably for railway materials and cotton textiles, the incentive to be masters of every latest technical advance became less sharp. Meanwhile, the concentration of the exporters of Germany on the markets of the European countries, with their more complex demands, acted as a powerful technical spur to their industries. British manufacturers could often get by without the extra effort. It would be pleasant to think that the recent reorientation of British commercial policy towards Western Europe was the prelude to a successful effort to recapture the industrial drive of the 1850s and '60s. Indeed, it is arguable that the whole historical trend of the last seventy years or so, subjecting British commerce increasingly to the influence of the imperial idea, has in the long run done British industry a great deal more harm than good.

When one is looking at a long-term trend of this kind, it is hard to be quite sure that one has sorted out cause and effect in the right order. Was it the technical deficiencies of British industry which caused the great slow-down, and also resulted in the failure to capture trade in the advanced industrial area of Western Europe, or did the change in world trading conditions, and in the geographical direction of the main British effort, lead to the technical weakness? Whichever way it was, there is no doubt about one basic fact, which is closely relevant to the argument of this book – that the end of British technical supremacy was associated with a decline in the tempo of investment at home. And that in turn coincided with the great surge of British investment overseas. The failure to invest in British industry on a sufficient scale was not caused by any lack of saving here. The British people were saving like mad; but between 1870 and 1913, it is estimated that as much as 40 per cent of all that they saved went into the development of capital assets abroad.[5] The demands of overseas investment were particularly heavy during the years just before the First World War. In 1907, not an exceptional year, British savings reached the high figure of over 20 per cent of the national income, but only 10 per cent of the national income went into fixed capital investment at home.[5] Most of the remainder was sent overseas. It was indeed this British capital which helped to sustain the demand for British railway materials and other products in overseas markets. The mood has changed dramatically in the half century since Palmerston said: 'It has hitherto been thought by the successive governments of Great Britain undesirable that British subjects should invest their capital in loans for foreign governments instead of employing it on profitable undertakings at home.'

Professor W. A. Lewis sums up the whole process as follows:[6] 'The Germans had the irresistible urge to invest in steel, machinery, chemicals, and such in the last decades of the nineteenth century, and broke into export markets, using whatever techniques were necessary. The British, by momentum and tradition, were otherwise occupied. In earlier decades they had had an irresistible urge to invest in cotton and in iron, which had carried them breaking into world markets with the necessary techniques. The rate of expansion which this permitted slowed down after 1860, but rather than invest at home at the old rate in the newer industries, they slowed down home investment to the pace of cotton and iron and put their money instead into foreign investment in agricultural countries, where it financed sales of cotton and railway materials without adding to Britain's productive capacity.'

A FIVE YEAR PLAN

After the enumeration of the handicaps, from which Britain began to suffer so long ago, it may be felt to be a cause for wonder that British industry still manages to hold its own pretty well in the middle of the twentieth century. Indeed, some readers may be content simply to point at this evidence of continuing industrial strength, and throw out the whole of the preceding analysis as a gloomy historical fancy. It should be observed, however, that the historical picture covers a broad complex of economic activity, containing a variety of industries and trades; among these, there are many which managed to maintain the highest technical standards. It would be remarkable if a national tradition of industrial efficiency died overnight. There is, besides, the advantage of having started earlier than anyone else on the road of industrialization; this may mean that at a subsequent stage, some of your equipment is technically antiquated, but it also means that you have a great accumulation of capital assets of all kinds at your disposal, which the late starters still have to build up. Even if they grow faster and achieve spectacular successes in individual industries, it takes a long time for them to catch up over the whole front. That is another way of saying that Britain was so much richer than a country like Germany at the end of the nineteenth century, that even if the Germans devoted a higher proportion of their wealth to the expansion of their industries, it would be a slow process to raise the volume of their capital assets and the annual income per head of population to the level of the British. Germany's national income per head – measured in Deutsche-marks converted into pounds sterling at the current rate of exchange – is only now coming up to the British. But if the recent comparative rates of progress of the two countries continue, the Germans will have got well ahead by 1960. A fifty-year start counts for a great deal; but the advantage does eventually disappear, unless you do something about it.

Meanwhile, the accidents of war and depression in the twentieth century have on the whole favoured industrial Britain, compared at any rate with the industries of continental Europe. In particular, the Second World War applied a powerful stimulus to the engineering industries. They came out of it in 1945 ready to contend with the world-wide demand for capital goods in a way which they could not conceivably have done before. There followed the deliberate attempt, during the early postwar years, to extend productive capacity and make good deficiencies in certain crucial sectors of industry. Steel and electricity are two examples which have already been mentioned. Others, for which private enterprise was solely responsible, are chemicals and oil refining. Then there was the special effort made, with the aid of public funds, in the two fields of aircraft production and atomic energy. In both, the initial stimulus was military, and for a long time the aim continued to be to keep one move ahead of any possible rival in the design of prototypes, rather than to obtain the maximum commercial return on a given volume of investment. It is extremely doubtful whether the many hundred millions of pounds of public money devoted to research and development in these two fields has paid off, on any straight calculation of profit and loss. The point is that it is not always commercially profitable to set out to be an innovator. Unless there is a vast surplus of funds available to finance the inevitable series of false starts, the innovators are sooner or later compelled to concentrate their resources and take a big scientific gamble. This is what has now happened in the aircraft industry and in atomic energy. Meanwhile, in the course of their development to date, these industries have absorbed far more of the country's research and development effort than is reasonable. If the public money that has been expended on them had been more widely distributed – some of it perhaps being used to foster technical education pure and simple – the commercial return would almost certainly have been far greater. But, of course, commercial considerations have played a very secondary part in the drive for supremacy in the aeroplane and in the atom during most of the postwar period. These things have been treated as objects of national importance in their own right – symbols of Britain's continuing status as a first-class power.

However, the main point is that all these examples of technical excellence together occupy far too narrow a sector of the industrial front. Moreover, the effort behind them is intermittent and unreliable. Even the hitherto sacrosanct atomic energy programme was reduced in the last series of investment cuts, in the autumn of 1957. That would not in itself be a cause for lamentation, if there were any sign that the Government was going to use the money saved there to speed up the process of re-equipment in other sectors of the economy, which are badly in need of it. Unfortunately, it is a cut pure and simple. What is now lacking in the British economic system is the basic equipment to sustain a high tempo of expansion. There is far too little capacity for making steel and for the manufacture of machine tools – to name just two basic needs – and the transport system is plainly quite inadequate as soon as one starts to think in terms of a rate of growth of the national product of anywhere around 5 per cent a year. (That rate of advance would still be only half as much as that achieved by both Western Germany and Soviet Russia recently.) The truth is that in one important sense the British economic problem today is the same as that of an under-developed country: it has to create the essential groundwork for an advance to a new and faster rhythm of industrial expansion. Of course, the technical problem involved in the transition from one tempo to another is much simpler here. The human resources required are readily available; they do not have to be laboriously nurtured over a long period of years. Moreover, there is already a great accumulation of capital assets, the heritage of a century and a half of industrial effort. That is why it seems reasonable to expect that one Five Year Plan only would do the trick.

When I speak of a Five Year Plan, I am not concerned with a particular span of years, but rather with a technique of mobilizing a country's economic resources, in order to achieve a number of clearly stated production targets. Normally, this is not an appropriate method for an advanced industrial nation to adopt. Its needs are too complex and subtle to be mastered by the planners' art – at any rate, with the rather primitive techniques known to the planners of today. Let me admit at once that I can foresee some quite forceful objections to the application of the Five Year Plan technique to Britain, on these grounds. The reason why, nevertheless, the method seems to me appropriate – not as a thorough-going plan covering every phase of economic life, but in the form of a number of production targets in a few crucial sectors of the economy – is that, in spite of the dangers of muddle and waste, it does offer a fair chance of shifting the British productive system into high gear. Once there, it will require no great effort to keep the engine ticking over at a satisfactory speed.

The waste which I envisage during this process is the inevitable concomitant of bureaucratic control over the distribution of scarce resources. It would not be just a matter of reintroducing building controls. Steel would almost certainly become acutely short, as soon as the Plan started to move forward in earnest. Ideally, the Government would exert pressure on private enterprise to work towards the production targets, by means of large-scale tax incentives of a discriminatory character – on the model of the German reconstruction period after the Second World War. But what with the need to limit the unavoidable strain which such a programme of expansion will impose on the balance of payments and the overriding priorities that will have to be enforced for the requirements of a series of crucial projects, whose timing will be all-important for the rest of the Plan, an allocation system for certain materials, for at least part of the time, is unavoidable. The consolations are that if there has to be bureaucratic intervention, the British bureaucracy is an exceptionally good one, and secondly, that it should not have to operate for more than a comparatively short period. The light will be showing from the other end of the tunnel right from the start.

I am in no position to suggest an order of priorities for such a British Plan. That is a considerable technical task. Having set the economists the problem of indicating the kinds of investment that would be required in order to double the rate of growth, a number of possible combinations would emerge, and it would remain for the politicians to make their choice among the alternatives put forward, in the light of other considerations, some of them ethical or emotional preferences, and some, no doubt, matters of pure political expediency. But presumably there would be some matters of priority on which there would be no serious argument. My guess would be that road-building and the improvement of transport generally would be regarded as tasks of the very highest urgency. Distribution services in this country are particularly cumbersome and there are big dividends to be obtained from a programme of investment designed to ease this bottleneck. It would not be a cheap programme. The movement of goods in British cities, and in the communications network between them, can only be radically improved by a process of tearing down, before building up again. However, it is, after all, part of the spiritual purpose of a Plan of this kind to increase the readiness to pull things down, when they no longer serve their purpose efficiently. Building afresh, with the aid of modern methods, is a great deal easier than it used to be. Standardization of basic parts and sizes would make it considerably cheaper too. It is part of the technique of political immobilism to make it appear that things are enormously costly to change. They rarely are.

MOBILIZING THE RESOURCES

Such a programme of industrial expansion would inevitably impose a strain on the balance of payments. First of all, we should need much larger imports of basic materials – steel being the outstanding case – and then, besides, we should go out of our way to buy a lot of up-to-date plant and equipment abroad, if this were not available, or available quickly enough, in Britain. It can be predicted with complete certainty that within a few months of the start of the Plan, the British capital goods industries would find themselves stretched right to the limit of their capacity. After all, the very nature of the Plan implies that this capacity is at present inadequate to sustain a high tempo of investment. (In the language of Soviet planners, we have failed to give sufficient attention to 'heavy industry'.) But if at this stage the British economy is not to lapse into the familiar coma of a three-year order book, large quantities of equipment will have to be bought from foreign suppliers. At the same time, some exports of British-made capital goods will be diverted to the home investment programme. The general effect will be that while our import bill becomes considerably larger, our export earnings will tend to become smaller. Here are the makings of the familiar crisis of a country trying to get ahead 'too fast'. The problem is to ensure that this country will be able to continue to move forward for a few years at this excessive speed, regardless.

Britain is, of course, much better placed to cope with this kind of problem than any of the relatively undeveloped countries, which have embarked on five year plans during this century. First of all, it would be clear to everyone that the process here would be short. The investment effort required would probably be of comparable magnitude, in relation to the national income, to that of Western Germany from 1950 to 1956; and the resources which Britain can command for such an endeavour are larger than those which the Germans had at their disposal during most of this period. It should be possible to obtain short or medium-term foreign loans on commercial terms to meet some of our additional import expenditure. The second point is that once Britain were seriously engaged in such a plan of expansion, its attractions for foreign investment capital, which are already considerable, would be much enhanced. After all, the ultimate aim, once the period of intensive seeding is over, is to ensure that the British standard of living rises at an accelerated pace. That prospect would offer a powerful magnet to foreign enterprise. There is little doubt that British industry could obtain a lot more private American investment to finance the expansion of plant, if it were so minded. A number of British companies are already familiar to Wall Street, and many others would be able to obtain ready access to this source of funds, as 'growth stocks' with good long-term prospects. A selling point for the Americans would be that much of the money being subscribed would be employed in the purchase of American machinery and equipment.

But more important than Britain's potential as a borrower of money abroad, are the country's own usable resources of foreign exchange which are being dissipated. They should be clawed back for domestic use. The two items in the foreign exchange budget on which major economies can be made are military expenditure abroad and overseas investment. We saw in Chapter Five that the special political expenses incurred abroad by Britain, including such things as subsidies to foreign governments and grants to assist budgets of certain colonies, came to a total of £200m a year. Long-term investment overseas, mainly in the Commonwealth, amounts to £150–200m a year.* All told, there is thus over £350m–£400m of overseas expenditure of a political, philanthropic, or purely prestige character, which has to be met out of British export earnings. If the purely philanthropic element in this – the grants to the colonies and the small amount of investment going into the really poor countries of the Commonwealth – were preserved intact, that would still leave something around £300m, from which to make economies. My proposal is that these economies should be of the most thoroughgoing kind. They would include a five-year stop on all private investment overseas – the philanthropy to the Commonwealth would be Government sponsored – and the liquidation of all military establishments overseas, other than those which are urgently required in the interest of the Western alliance. Where they are so required, the other allies will have to bear a fair share of the cost of upkeep and of the garrisons.

The net gain to the British balance of payments of a policy of this kind ruthlessly pursued might well be of the order of £250m

* See Chapter 4.

a year. In addition, it is open to the British Government, under the agreement of 1957, to postpone paying the annual instalment of £60m on the American postwar loan for another five years. That would bring the total annual saving of foreign exchange to over £300m during the short period of extremely high investment, which is envisaged. Commercial loans from abroad to Government or privately-owned industry, plus direct investment here, might well bring the total net addition to the country's foreign exchange resources to £400m a year. That would be quite a useful cushion – over a five-year period, it would add up to double the amount of the original American postwar loan to Britain.

None of this could, however, be had painlessly. The forces of national sentiment and imperial nostalgia will fight powerfully for every corporal of every garrison from Bermuda to Hong Kong. Then, the financial measures required to stop the export of British capital will mean that transactions between Britain and the rest of the sterling area will have to be subjected to exchange control. This would represent a radical departure, and the sterling area would probably never be the same again after it – though it is only fair to point out that nearly all the outer sterling area countries control the export of any of their funds to Britain. It is only Britain which has hitherto regarded it as a point of principle to keep the outward flow of funds absolutely free. The other point that is worth noting is that the present freedom benefits a few chosen countries only, and provides no significant help to the really needy members of the Commonwealth.

There are, in any case, strong reasons for advocating the imposition of exchange control over capital movements into the sterling area, quite apart from any plan of British domestic investment.[7] It has become increasingly apparent that the various external demands being made on the limited supply of British savings are excessive. The Government's decision to liberate Overseas Trading Corporations completely from any form of British tax liability in the Budget of 1957 was a strangely quixotic act, which added further to the strain. It means that British firms now have a positive incentive to set up manufacturing plant in most of the countries to which they export, rather than to develop their factory production here. That is because the taxes on business abroad are in general lower than in Britain, so that if other things are equal – which fortunately they often are not – the net profit on a given amount of investment will be greater on British capital applied in foreign parts. The invitation to capital flight from this country could not be more open. What is required to help the finance of the Five Year Plan is precisely this tax concession in reverse. There should be discrimination against investment in overseas enterprises, on the straightforward ground that they generally add considerably less to the national income than an equivalent amount of investment at home. The profit on an overseas enterprise has to be exceptionally high to make it worth while from the national point of view.* Such exceptionally profitable businesses would be able to absorb the cost of a U.K. differential tax on overseas investment, and still carry on. But for the ordinary concern with normal profits, the extra tax liability would, especially if it were combined with generous tax allowances for investment in domestic British industry, create an inducement to repatriate capital from abroad. It would be admirable if for a matter of five years British domestic investment could be sustained by a return flow of funds, derived from Britain's investment effort in the rest of the world over a century and a half.

In practice, however, a large part of these overseas investments is likely to be required by Britain for another purpose. Having blocked the opening for the flight of capital out of Britain itself, the problem would remain of preventing a general movement out of sterling abroad. The total amount of such sterling, held mainly by overseas governments, is around £3,500m. The British gold and dollar reserve, in the course of its fluctuations over the last five years, has rarely amounted to much more than a quarter of the size of these sterling balances. Our condition appears to be one of acute insolvency. And that is one of the reasons sometimes advanced for continuing at all costs with the sterling area, as a kind of bankers' hoax: it does at least, so it is suggested, stop people from asking for their money back. But the British balance sheet of foreign assets and liabilities is, in fact, much sounder than this. It must be rare in the history of business that confidence in a concern has been so wilfully damaged by mismanagement in the

* See Chapter 5.

presentation of its accounts. To begin with, the published figure of the gold and dollar holdings does not include the considerable block of American dollar securities held by the Government itself, nor the large holdings of American investments in private hands, which could be mobilized in case of an emergency. A realistic assessment of our assets would raise the officially published figure of gold and dollars by at least 50 per cent. The next point concerns the manner of calculating the size of Britain's sterling debt. The balances owned by foreign governments and banks, of which a large part are held in the form of gilt-edged securities in this country, are shown at their *nominal* value, not at the price which they would fetch if the owners tried to sell them in the market. To take an extreme case, the market price of $2\frac{1}{2}$ per cent Consols is under half of its nominal value. There is no means of knowing how large a proportion of the sterling balances are held in the form of such depreciated securities. But the amount is almost certainly fairly substantial. This means that the actual sum of effective sterling currency, which these foreign holders could command, if they decided to engage in a flight from the pound, would be less than £3,500m.

Finally, on the other side of the balance sheet, there are the British holdings of foreign assets of all kinds, which might be used to counter a flight from sterling by foreigners. Characteristically, there is no complete inventory of our resources, only of our debts. The nearest indication is a partial estimate, omitting certain important categories of property, made by the Bank of England for 1955, which works out at a total of £2,137m. By far the greater part of these British-owned foreign assets are made up of direct investments in factories, mines and commercial enterprises. The market value of these concerns – what they would actually fetch if they were offered for sale – is very considerably in excess of the nominal value of their share capital. In other words, British overseas assets are, in the main, investments which have substantially appreciated, while the gilt-edged holdings of Britain's creditors have depreciated in value. The market value of all this British capital abroad is certainly a good deal more than the total value of sterling balances. Indeed, Britain's annual income from this source is one-third larger than all the income of foreigners from property in the United Kingdom, including the profits from the extensive foreign-owned commercial enterprises here, as well as the interest paid on sterling balances and the like. This provides a fair indication of the corresponding capital values.

Unfortunately, the problem cannot be neatly solved by offsetting our claims on each other. Would that it could be! For it is in large part this accumulation of sterling outstanding abroad which is the source of the periodic waves of speculation, which have rocked the pound since the war, and with it the economy of the United Kingdom. It would be well worth the sacrifice of a corresponding amount of overseas assets, in order to rid ourselves, once and for all, of the menace of this recurring nightmare. At the moment, we have manoeuvred ourselves into a position where our liberty of choice as a sovereign nation in the field of social and economic policy is constricted by the views of a marginal holder of sterling in Zürich or some other foreign capital. Worse still, since there is little accurate factual knowledge about his views, the decisions of the Government are guided by fears of what his reactions *might* be. Hence the tragedy of the autumn of 1957, when the Chancellor of the Exchequer adopted as his guide to action the slogan: 'I must be hard-faced enough to match the mirror-image of an imaginary hard-faced little man in Zürich.' It is tough on the Swiss that William Tell should be displaced in English folklore by this new image of a gnome in a bank at the end of a telephone line. But it is tougher still on the British that their efforts to create more wealth for themselves by means of increased investment should be frustrated time and again by the reverence of our authorities for this creature. Nothing can be done until they cease to be in thrall to him.

FREEDOM FROM ZÜRICH

In order to achieve this, I would propose the following measures:

(1) The stock of foreign exchange at the Government's disposal should be substantially increased by taking into the currency reserve the readily realizable securities in British ownership. The major part would be U.S. and Canadian dollar securities, but

there is also a valuable British holding of many highly saleable Continental stocks. These enlarged foreign exchange reserves should be *used* – not just held – in order to meet any deficit in the balance of payments caused by the Plan, and also to buy back the most troublesome sterling balances, in the main those held in Western Europe and North America, when the owners show a desire to sell.

(2) There is no need, however, to buy these balances back on the highly expensive method, which the Bank of England has been following since 1955. The decision taken in February of that year, it will be remembered,* was to give the Bank the task of maintaining the selling rate for the pound in the unofficial markets for transferable sterling in Zürich and New York. The practical consequence of this move has been free convertibility into dollars for transferable sterling, paid for out of the British gold reserve, at a discount of little more than 1 per cent. There is no reason why this prestige policy of 'supporting' the pound should go on, once the Government gives up the objective of bringing sterling into wider international use as a medium of exchange. As Alan Day has pointed out,[8] it acts as an additional drain on the gold reserve, and ought to be stopped. If people insist on turning the transferable pounds sterling, which are issued as inconvertible, into dollars through unofficial channels, then let them do it the hard way. Let the market rate in Zürich drop until the British authorities are enabled to acquire back cheaply some of the constantly renewed stock of this volatile sterling. The stock of sterling in European hands is not all that large; the difficulty arises, when it is fed from sterling balances outside.

(3) To counter this, it would be worth following another proposal made by Mr Day – to offer to governments holding sterling balances a long-term guarantee of the exchange rate, in return for an agreement to keep their withdrawals of sterling in any one year down to a specific figure, which would not strain the British balance of payments. This would for practical purposes be a return, in a slightly modified form, to the system of blocked balances, which operated from the end of the war until 1952. Only now it would be extended to cover the sterling balances

* See Chapter 8.

of countries like Australia and New Zealand, which were never blocked under the postwar arrangements. There would, of course, be a special danger, once the export of British capital into the rest of the sterling area was stopped, that some countries would wish to draw much more freely on their sterling balances, in order to make up for the lost supply of funds. Thus Britain would still find its own resources strained to meet the capital requirements of foreign countries; the sole difference would be that for book-keeping purposes, it would represent the cancellation of existing sterling debt, rather than the provision of new credit.

(4) There would undoubtedly be strong objections to a policy of limiting withdrawals from the sterling balances, at the same time as the outward flow of British investment funds came to an end. But that should not deter Britain from pursuing the reasonable aim of limited liability overseas, as the means of sustaining the expansion of its own production at home. The case of Australia serves well to illustrate both the difficulty and the possible way to a solution. The Australians have, at the time of writing, holdings of sterling in London amounting to around £400m. This is, in effect, their foreign exchange reserve, and they naturally like to feel quite free to use the whole or part of it for whatever purpose at any time of their choosing. On the other hand, this demand for total liquidity is not a privilege that can be accorded to one side only. After all, the actual British holdings of Australian assets are far bigger than the Australian holdings of British assets. Indeed, the amount of British money invested in Australia during the past ten years alone, mainly in manufacturing industry, comes to over £300m. The Australians tend to accept it as part of the order of nature that their assets in London will always be liquid, while all British assets will remain frozen into solid and immovable blocks of financial ice. A British Government, with powers to mobilize and control the investments owned by its nationals in overseas countries, would soon be able to acquire a lot of liquid Australian pounds, if it so desired. The main purpose that this would serve would be to demonstrate, as a last resort, that Britain really has a strong bargaining hand in any negotiation about the use of the sterling balances. It is not just a matter of begging the various members of the sterling area to do us a favour.

But on the other hand, it would be no part of the programme envisaged in the British Five Year Plan to hold back the development of other countries by extinguishing their foreign exchange resources. That would happen, for instance, if British investments in Australia were sold to Australians, who drew on Australian sterling balances held in London to pay for them. At the end of it, Australians would be left controlling more of the assets in their own country, but with no foreign funds left to finance further development. The only way in which Australia's economic interests could be secured, while at the same time limiting the strain on the British balance of payments, would be through a financial arrangement with a third country. If it were agreed that the Australian drawings on their sterling balances would be limited to, say, £150m over a five-year period, then Britain might arrange to sell enough of its Australian investments in the United States or in other international capital markets, to produce that sum of money during the period. Of course, the consent of the Australian authorities would have to be obtained for any such large-scale transfer. If they did not like it, it would always be open to them to reduce their demands on Britain by spending less of their sterling balances.

(5) There are varying degrees of assistance which might be forthcoming from the U.S. and other countries with a capital surplus available for lending or investment abroad, in order to ease this situation. The most convenient thing from our point of view would be if they put up some of the money required as a loan to these sterling area countries, against the pledge of an equivalent amount of British-owned investment overseas. But it is probably too much to expect that other countries will be ready to go out of their way to establish quite so comfortable a moratorium on withdrawals from the sterling balances for our benefit. On the other hand, there is reason to hope that some help will be forthcoming from the United States in setting a temporary limit to Britain's financial commitment to the sterling area, during a period of strain on our domestic economy. It is, in any case, essential that there should be the maximum amount of international consultation in the approach to the British Plan. For, unfortunately, the main general effect of the British economies in overseas spend-

ing will be to take money away from the less developed countries, while the benefit of the increased British spending on imports will go chiefly to the developed industrial countries. It will fall to the United States and Germany, in particular, whose export earnings are certain to be further enhanced in the process, to do something positive in the interim period to help to redress the balance in favour of the undeveloped countries. In the long run, Britain itself will be in a better position to make an effective and sustained contribution to this end than it has been hitherto. But in the short run, there will be an urgent need for something to replace the functions which have been performed by the sterling system in the finance of international trade. It will not be easy. An extension of the European Payments Union points the way to one possible solution.

(6) While measures are taken to halt the flow of British long-term capital investment overseas, a special effort should be made to restrict the present very extensive use of short-term credits provided by London for trade and financial transactions. This is a hang-over from the nineteenth century. As was discovered in 1957, when the authorities belatedly started to tighten up these facilities a little, they are widely used by foreigners, during periods of emergency, to speculate against sterling itself. There is no reason, in any case, why foreign exporters should not provide some export credits to British customers, instead of there always being a one-way traffic. That could make a big difference to the country's foreign exchange position in the short run.

(7) Finally, the exchange controls over all transactions in foreign currency should be tightened up. They have been allowed to grow lax over the years. The most important need is to stop the outsize loopholes which now exist for the flight of capital abroad. In addition, the timing of the actual payments for British exports and imports ought to be subjected to much more careful scrutiny. It is notorious that the major element in the succession of speculative crises against sterling has been the combination of British importers hurrying to pay out foreign currency to their suppliers ahead of time and customers for British goods abroad lagging over the settlement of their debts. There is no reason why the British authorities should passively accept this situation.

There are means of pressure at their disposal. They should be used.

TOWARDS A WAGES POLICY

Thus armed, Britain would be able to face the dangers of a run on the pound, without panic. The three main measures of defence, first, the blocking of the greater part of the sterling balances, second, the mobilization into the country's foreign exchange reserve of a mass of realizable assets in North America and Western Europe, and third, the tightening of controls on all foreign credit and exchange transactions, should provide Britain with room to breathe. They should be enough to allow us to carry through a programme of steady expansion at home over a period of five years or so. But it is important to make the political choice quite unequivocal right from the start: if by ill-chance the pound sterling were subjected to more speculative pressure than it could bear or the strain on the balance of payments proved to be greater than had been envisaged, then the Government should be prepared to let the currency be devalued, if need be. The danger of a drop in the international value of the currency should not be used as an excuse, once more, for stopping everything dead. There are many worse things than devaluation. Stagnation is one of them.

At home, the process of mobilizing Britain's external resources for a great once-and-for-all effort with a simple tangible objective at the end of it should have a useful effect on the political climate. Above all, it should help to make the professionally warring group interests more willing to negotiate forms of temporary compromise. The national ethos still responds most readily to the cry: 'Hands to the pumps!' Only it must be a real emergency. The British people are by now wholly unimpressed by the sham life-and-death struggles conducted every couple of years over the balance of payments. Governments have shouted 'Murder!' and 'Mass unemployment!' a bit too often. Rightly or wrongly, the ordinary newspaper reader no longer believes a word of it. But a plan to double the standard of living in a couple of decades – a refrigerator in every kitchen and a car in front of every second house, an extra year at school, and a real pension to live on comfortably after retirement – would be quite different. The problem would be, as in wartime, to achieve the maximum restraint in consumption over a short period of years. But the advantage over a similar wartime endeavour would be that under the Plan it would be possible to state the exact number of lean years in advance. It would also be possible to promise an immediate bonus from the rich harvest that would come at the end of them.

The ideal solution to the problem of the lean years would be to pay part of current wage and salary earnings to people in the form of deferred credits. Unfortunately this device, at any rate in its simplest form, has acquired the reputation of a high-grade swindle, as a result of the fiasco of the 'postwar credits'. There are, however, many varieties of pressure that the state is able to exert in order to bring about a postponement of spending. Forced saving, with the promise of tax refunds later, on the lines of the postwar credits, is only one of them. The Government might, for instance, offer to reduce or forgo income tax altogether on any income put into certain recognized types of saving, on condition that it stayed there for the required minimum period of years. It would, of course, earn interest in the ordinary way during that period. Creating nest eggs of this kind would be still more attractive, if there were a real prospect that things would be cheaper and easier to buy later on. One form of guarantee that should be offered to the deferred spenders is an automatic adjustment in the value of their savings to movements in the official index of retail prices. Another device for ensuring that the deferred spender really benefited from his patience would be to raise the purchase tax extremely high at the start of the Plan with the clear promise that it would stay there for a specified period of time. A timetable should be set out for its reduction by steps after that, leading to its ultimate elimination. The same kind of principle could be applied, in order first to cut down, and later enlarge the facilities for hire purchase.

But the central problem is to secure agreement on a rational wages policy. It is assumed that the Trades Union Congress would be a strong supporter of the programme of industrial expansion, indeed that the programme itself would have been prepared with its active collaboration. Unfortunately, whatever was said by the leaders acting as the General Council of the T.U.C., it would still be possible, given the structure of the British trade union movement, for wage claims to go forward, which implied a substantial increase in spending power at the cost of the agreed investment plan. It would never be put as a straight choice like that, but that is what it would come to. The most hopeful line of progress, as we saw earlier*, lies through an increase in the effective power wielded at the centre of the trade union movement. In this way we might approach something like the Swedish arrangement of negotiating for a year ahead an overall level of wages, fixed in relation to the prospective size of the national product and the amount of resources required for investment. Critics of the Swedish experiment, and of similar experiments in Holland since the war, point out that in the long run excessive wage demands do assert themselves, and the rule of reason is shattered. But even if this is necessarily true, which I doubt, the problem in this country is concerned with the comparatively short run; it would be enough to give the Plan a flying start, if reason triumphed for a matter of three or four years only.

The main issue is to reach agreement with the representatives of organized labour about the level of investment that the country should aim at. This question – which is the same thing as asking how much ought to be withheld from the nation's spending power – is the most important single bone of contention. Most of the other major decisions about the distribution of resources follow from it. But of course there are plenty of smaller matters concerned with the division of the spoils among individual group interests within the working class, which could still cause a great deal of trouble. The amount of noise and the fury of the struggle are not always related to the size of the bone. That is one of the compelling reasons why the T.U.C. needs to be strengthened – in order to assert effectively the interests of British wage-earners as a whole. The prospect of doing so is not quite so hopeless as it might seem at first sight. The individual unions belonging to the T.U.C., who have hitherto been so intransigent in the assertion of their particularist rights, are beginning to look over their shoulders with some anxiety at the problem of rising costs: a union

* See Chapter 2.

cannot be run efficiently any longer on the traditional scale of expenditure, nor can it hope to attract talented people into official positions at the salaries offered. At the same time, there is a reluctance to ask for an increase in membership dues, sufficient to meet the cost of an up-to-date trade union. This is not a period of working class militancy, when leaders feel that members would willingly contribute more. Indeed, much of the failure of the British trade unions to maintain close touch with the rank and file of their members in recent years, and the consequent rise of the shop steward to a position of dangerous pre-eminence, has been due to the inadequate number of full-time officials available to deal with disputes on the spot. Equally, the resources required nowadays to carry through an effective strike are much greater than in the past, when the workers were prepared to maintain an attitude of defiance on a level of strike pay, which still left them hungry. The strike funds of the trade unions are no longer commensurate to the task.

All this seems to point to one obvious measure of economy – the centralization of certain common services for the trade union movement as a whole and of its various emergency funds. Union dues will have to go up anyhow, but the rise will be moderated, if instead of each individual union trying to be completely self-reliant in all matters of finance, a central strike fund were established to provide additional assistance during an emergency. The arrangement might start as a straightforward measure of collective insurance. But it is plain that if there were a move in this direction, the balance of power within the trade union movement would change. I do not wish to pitch the hopes of such a development too high. On the other hand, it does seem quite likely that events will push in this direction. But they need a further powerful shove to get there; and this will only come from the recognition of the failure of the trade union movement as at present constituted to represent the collective interest of all British wage-earners, and from the positive will to centralize. That must probably wait on a change of leadership in the T.U.C. itself.

For the purposes of the Five Year Plan, the important point of principle, which ought to be made clear from the start, is that once agreement has been reached on the level of investment in the

British economy, the success or failure of the trade unions in controlling their members will determine the level of prices – and nothing else. If wages go up, and consumer demand increases excessively, resources will not be diverted from the task of investment to consumption. The investment programme will go on. The increased money incomes available, chasing the same number of goods, will simply push up prices by the corresponding amount. If the price level went beyond a certain point, British goods would no longer be able to compete in export markets, and the pound would have to be devalued. It is not over-optimistic to suggest that the present generation of British trade union leaders would be willing to do a great deal to avoid this process, once the issues had been made unmistakably clear. It is not the will, or in most cases the understanding, that is lacking; it is the means to make their will effective, without a violent wrench in the central structure of the British trade union movement.

THE ROLE OF GOVERNMENT

It goes without saying that a Government which embarked on the plan of expansion would have to be prepared to intervene directly, by orders, by threats, by incentives, and by exhortation – whichever happens to be the most promising technique – in the private sector of the economy. It might be thought that this role of active state intervention would be most appropriately fulfilled by the Labour Party. But on the other hand, the exceptionally rapid growth of production which is envisaged will inevitably, in a mixed economy where private enterprise remains the dominant partner, create exceptionally high profits for some of the lucky firms. That should be accepted and welcomed. To achieve the kind of commercial momentum necessary for success, the atmosphere created here should be something like that of a frontier boom town. The frontier would happen to be a technological one. But there should be the same feeling of big money waiting to be picked up by people ready to engage in certain activities, for which the demand is temporarily insatiable. This should apply at the level of the wage earner, e.g. to people bettering the time schedule on a key constructional job, as well as to entrepreneurs using their initiative to break through some of the innumerable bottlenecks that will suddenly present themselves, as soon as the economy begins to stir. Whereas the task of active state intervention could probably best be fulfilled with the Labour Party in power, the use of the profit motive in an active and flexible fashion would come more easily to the Conservatives.

What would really be required of the Labour Party, in order to make a success of such a programme of expansion, would be the equivalent of what Lenin's New Economic Policy of 1921 was to the Bolsheviks. The slogan for the businessmen who do the things required by the Plan should be: 'Enrich yourselves!' The whole scheme depends in the long run on the initiative of entrepreneurs. The state's part, outside the nationalized industries, is to create the conditions in which this initiative receives a proper stimulus and is then allowed full scope. It should be recognized from the beginning that the role of private enterprise is primary. The Labour Party would only be able to carry out the task, if it offered plenty of carrots, along with the sticks which it proposes to apply to the capitalist. Moreover, no government will be able to set about the real business of the Plan, which is to release a dynamic movement of production *against* the traditional forces of resistance in the British economy, if its main concern is with the minutiae of social justice in the process. If the forces of private enterprise are really set to work on a programme like this – rather like a wartime programme, but without the restraint of powerful patriotic emotions on the making of the very highest possible profit – the result, in terms of the distribution of the big prizes in the short run, is bound to be unfair. The fact should also be squarely faced that during the first phase of rapid expansion, capital is bound to do better than labour. The aim, after all, is to hold back consumption, while the capital assets of the country grow at an enormous pace. The active entrepreneur, and even the inactive but intelligent investor, is likely to come out at the end with his capital wealth considerably increased.

This is not to say that the state should hold back and fail to insist on obtaining a reasonable share of the fruits of economic growth for the rest of the community. It will, by means of its generous tax concessions for new industrial investment, have assisted the capitalists very largely in the process of expanding their assets. There is no reason why the state should not exact a capital gains tax or a straight tax on wealth, when the investments mature and produce greatly increased personal riches. The administrative details will obviously depend very much on which party happens to be responsible for carrying out the plans of expansion. There is little to be gained by trying to lay down rules in a field where ideology is bound to be a major influence.

All that I am concerned to do is to assert, first of all, that a conscious and major effort is necessary to lift Britain to a higher tempo of expansion, and secondly, to show that the effort is within the compass of our material resources. However, it does require the spiritual upheaval of a policy of deliberate retreat from a number of positions of high international prestige, which Britain has traditionally held. That, in my view, is the most testing political task ahead. Where is the political leader who will frankly proclaim the need for a policy of steady retreat over a period of years, as a prelude to attaining for Britain a position of strength and some room for manoeuvre?

NOTES

1. Mr T. R. Fyvel, *Socialist Commentary*, July 1957.
2. Professor A. K. Cairncross in *Progress*, September 1957.
3. Professor Phelps Brown and Mr Handfield-Jones, *Oxford Economic Papers*, October 1952.
4. Mr D. J. Coppock, *The Manchester School of Economic and Social Studies*, January 1956.
5. Professor A. K. Cairncross, *Home and Foreign Investment 1870–1913*.
6. Professor W. A. Lewis, *American Economic Review*, May 1957.
7. Mr R. R. Neild, *District Bank Review*, December 1957.
8. Mr Alan Day, *The Listener*, 21 November 1957.

THE GROWTH OF CAPITAL WEALTH: PRE-WAR AND POST-WAR

(£ million at constant 1948 prices)

	1938	1948	1949	1950	1951	1952	1953	1954	1955	1956
Total U.K. net fixed investment	**724**	**541**	**642**	**683**	**648**	**648**	**787**	**888**	**967**	**1,055**
By type of asset:										
Dwellings	332	167	157	147	138	196	307	329	288	284
Other buildings and works	212	61	129	177	159	173	194	229	284	355
Plant and machinery	134	182	214	262	299	247	236	279	330	330
Vehicles, ships, and aircraft	46	131	142	97	52	32	50	51	65	86

SOURCE: *National Income and Expenditure 1957*, Blue Book.

BRITAIN'S ASSETS AND LIABILITIES (£ million)

	ASSETS: Gold and Dollar Reserves	STERLING LIABILITIES*: Total	To Sterling Area Countries	To Others
31 August 1938	864†	760	‡	‡
31 December 1951	834	3,809	2,791	1,018
31 December 1956	762	3,421	2,856	565
30 June 1957	850	3,494	2,925	569

* Excluding sterling liabilities to international organizations.
† Including estimated private holdings of gold and dollars.
‡ Information not available.

SOURCE: Pre-war figures from *Statistical Material presented during the Washington Conference* (Cmd 6707); post-war figures from Balance of Payments White Papers.

CURRENT BALANCE OF PAYMENTS (£ million)

	1952	1953	1954	1955	1956
U.K. Earnings:					
Exports and re-exports of merchandise	2,827	2,672	2,820	3,070	3,403
Other exports of goods and services	777	725	788	857	961
Interest, profits, etc., received from abroad	465	521	612	626	667
U.K. Expenditure:					
Imports of merchandise*	2,944	2,888	3,006	3,429	3,462
Other imports of goods and services	587	554	590	711	806
Interest, profits, etc., paid abroad	372	358	387	466	489
Other current transfers (net)†	−81	−70	9	26	41
Current surplus (or deficit−)	247	188	228	−79	233

*F.o.b.
†All other items entering into the current balance of payments, e.g. Government outgoings and receipts.

SOURCE: *National Income and Expenditure 1957*, Blue Book.

WHERE THE SURPLUS WENT
(£ million)

	1952	1953	1954	1955	1956	First half 1957	Total 1952 to mid-1957
Current balance of payments without American aid	126	86	180	−124	219	107	594
Current balance of payments, including U.S. defence aid*	247	188	230	−78	245	125	957
Net foreign investment, repayment of debt, and other capital items	92	175	237	18	251	128	901
U.K. sterling liabilities: borrowing (−), repayment (+)†	+330	−227	−94	+133	−11	−91	+40
Increase (+) or decrease (−) in gold and dollar reserves	175	+240	+87	−229	+5	+88	+16

* These figures are taken from the latest Balance of Payments White Paper; they allow for corrections, which are not included in the analysis of earnings and expenditure in the previous table.

† This item is mainly made up of the sterling balances held by overseas governments in London; it also includes the outstanding British debt to the European Payments Union, the sterling held by the International Monetary Fund, etc.

SOURCE: Balance of Payments White Papers (Cmd 122 and 273).

THE DIMINISHING DOLLAR GAP
(£ million)

	1952	1953	1954	1955	1956	First half 1957
Total U.K. Dollar Earnings	**494**	**563**	**607**	**700**	**883**	**455**
Exports and re-exports of merchandise	410	444	423	495	622	330
Shipping	83	79	86	95	108	55
Interest, profits, and dividends received	57	58	57	64	76	39
Travel	27	31	34	39	42	18
Other (excl. defence aid)	−83	−49	7	7	35	13
Total U.K. Dollar Expenditure	**789**	**669**	**729**	**952**	**932**	**505**
Imports of merchandise*	606	517	556	732	761	412
Shipping	74	55	54	75	76	43
Interest, profits, and dividends paid out	88	81	97	110	70	30
Travel	5	5	5	5	5	3
Migrants' funds, legacies, and private gifts (net)	7	2	8	15	6	10
Other	9	9	9	15	14	7
BALANCE	**−295**	**−106**	**−122**	**−252**	**−49**	**−50**
DOLLAR ACCOUNT OF REST OF STERLING AREA:						
Exports and re-exports	461	410	402	463	460	249
Imports	601	428	438	494	555	349
Other net†	177	105	63	54	94	167
BALANCE	**37**	**87**	**27**	**23**	**−1**	**67**
Plus Gold sales to U.K. (net)	**72**	**78**	**138**	**176**	**220**	**105**

* F.o.b.

† Includes capital transactions, drawings from and repayments to the International Monetary Fund, and all gold sales other than to U.K.

SOURCE: Balance of Payments White Papers (Cmd 9430, Cmd 122 and 273).

INDEX

Index